A CHORUS of COCKERELS

WALKING ON THE WILD SIDE IN MALLORCA

ANNA NICHOLAS

summersdale

*For the one and only 'EC1' –
my irreplaceable sister, Cecilia*

ACKNOWLEDGEMENTS

This latest book has afforded me the luxury of setting off on a magical journey around the beautiful island of Mallorca, my home, visiting favourite haunts and discovering new ones. In truth, this voyage of the senses would not have been complete without the generosity, kindness, humour and good faith of the many extraordinary, talented, and engaging individuals I became acquainted with along the way.

I very much appreciate my enduring relationship with the Summersdale Publishers team and would like to give a special mention to Abbie Headon, commissioning editor, and my editor, Debbie Chapman, for their professionalism, encouragement and enthusiasm.

Once again I would like to give a verbal hug to Alan, my long suffering and supportive Scotsman, and Ollie, my son, for their unwavering faith in me and for their patience in coping with my relentless zeal for local culture and history. I would also like to extend a huge *graciès* to the Sóller community for preserving the island's traditions and way of life in our special valley, and for its continuing friendship. Last but not least, I offer a virtual trug of golden lemons to my wonderful readers for having so kindly supported my work.

CONTENTS

AUTHOR'S NOTE

Most of the local vernacular used in this book is in the Mallorquí dialect. Although it is derived from Catalan and is believed to have been spoken for more than five or six centuries, it varies greatly when written. During the Franco era, this local dialect was forbidden in Balearic schools and this has made it an oral language, reliant on Catalan when transcribed to print. Thankfully *Diccionari Català-Valencià-Balear* compiled by historic Mallorcan writer, Antoni M. Alcover and collaborator, Francesc de Borja Moll, still exists today in online form and is an etymological jewel. Catalan is the main language used in the island's schools, closely followed by Castilian Spanish, while the Mallorquí dialect is spoken socially and in the home. The vocabulary and spelling often varies greatly from village to village in Mallorca. I have taken advice from local language experts and so hope to have accurately transcribed the Mallorcan language, where used, to print. However, I apologise unreservedly to any fervent linguists who may care to differ!

One

THE HILLS ARE ALIVE

There it goes again. I rush over to the open first floor window and peer down into the tranquil pond below, my ears straining to hear the familiar sound above the buzzing of bees and chattering cicadas. My eyes search the water's hazy surface, clumps of tall reeds and craggy rocks, in the hope of alighting on a small and rotund amphibian form – but it's not to be. A large bluebottle lands on my face. In some irritation I flick it away and keep up my vigil for a few more minutes. Nothing.

'Bother!'

I hear the heavy crunch of boots on gravel and suddenly a face looks up at me from the patio below. 'What's up?'

I give a tut. 'I could have sworn I heard Johnny's throaty cackle but I must have imagined it.'

Alan – better known as the Scotsman – sniffs the air. 'I haven't heard a croak from the old toad yet, nor the frogs. Still on their hols, maybe?'

'It's March. How long do amphibians need to vacation, anyway?'

He shrugs nonchalantly and, with a smile, triumphantly holds up his trug. It's full to the brim with plump oranges. 'Not a bad crop, eh?'

'Wonderful. Have you planted the beans yet?'

'Give me a chance. It's not even eight-thirty!'

A tiny puff of smoke escapes from behind my husband's back and momentarily smudges the air.

I sigh deeply. 'Unless you're secreting a baby dragon in your jacket, I'd swear that was cigar smoke.'

He puts down the trug of his prize oranges and expansively sweeps the air with his hand. 'No, it's just bonfire fug. You know what it's like at this time of year. Every pyromaniac in the valley comes out in the spring.'

As bonfires are banned during the long summer, many locals make the most of a good spring clean in advance of the season, sprucing up orchards, burning debris and getting their gardens ship shape.

'Hm. Show me your other hand. The one hidden behind your back.'

With a guilty chuckle he grasps the trug once more and beats a hasty retreat across the lawn of the front garden without revealing his smouldering prize. 'Must get on!'

The Scotsman and I rarely see eye to eye about his penchant for *puros*, the chubby Havana cigars that he squirrels away in his man cave, the *abajo*, in the lower orchard and field.

I walk away from the window and give a cursory glance at the piles of papers and books cluttering my desk before deciding that I really should change out of my running gear and shower before tackling any work. Since merging my PR business with Dynamite, a larger London-based communications company some years ago, I now devote much of my time to journalism and freelance consultancy work. As I slip out of my airy office, snuggled in a corner of the upstairs tier of our house, and pass through the cosy TV room, I hear the front gate's shrill buzzer. Surreptitiously I look through the slats of the room's closed shutters and see the telltale flash of Jorge the postman's yellow *moto*, his motorbike.

I smile, remembering when some years ago I'd asked my elderly Mallorcan friend Neus why she always kept her wooden shutters closed even when the sun wasn't beating down. She had shaken her head despairingly. 'To spy without being seen, of course!'

I press the button on the entry phone and hear the electric gate opening lethargically. It rolls slowly on its rail, making a groaning sound that could almost be mistaken for a yawn. Even inanimate objects appear to suffer from a bit of *mañana* fever on this island.

Jorge greets me with an impish grin. 'I like the outfit!'

Earlier, in my alacrity to kick off my trainers on returning from a run, I had suddenly felt chilled and thrown an old fluffy pink jumper over my sports gear and donned a pair of my son's, Ollie, old blue Crocs, a vestige from his childhood.

'Style is my calling card, Jorge,' I reply with a wink, performing a playful twirl.

He raises his eyebrows. 'Isn't your next marathon coming up soon?'

'Sadly it is and I don't feel very prepared.'

'It's Prague, isn't it?'

I nod.

'Lucky you. I hear the beer's really good there.'

He yawns and hands me a heavy rectangular box wrapped in brown paper.

'Been buying new shoes?' he asks.

'Good grief, no. I'd never buy shoes by post. How would you know if they fit?'

'My Beatriz is always buying things by post, including shoes. More's the pity.'

'We all need the odd treat, you know.'

He flicks back his long mane of wavy locks and knits his brow. 'What's inside, then? It's got a London postmark.'

'I'm afraid my psychic powers aren't working, Jorge. I take it you want me to open it now?'

He shrugs. 'Well, I admit I'm a little curious.'

I rip off the paper and see the familiar gold logo of Havana Leather imprinted on the box's burgundy lid. This swanky leather emporium, based near Mayfair in London, is owned by my long-standing maverick client, Greedy George; well, that's what I call him, anyway. What on earth has he sent me now? I have an unnerving flashback to the time when he posted me a novelty leather lizard infused with fragrance, which served as an air freshener. My hand plunges into the inky-blue tissue paper within and discovers a fat chicken. It's not a real one, thankfully, but a squashy, brown, polished leather version with a label tied to its neck and yellow Post-it sticker on its back that reads: DO NOT EAT!

Jorge is frowning. 'What does the note say?'

'It says that you can't eat it.'

He shrugs incredulously. 'Even a halfwit would know that!'

'It's just my client George's idea of a silly joke,' I examine the printed label and laugh. 'It says the hen is called Pertelote and that she's "full of beans".' Oh very funny. 'It's a beanbag doorstop, Jorge.'

He looks disappointed. 'Why not just use a rock or lump of wood like everyone else?'

'The sort of customer my client fetes would probably much prefer novelties of this kind.'

He sits astride his bike and, whipping his hair over his shoulder, secures the strap on his helmet. 'Each to his own. Besides, what a ridiculous name for a hen!'

'Actually, it's rather a good choice. It comes from a popular Chaucer fable, *The Nun's Priest's Tale*. In the story, Pertelote was married to Chanticleer, a vain cockerel who very nearly came to a sticky end.'

He revs the engine and shakes his head despairingly. 'You and your books! So what happened to Chanticleer?'

'He nearly got eaten by a fox.'

'If he'd lived in Mallorca he wouldn't have had a problem as we don't have foxes.'

'Yes, indeed.'

His *moto* heads out of the gate pop-popping up the stony track in a haze of acrid smoke. For a moment I stand in the courtyard, my head tilted up to the warm sun. Spring is most definitely in the air. Tendrils of jasmine are already curling lovingly around the stone pillars of the front porch, their tiny white flowers opening up sleepily to the radiant blue sky above and exuding their characteristic sweet and pungent perfume. Among the shrubs bordering the front lawn a cluster of pretty Coronilla flowers catches my eye, their bright yellow petals and subtle scent contrasting sharply with the dry and aromatic odour of their nearest neighbour, a bush of wild, silvery-green rosemary. Today the Sóller valley is enveloped in a dense blanket of ghostly white vapour, a legacy of the early morning bonfires that mark the beginning of spring.

Breaking out of my brief reverie, I run up the steps to the porch and make for the front door, but not before a loud croak-cum-cackle assails my ears. He may be playing hide-and-seek, but happily I am now certain of one thing: Johnny, my beloved and corpulent toad, is definitely back.

I'm upstairs, rootling around our cluttered walk-in wardrobe looking for a favourite old jumper, when I come across a row of suits squeezed behind a rack of the Scotsman's shirts. They are the vestiges of my former life in London where, for nearly two decades, I ran a busy PR company in Mayfair. I wonder at the extravagant fabrics, fine wools and silks weaves, trying to imagine myself ever donning such attire again. In truth, these days I'm more likely to be found wafting around the terrain in an assortment of gear that wouldn't go amiss at a village jumble sale. The days of having to wear sharp suits and elegant separates, a kind of acceptable London battledress, are thankfully long gone, and now I can just please myself and wear a tea cosy on my head if I so choose. A voice booms behind me.

'What are you doing hiding in here?'

I look round to see my friend Catalina staring at me, with hands placed firmly on her hips. 'Lazy woman! Haven't you any work to do?'

My friend Catalina is regarded by many as the ears and eyes of the valley. Aside from helping me with cleaning and ironing a few times each month, when she and her assistant Miquela have time, she keeps an eye on the holiday rental properties of several expats in the valley.

'I didn't hear your car,' I reply, stepping forward to kiss her on both cheeks. 'I was just looking at all my old suits.'

'Why are you keeping them anyway? You could give them all away. Our local Red Cross is desperate for clothes for people who've fallen on hard times.'

'Do you honestly think they'd be of use to anyone here?'

She nods emphatically. '*Si*. Maybe a local woman could wear one for work or to look smart for a job interview or perhaps a wedding. It could make all the difference.'

For a moment I hesitate, a surge of nostalgia overwhelming me, before I pull myself up sharp and decide that now is definitely the time to wave adios to such items for good.

'OK. I'll take them in tomorrow.'

She puffs out her cheeks. 'Now are you going to make us both a coffee or do you plan on staying in the cupboard all day?'

Downstairs, the Scotsman is fussing around the coffee machine. 'This damned contraption isn't working again!'

I elbow him out of the way. 'Patience is a virtue. You have to let it warm up first.' I inspect the machine. 'In fact, switching it on first might be a good idea.'

Catalina sniggers as she sits at the kitchen table, munching on one of my blueberry muffins. She inspects the trug of oranges sitting before her and turns to the Scotsman.

'I hope you've already started planting your beans and potatoes. And what about the beetroot?'

'Don't you start.' He rolls his eyes and sits down heavily on a chair. 'I've had a very vexing morning starting with those wretched cockerels waking me up at four o'clock. And if that wasn't bad enough, I've had to contend with the hens digging up my newly planted pea seeds.'

'You need to protect them with netting,' Catalina replies.

'That's precisely what I've been doing in the field just now. I could hardly hear myself think with the noise of my wife's swarm of hens filling my ears.'

I place steaming coffees down in front of them both. 'My hens? I like that! I notice you don't object to scoffing their eggs.'

'How many are there now?' asks Catalina.

The Scotsman gives a grunt. 'At least thirty and eight cockerels. One of them – Ferdinand – is a real terror and his brother Franco isn't much better. He tried to peck me this morning. A very aggressive blighter.'

'Surely not!' I protest. 'He's just being inquisitive.'

He ignores me. 'As I say, they're completely out of control, but will she listen?'

'You should have some of them slaughtered,' Catalina says matter-of-factly.

'Heavens, we can't do that. They're pets. I mean, they all have names,' I protest.

She gives me a long look. 'That's not normal.'

'As you know, normality and my wife don't go together,' answers the Scotsman dryly. 'Somehow she's even brainwashed me into calling them by name.'

'I love the hens,' I counter. 'They follow me around each day and chat with me in the corral. And their eggs are so delicious.'

'Well perhaps you can ask them to keep their beaks shut tomorrow.' The Scotsman gets up and strides over to the open door. 'What a cacophony this morning. Now the dogs and donkeys have started!'

Catalina laughs. 'The next-door gardener drove up as I was parking. He told me that he's about to start trimming your neighbour's hedges.'

'More noise,' he groans.

Minky, our glossy brown cat waltzes into the kitchen, his fluffy grey brother, Orlando, shadowing him. They have guilty looks on their faces.

The Scotsman upbraids them. 'Ha! I want to have words with you two about uprooting my saplings. As if I haven't got enough to do, you have to disturb all my pots.'

Orlando eyes him warily and pads off in the direction of Ollie's bedroom, while Minky yawns and stretches out his long body in a shaft of sunlight on the terracotta tiles.

Catalina thumps down her cup. 'Well, I'd better get on with some ironing.'

There's the sound of a car crunching across the gravel in the courtyard.

Catalina smiles. 'That'll be Miquela. She's running late today. I'll get her started on the hoovering.'

The Scotsman shakes his head. 'So much for a quiet life. I'm off to my *abajo* to get on with some urgent tasks.'

I grin across at Catalina. 'To smoke a *puro*, I think he means.'

She offers me a conspiratorial wink. '*Exacto!*'

While Catalina and Miquela take charge of the weekly clean, I seek refuge in my office upstairs. Ever since my husband, Ollie and I upped sticks from central London for a new life in rural Mallorca some thirteen years ago, Catalina has been a firm friend. Originally she worked as an au pair for my sister, Cecilia, in Kent, before eventually heading back to the island where she married and settled down with her husband, Ramon, and their twin daughters. Having urged us to holiday in the rugged north-west where she lived, we soon fell in love with Mallorca and returned often. In fact, it was during one extended holiday, staying in a rented villa in the area, that we met an enthusiastic local estate agent who persuaded us to view some old properties on his books.

Although we had no intention of buying a second home, when we viewed the final smallholding on his list, a dilapidated three-hundred-year-old *finca* – a country house – tucked away at the end of a private track, we were smitten. The house might have had a sunken roof, no bathroom, gaping windows with no panes and a wild and untamed garden, but we felt that with a little loving care, it could be restored to its former glory. As we looked out over the magnificent pewter-hued Tramuntana mountain range that formed a backcloth to the lower gardens and lemon and orange orchard, we were mesmerised by the panoramic views over the Sóller valley. As a fervent gardener, the Scotsman had already set his sights on tackling the unruly terrain and turning it into his own terrestrial version of the Garden of Eden.

Following our move to the island, not long after the new millennium, the house resembled a building site as we installed new ceilings and staircases, extended bedrooms and, some time later, built a pool. The years may have swept by but there still seems to be a never-ending list of tasks to be fulfilled – both in the house and gardens. During the November storms, *bancales*, stone-hewn walls are want to collapse and when the wild winds and rains tap dance across the roofs, tiles and guttering loosen. As my elderly neighbour Margalida once remarked when we first moved to the track, 'an old *finca* is like a child and will forever need your love and support.'

As I sit down at my desk, the mobile phone hollers. I call it Judas because it's always betraying my whereabouts to my most tiresome clients. To my relief I hear the friendly voice of Rachel, once the managing director of my PR firm in Mayfair, but now running her own communications agency in Yorkshire.

'How's life in the madhouse?' she trills.

'Much the same. Few sane heads under this roof. And you?'

'Busy, and needing your pearls.'

I brace myself. 'Fire away.'

'Our local elderly farmer has a sister who runs a small charity based in a village near the Sussex Downs and he's asked for my advice. Basically, what his sister wants is a bit of a tall order: someone with charity experience who understands rural matters and loves hens to help her with a promotional charity stunt. Naturally it's not my bag but then I had a eureka moment and thought of you!'

'Hm. What kind of help does she need, exactly?'

'She runs an enterprise called the Chanticleer Chicken Trust, known as CCT.'

'That's strange,' I reply. 'I was just talking with my postman about Chaucer and his tale about Chanticleer the cockerel.'

'Really? Evidently a sign that this will be a match made in heaven.'

'Steady on, Rachel. I smell a rat. Is this woman remotely nutty?'

'Henrietta Driscoll? She's as sane as you and me.'

'I don't find that very reassuring.'

She giggles. 'Look, she's setting up some kind of knitathon for chicken jumpers early next year in London...'

'Whoaaaa! Chicken jumpers?'

Rachel clears her throat, trying to fool me with a touch of gravitas. 'Well, basically the CCT rescues maltreated and old battery-farm fowl. A lot of them have lost their feathers so need knitted jumpers to keep them warm until they grow back.'

'Hang on, I'm just checking my calendar in case today is in fact April the first.'

Rachel bursts into laughter. 'Look, will you hear me out? I'm not pulling your leg. These hens really do need jumpers. A cold British winter can be harsh on them.'

I give a sigh. 'Well if that's the case, my heart goes out to the poor little things.'

'There, you see, I knew you'd buy into it. Anyway, I've got to go.'

'But I need to know a lot more.'

'Henrietta Driscoll's just left for Baltimore where she's guest speaker at a fowl convention and won't be back for a few weeks. She told me that she's doing a tour of hen refuge centres over there.'

'You mean they have them all over the States, too?'

'So it seems. Anyway, she'll be in touch directly as soon as she returns.'

I give an outraged sniff. 'You've already passed her my details?'

Her voice tinkles with mirth. 'Of course. I know what a sucker you are for broken wings! Toodle-pip!'

Rachel is off the line before I can remonstrate with her. Somehow, I have a funny feeling that Henrietta Driscoll of the CCT is going to prove a strange old bird.

As I wave goodbye to Catalina and Miquela, relishing the pristine appearance of the airy *entrada*, our large hallway-cum-living room with its freshly mopped and polished stone floor, I hear a loud and throaty croak. That's it. I march into the front garden, lean over the edge of the pond and carefully study the dark water, searching for our resident toad who speaks with an American twang. Of course some foolish folk think that a talking toad is a figment of my imagination. Luckily I know better.

'Johnny, where are you?' I hiss.

Silence.

'OK, if you want to play hard to get, that's fine by me, but I think it's a pretty poor show given that months have elapsed since we last spoke. Your holidays seem to get longer each year and...'

There's a loud plop and a pair of large glassy eyes survey me from behind a rock. 'Jeez! Still complaining about my vacation? Me and the boys toil all year, singing our hearts out and keeping watch over wildlife in your pond and when we take one short, well-deserved annual break, all we get is grief.'

'I'd say five months is a fairly long holiday.'

'Give a toad a break! For one thing, it's not just a holiday. Me and the boys also help out at an amphibian refuge centre in France.'

'Don't be absurd.'

'You don't believe me? Well, what if I told you that there are a heck of a lot of valiant toads and frogs out there that have been maimed and abused by brutish beasts like your four feline monsters or predatory herons and eagles? And what about all those casualties of French restaurants? The lucky ones wind up on crutches. I tell you, some haven't even got a leg to stand on.'

I shake my head. 'So where did you holiday this year?'

'Nowhere special. We just hung out in the cool ravines of the Tramuntanas and hooked up with a couple of Midwife toads and their families. Boy! There's a lot of human activity going on up there. The toad community isn't too happy about it.'

'What do you mean?' I ask. I'm a great fan of the tiny Midwife toads of Mallorca that live in the highest ravines and are now a protected species.

'Some photographer guys have been snooping about, taking lots of happy snappies and there are groups of boring suits with clipboards.'

'I wouldn't worry. The Tramuntanas have just been declared a UNESCO World Heritage site so there have probably been a lot of officials and local politicians inspecting the terrain of late.'

He puffs out his cheeks. 'Hard to get any peace in this valley.'

'Well I'm happy that you're finally home, Johnny. Are the frogs with you?'

'Sure thing. Me and the boys arrived at dawn. Been lying low to get the lay of the land. I see you've got new reeds. That's an improvement.'

'We thought they might give you greater protection from that pesky heron.'

'Good call, but I have got a bone to pick with you. None of us boys could get a wink of sleep. What's the deal with the roosters?'

'You don't like them?'

'Are you kidding? They're a nightmare! Apart from the unholy row at four o'clock in the morning, they come grubbing around the pond with their fancy bits, those coquettish hens, rustling their feathers, cooing and scratching in the dust.'

'They escape through the garden gates.'

'Then keep them shut, missy!'

His head disappears below the water just as my mobile rings. It's Ollie.

'Darling! I was just this minute catching up with Johnny.'

'Ah, your imaginary little friend, mother? I'm delighted for you.'

'So how's boarding school life?'

'Dreadful as usual.'

'How about your studies?'

'Boring as hell.'

'Excellent, and the weather in England?'

'Hideous.'

'Wonderful. Any news?'

'None whatsoever.'

'Great. And do you need any pocket money?'

'Now you're talking, mother!'

When I've finished the call, I contemplate life for my son back in the English countryside. He is studying for his A levels at a

British school, which he has been attending for the last four years. He had spent a blissful sojourn at a local Spanish school until aged thirteen, when he began to long to experience England. Neither the Scotsman nor I were remotely interested in relocating back to the UK, nor Ollie, come to that, so he himself suggested boarding school for a few years and we went along with the plan. Although at times I miss him dreadfully, I have to admit that the whole experience has made him far more confident and independent, and it makes holiday periods all the more special for the three of us.

It's early evening when the front door swings open and the Scotsman strides out, wearing the ear protectors he uses when trimming hedges. When he sees me, he lowers them onto his neck.

'What on earth are you wearing those for?'

'To enjoy a little solace away from the sound of baying dogs, shrieking cockerels, tractors, donkeys, complaining cats, hoovers, lawnmowers and frogs!'

I stifle a guffaw. His attention is diverted to the olive tree in the centre of the lawn. 'Is that Sergi Squint up there?'

A rotund and stealthy Siamese with a wonky eye has been stalking our land of late, much to the consternation of one of our cats, fat Doughnut, or 'Do Not', as the Scotsman refers to him. The smoky-beige-hued creature peers down at us through the sparse silvery leaves before making a dash for freedom. He claws his way expertly down the rough trunk and disappears behind a patch of tall Echiums. There's the busy purr of an engine and we both look up to see a large truck waiting at the gate.

'What now?' exclaims the Scotsman.

As we wave the driver into the courtyard, I realise with some excitement that he is delivering the traditional wooden nesting boxes for our chickens that I ordered from a farm in England. Helpfully he piles them up on the gravel drive, gets me to sign the delivery note and, with an *adeu*, goodbye, jumps back into his vehicle and drives off along the track. The Scotsman gives me a wry grin. 'So you've ordered more laying boxes so that our hens produce even more eggs or chicks?'

I scratch my chin. 'That's a bit of a chicken and egg conundrum. My thought was to encourage the wild fowl that land in our field to lay eggs in the boxes rather than bury them in the orchard.'

He squats down on the gravel to inspect them. 'We've got to be careful. If we breed any more hens and cockerels, we might be overrun.'

I give him a reassuring pat on the back. 'There's plenty of room in the field. I don't think we'll have a problem.'

'Hm, famous last words.'

We move the boxes over to the patio and discuss where we're going to house them in the field. With only two nesting boxes, our hens are currently queuing up to use them each day.

The Scotsman shakes his head. 'If we're not careful, we'll be running a battery farm soon.'

'Over my dead body!' I shriek. 'Rachel's just been telling me about a charity in Sussex that gets volunteers to knit jumpers for featherless hens that have been abused at battery farms.'

'What on earth are you talking about?'

'Remember the film, *Chicken Run*, with all those poor hens trying to make a bid for freedom?'

'Fortunately not.'

'Well the charity is holding a knitathon and I might get involved in promoting it. I thought I could make a few jumpers, too.'

'You knit?'

'I used to make woolly scarves when I was young.'

'God help us!' He rubs his eyes and stares out at the ruby-hued Tramuntanas. In the early evening, a rosy glow flushes the flanks of the mountains, a sight I never tire of. The hens have quietened down and are roosting in the trees and in the corral and Minny and Della, our two donkeys, have disappeared into their hut for the night. Even the gardener next door has packed up and gone home.

'Ah, bliss,' sighs the Scotsman as he rubs his hands together. 'Silence at last.' He examines his watch. 'Seven-thirty already. Time for a welcome snifter, I'd say.'

He turns towards the house just as a fierce rumbling and banging can be heard from the mouth of the track.

'What on earth is that?' I ask.

The noise gets louder and louder and soon a lorry appears, a sizeable mountain of gravel sitting on its open deck. The Scotsman shakes his head in disbelief. 'What a chump! I forgot that I ordered the gravel today.'

'What's it for?'

'I need to bolster the paths in the lower gardens. The gravel on them is getting pretty thin.'

Before the driver releases the huge load onto the drive, I give a quick wave and scuttle as quickly as possible into the house. Through the front door I can see the Scotsman standing stoically by the truck, his mufflers firmly replaced on his ears. And then, in just a matter of moments, when the load is released with a great roar, my jolly Scotsman disappears, quite literally, in a cloud of dust.

Two

BIRDS OF A FEATHER

I'm sitting at my desk upstairs, listening to the comforting murmur of trickling water from our pond and the occasional sharp and repetitive croak of our frogs. Johnny is, as ever, keeping a low profile, no doubt lurking in his favourite hole in the pond's craggy stone wall. The urgent cry of Athena, our resident Eleanora's falcon that lives with her brood in a tree in the back garden, ripples in the breeze. She is unusually maternal of late, rushing back and forth to her nest with titbits for her young offspring. Much as this is all very touching, I fear for our baby chicks in the corral, who are often at the mercy of both Athena and a powerful eagle we've christened Hercules, who flits over the orchard each week in search of prey.

I take a gulp of coffee and look at my watch. It's ten o'clock. Ollie is home from school for Easter and I've promised to take him to Sóller port for breakfast and to pop by the studio of Toful Colom, a local sculptor friend. First I must call Henrietta Driscoll, who has sent me a long e-mail all about her forthcoming fundraising knitathon. It all sounds a bit lacklustre and, from what I can glean, the event is going to need some commercial sponsors. There's a strange crackle on the line that sounds rather like a gurgling crow and then a loud voice booms in my ear.

'CCT. Who is this?'

I proffer my name, explaining that I'd like to speak with Henrietta Driscoll and suddenly the woman grows animated, her cut-glass accent filling the air waves.

'Do call me Hennie! How wonderful that you've called. Are you going to help with our knitathon?'

I explain diplomatically that I can only offer limited assistance given my location but am happy to help with promoting the event which, she reliably informs me, will culminate in London the following February.

'Do you have any commercial partners?' I ask. 'I presume you're planning to have a media reception for the event?'

'Oh dear, yes, we could do with some more financial backing. It's something I'm working on.'

'Any celebrity supporters who could introduce the event?'

'I'm already in touch with a few celebrities who donate to our foundation and I'm sure Joanna Lumley might help out.'

'That would be wonderful. Does she like chickens?'

'I really can't say but she looks like a good egg so she simply *must* like chickens! Nicholas Parsons seems like a very nice man so I might send him a letter.'

The woman is evidently mildly bonkers, which isn't necessarily a bad thing.

'Do you actually know either of these celebrities?'

'Not exactly but I know we'd all get on like a house on fire. If it helps, I know two bishops and a cardinal.'

I close my eyes and visualise aiming a pea-shooter at Rachel. I should have trusted my instinct. Hennie Driscoll is as dotty as I'd suspected.

'Have you thought of calling your knitathon something a little more catchy?' I hazard.

'Such as? I thought these something-athons were all the rage these days. There are always charity something-athons on TV, aren't there?'

'I don't watch TV very much,' I confess. 'What about a slightly more memorable title, such as Chick-Knit? You know like chick-lit?'

She screeches like a demented cockerel. 'Oh how super! I love it. Chick-Knit. Why didn't I think of that?! And what, pray, is chick-lit? A reading scheme for hens?'

'Not exactly. It's a literary term used to describe novels that appeal to young women.'

'A shame, but in truth, none of our hens can read. At least I've never *seen* them reading.'

'Don't you believe it. By night they're probably reading copies of the ancient folk tale Chicken Licken and Chaucer's tales by torchlight in their corrals.'

'Golly gosh, what a thought!' she squeaks in delight.

After I've managed to get Hennie off the line, I put a quick call through to Ed, one of my closest old university chums, who happens to be one of life's most fervent hypochondriacs with a penchant for courting disaster at every turn. Ed lives in London with his serene and beautiful fiancée Rela and I am ever hopeful that one day soon they will tie the knot. After having been made redundant from his long-standing job at the BBC, and trying his hand as a computer consultant, Ed has recently started work in the technical support department of a large comprehensive school. It involves early starts, low pay and coping with complicated equipment. In short, my idea of the job from hell. His most recent text, sent to me at some godforsaken hour of the night, was cryptic, to say the least. It simply read: 'Bummer day, Scatters. Please call urgently.' Ed still refers to me by the old university nickname he once gave me.

He whispers into the receiver. 'Is that you, Scatters? I can't be long. Members of staff get into trouble if they're caught speaking on their mobiles.'

'You did ask me to call,' I remonstrate.

'Yes, I know. It's just that I'm in a bit of a pickle. I don't think my department boss likes me.'

'Now don't get paranoid. You've only just started in the job. Go with the flow and try to be diligent and nice to everyone until you get a handle on the place.'

'But yesterday my boss told me I was an idiot.'

I frown. 'Indeed, that's not very friendly but did you do something to annoy him?'

He emits a long sigh. 'If you count accidentally dropping the keys to the music room down a drain.'

'Hm. Not a great start. Did you manage to get them back?'

'Well I had a slight panic attack when it happened so I rounded up some pupils to come and help. They were brilliant. One of them used a coat hanger to draw them up.'

'That doesn't sound so disastrous then.'

He hisses into the receiver. 'The problem is that the pupils should have been in their lessons and, instead, spent thirty minutes helping me. Staff members were looking high and low for them. It never crossed my mind that they should have been in class.'

'You are working in a school. That should have given you a clue, Ed.'

'I suppose,' he says gloomily and then his voice brightens. 'Anyway, I have some very good tidings, too. Rela and I have set a date for the big event. We're getting married in July. I trust you'll come over.'

I am elated. 'Wild dogs couldn't stop me.'

'Lord, I hope you don't encounter any of those on the way,' he says fretfully.

I am distracted when I hear a loud clucking and tut at my office door and see Cordelia heading towards me. 'Must go, Ed. My hen, Cordelia, has appeared and is eyeing up my trainers. She thinks the laces are worms.'

He gives a small shriek. 'How ghastly! What on earth is she doing in the house? Your livestock situation is getting completely out of hand.'

I'm laughing too much to reply. I end the call and bend down to stroke Cordelia's head as she pulls valiantly at one of my laces, disappointment dawning on her face when she realises that it isn't edible. 'Come on old girl, let's get you some porridge and raisins.'

She looks up at me expectantly and clucks something in hen dialect, flapping her wings behind me as I stride out of the office. I pick her up and, descending the stairs to the kitchen, place her outside the back door. She waits until I deposit a bowl of warm oats in front of her and ruffles her feathers in excitement before pecking at her private feast. Of course I shouldn't single out Cordelia for special treatment, but she is the last survivor of our original flock and is more of a dog than a fowl. She is my constant shadow and often sits watching me as I work at my desk. Our four cats vie for my affections, too, so it is not unusual to find the desk littered with slumbering felines while Cordelia keeps guard at the office door. I sit at the kitchen table and contemplate Ed's less than glorious start to his new job, hoping that it will all come good in the end, just as his union with Rela has proven such a resounding success. My mind floats back to my earlier conversation with Hennie and I smile, thinking what fun it will be to work with her on the Chick-Knit event. Somehow I think it will be a far cry from the kind of joyless relationship poor Ed currently appears to have with his boss at the school.

Ollie wanders barefooted into the kitchen, wearing skinny grey jeans and an old white T-shirt. At the sight of Cordelia, he raises his eyebrows before pulling a can of lemon Fanta from the fridge. He takes a long draught and yawns.

'I thought you'd be impressed that I'm up so early.'

'It's nearly ten-thirty, which I suppose is the crack of dawn for you.'

He nods and offers me a wry grin. 'I think I could do with a strong coffee, scrambled eggs and some fresh air.'

I take the hint. 'Come on, let's go. I promised Toful we'd pop by in half an hour.'

He glugs down his drink. 'Have you been for a run this morning?'

'No. I had some urgent work deadlines. I'll go out later.'

He strikes a warning note. 'The marathon's not far away now. Got to keep up the pace, mother.'

My son has an uncanny knack of pricking my conscience. Of course he's right. I should be hitting the road more frequently now. 'I've got more than a month to go.'

'Is that all?' he taunts.

I tap his head with the day's copy of the *Majorca Daily Bulletin*, the expat daily newspaper for which I pen a column every Saturday. 'Come on, let's hit the road.'

As the car rumbles along the track, Rafael, my neighbour, appears at his porch, munching on an orange. He comes over and slaps the bonnet.

'Hey, running girl! When you do the marathon?'

'Soon. Don't remind me.'

'Lots of kilometres, eh? I tell Ollie yesterday, at your age it's good to run every day.'

Ollie stifles a smirk. '*Si, si*. I keep telling her, Rafael.'

'You know it's San Jordi day soon? Lovers give each other books and roses. It's nice tradition. Your *senyor*, Alan, maybe buy you a rose!'

I roll my eyes. 'Ha, you must be joking. Anyway, I think I'd opt for a book.'

He leans in at the driver's window. 'I prefer a rose. I don't have time to read.'

Throwing his orange peel into his orchard, he shoos away the assortment of hens and cockerels outside his front door and offers us a wave. At the mouth of the track, we find ourselves kissing bonnets with our eighty-year-old neighbour Pedro and his cheery wife Silvia, who are attempting to reach their *finca* close by. Chivalrously Pedro reverses while I manage to manoeuvre the Mini through the narrow gap. He pops his head out of the driver's window.

'Are you going to the *Setmana Santa* procession tomorrow night?'

'Of course,' I reply.

He nods contentedly.

In truth, I am always rather unnerved by the Easter-week processions of *cofradías*, religious fraternities, whose penitent members, known as *caperutxes*, wear long robes and hoods shaped like upturned ice-cream cones. Eye-slits are cut into the hoods' fabric, making it impossible to recognise any of the participants, which is why some uneasy visitors compare them to the masks once worn by the Ku Klux Klan. All the same, the various processions taking place island-wide from Maundy Thursday to Easter Sunday are truly mesmerising and an important feature of the season's festivities.

'And what about your husband? Has he started planting his tomatoes yet?' he asks.

'It's on the list. We've got to deal with the artichokes and broad beans first. I'm bottling them later.'

'Tell him not to leave it too late,' he persists.

He potters back to his car and offers me a salute as we turn in the direction of the port.

'Nothing like putting pressure on poor Al,' sighs Ollie, using his affectionate nickname for the Scotsman. 'I shall enjoy winding him up when we get back.'

The road to the port is unusually quiet but it's not long before I hear a familiar hooting and see Gaspar, the newspaper delivery-man, flashing the lights of his *moto* behind me. I slow down before turning towards Can Repic beach. I roll down the driver's window.

'*Hola*! How's life, Gaspar?'

'*Bien*,' he shouts above the noise of his engine. 'I've started a new diet. All you eat is meat and fish.'

'Are you sure that's a good idea?'

He beams at me. 'Just wait and see. I'm going to be as thin as a chorizo stick.'

As he speeds off, Ollie smirks at me. 'Yeah, right. I can just see that happening.'

Gaspar's girth has been expanding of late to the extent that he has difficulty mounting his *moto*. Now in his late thirties, with thinning hair and little interest in his appearance, it's apparent that he is becoming a firm bachelor, perhaps enjoying his beloved mother's cooking and his parents' comfortable home a tad too much. At times the bike seems to wobble precariously under his weight and visibly sinks onto its tyres when he plonks heavily down on the seat. It's rare not to see him munching on an early morning *ensaimada*, the island's famed spiral-shaped pastry, or tucking into a huge pasta or rice dish at Café Paris, one of my favourite haunts in Sóller town.

Toful is working on a sculpture near his front gate and rushes over as I turn into his drive. His studio is a brisk five-minute walk from Can Repic beach and faces the Tramuntana mountains on one side and orchard land on the other. Today, a tangerine sun beams down on the contemporary metal creations that adorn the long strip of garden at the side of his home. We follow him into the studio where his latest works are exhibited. Most of the sculptures follow an aquatic theme and are created from recycled metals, although wood is employed in his designs, too. Ollie picks up a craggy-looking, bright-pink fish on a stand and admires it.

'You like that? It's one of my new designs. It's Mallorca's Cap Roig fish.'

'Ah, of course,' nods Ollie. 'Is that mermaid new?'

Toful nods enthusiastically. 'It's going to be displayed at a new exhibition I'm holding at Aimia Hotel in the port. I've been experimenting with an octopus design, too.'

I study the carefully crafted creature honed from wrought iron and smile. 'Where's the *pièce de résistance*, my artichoke?'

He laughs and beckons us outside. Sitting cheek by jowl with an abstract sculpture in what Toful refers to as his 'sculpture park' is a huge, spiky, wrought-iron artichoke. As my favourite vegetable, it's no wonder that I have a fondness for the piece. Back in Toful's workshop I help him with the English wording for a new sign for his gate. He is keen to attract holidaymakers to view his works but is worried about his limited English.

'I must take lessons,' he tells me. 'It's all very well you writing the signs for me but when English people enter my workshop, I won't be able to understand them.'

I look round at all his creations. 'It's simple. Just place price cards by each one and conversation can be kept to the minimum.'

He shrugs. 'I suppose so. By the way, you asked to see my works within the old naval base and to have a peek at one of the underground tunnels there. The *comandante,* the commander in charge of the base, has given me permission to give you a tour one day.'

I smile. 'That would be fun. Let's make it a date.'

Two of Toful's sculptures, an abstract design of a man with a fishing rod in honour of local fishermen and a giant cross, have been erected on rocks at the far end of the naval base and are viewable from the sea. The base is out of bounds to the public but occasionally opens its doors for events. It is well known that there are vast underground tunnels there, rumoured to have been used during the Spanish Civil War to store torpedoes. I have always been curious to visit them. Toful's other most notable sculpture is the giant metal prawn that adorns the port's main roundabout. It was created in celebration of Sóller's heavenly and highly prized *gamba roja*, the sweet pink prawns that come at a price but are worth every *centimo*.

After a grand tour of Toful's latest works, Ollie and I jump in the car and are about to drive to the port when he knocks on the passenger window and passes Ollie the little Cap Roig fish sculpture.

'A little gift since you liked it so much.'

Ollie smiles in delight. 'It'll take pride of place on my chest of drawers.'

Toful nods and pats the roof of the car as we head off. We park near Es Port Hotel and walk along the sunny promenade, feasting our eyes on the tranquil sea with its glistening, pearlised waters. The blue expanse is dotted with small fishing vessels and elegant luxury yachts, while white, garrulous gulls duck and dive overhead cawing excitedly. Ollie points to a beautifully restored honey-coloured boat anchored in the harbour. It sports a bright blue border and has the name *Bonnie Lass* painted on its side.

'The Scotsman would like that,' he says with a smile. 'It's a lovely old classic.'

'Indeed he does.'

I tell Ollie how Alan and I had recently met the captain, Peter Lucas and his wife, Roo, and thought they were thoroughly good eggs. Their boat is a fishing vessel that was built in East Lothian in Scotland in 1949 and, in its newly refurbished state, they have conducted all sorts of chartered trips around the coastline. More importantly, out of season, they offer the boat as a research vessel to ondine and oceanic associations that protect local marine life in Balearic waters.

'Oh you're not going to start bashing on about sea turtles eating plastic bags, are you?' he groans.

'Someone's got to,' I retort, warming to my theme. 'Anyway, they're doing a fine job without my intervention.'

He nods. 'Yeah, I remember they sent a guy to my old school here trying to get us to help clean up the beaches.'

'Such a great idea. Tourists could help, too.'

He laughs. 'I think they'd rather be relaxing on their sun loungers, to be honest.'

We sit at a table outside La Vila Café and are soon tucking into delicious scrambled eggs, fresh bread and strong espressos.

Ollie bites into some chunky toast. 'What happened to your chum Isabel Moreno, who used to head up biology at the local university? I thought she was involved in marine conservation?'

'She still is despite having officially retired a few years ago. In fact, I'm meeting up with her next month. She's just published a book about her adventures overseas as a marine biologist. She went to the Antarctic three times, which is pretty impressive.'

'For a woman,' he goads with a wink. Ollie enjoys pulling my leg about my apparent feminist cheerleading for womankind.

Abdul, the happy and well-liked waiter at La Vila, comes over for a chat.

'It was quite choppy earlier but now look at it. I predict a fine afternoon with moderate sun and a gentle breeze.'

'I hope you're right, Abdul,' says Ollie. 'I've got a tennis match in Deia later.'

'Mark my words,' he replies. 'You'll have perfect conditions for a match.'

We head back to the car, stopping on the way to peruse a villa with half-filled plastic water bottles standing on either side of its front door.

'You know those are placed there to prevent dogs cocking their legs,' I say.

Ollie gives a snort. 'How does that work? The dog would surely pee on the bottles instead.'

'I've no idea, but my chum Tomeu Aloy, who teaches at the Calvia School of Languages, told me and as he's the font of all knowledge, I'll take his word for it. He says it's a bit of an old wives' tale.'

'A shaggy-dog story more like,' he replies dismissively.

Back at the house we discover the Scotsman at the kitchen table, surrounded by mounds of broad beans and artichokes.

He stands up and jangles his car keys. 'Ah, there you are! I've got everything prepared for bottling. You'll find the Kilner jars over there ready for sterilising and I've podded all the broad beans and washed the artichokes.'

'Are you going out?' I ask.

'I'm popping round the corner to Rafel and Cico's to arrange an ITV for the car.'

Our local garage is run by two cheery brothers, both of whom are dedicated mechanics. Rafel takes the Mallorcan spelling of his name, unlike our neighbour, Rafael.

'What's an ITV?' quizzes Ollie.

'The equivalent of a British MOT. It's an odd sounding acronym for a car service, isn't it?' the Scotsman replies.

'Easy to remember though,' shrugs Ollie and promptly slopes off to his bedroom.

His father drums the table with his fingers. 'I ought to get another corn sack and some tomato seedlings from Sebastian at Hens while I'm at it.'

When we first moved to the valley, we had no idea that Hens, the name of our local agricultural supplier, had nothing to do with poultry but was the brand name for a Dutch agricultural company. When Sebastian acquired the business back in the seventies, he kept its original name, even though it had long bitten the dust.

'Good idea,' I reply. 'As it happens, I bumped into Pedro on the track and he said you needed to get cracking with the tomatoes.'

He shakes his head in some exasperation. 'Why is everyone, including my neighbours, so interested in my planting programme? Anyway, Pep's popping round in a bit so I'd better go now before he arrives.'

I narrow my eyes. Pep and Juana are good friends but when the Scotsman gets to be alone with his partner in crime, that usually means trouble.

'So what does Pep want?'

'It's just a social call,' he says hastily. 'He needs to store some bottles in our cellar.'

'Why can't he use his own?'

'I've no idea. Maybe it's full.'

An hour later, as I'm mid-blanching baby broad beans and char-grilling artichoke hearts, in strolls Pep. He encompasses me in a bear hug.

'So, the little British housewife at her stove! How charming.'

I waggle my kitchen knife at him. 'Watch your step. So what are you up to?'

He opens his eyes wide and – ever the showman – raises his arms dramatically in the air. '*Hombre*! Whatever do you mean? Can I not pop round to see my old British friends without the Spanish Inquisition?'

'I hear that you need to deposit some bottles with us?'

He gives me a winning smile and pushes a hand through his thick grey hair. 'Ah, yes, I have been experimenting with some new formulas for my *herbes* liqueur and need to rest the latest batch somewhere secure.'

'In other words, you're hiding them from Juana?'

He pulls thoughtfully at his beard. 'Ever the cynic, but yes, she wouldn't be too happy. These days she has zero tolerance for my wine- and spirit-making.'

I give him a prod. 'That's because you always make such a mess and then vacuum up half the contents with your cronies in one night.'

The kitchen door opens and the Scotsman enters, beaming with delight at seeing his old chum. 'Ah, Pep. Just in time. I'm about to plant the tomato seedlings. Would you like to help?'

'You've got to be joking, *mi amic*! I hate gardening.'

The Scotsman shoots him a theatrical wink, which he doesn't think I notice as I toil at the work surface. I watch their schoolboy antics in the reflection of the window.

'But I could do with your help down in the field, Pep,' he replies labouredly.

'Ah, of course! I may not like gardening but I love planting tomatoes. Let's get going.'

They creep out of the kitchen and head for the Scotsman's *abajo*, no doubt for a chinwag over a clandestine whisky and plump *puro*. Meanwhile I begin filling my sterilised jars with slices of garlic, black and pink peppercorns, and sprigs of basil and thyme. Slowly I add the blanched baby broad beans that have been steeped in cider vinegar and add freshly squeezed lemon juice and virgin olive oil. I seal the lids and tie on labels with the date of production. Next I start the same process with the char-grilled artichoke hearts. I add rosemary to the mixture and breathe in the delicious heady fragrance of the combined herbs. Ollie suddenly appears in the kitchen and deftly manages to extract twenty euros from me before heading off to Deia village for his tennis match.

I sit down with a cup of tea and a slice of home-made almond cake and contemplate my next task – sweet cucumber pickle. The Scotsman and I belong to a local eco group, Va de Bio, formerly known as Aixo es Vida, meaning that's life, which supplies us with a scrumptious selection of eco vegetables and fruits each week. Within the group, we swap different home-grown vegetables, fruits, eggs and local goat and sheep cheese and now Va de Bio also produces pulses and organic meat. In my last box of goodies I received a large number of cucumbers so hit on the idea of pickling them with dill and onions.

I hear the buzzer at the gate and press the entry button. Toful and his brother wave at me from the front seats of a sizeable van. They jump out and open the back doors to reveal the giant wrought-iron artichoke that has previously graced Toful's sculpture garden.

'A little surprise for you!' says Toful. 'You've always admired it and I thought it would look good in your orchard.'

Words fail me. I call Alan and Pep and, between the four men, they manage to wrestle it down the slope that leads from the front courtyard to the orchard below.

'It's wonderful, Toful. I really can't thank you enough.'

Pep puffs thoughtfully on his cigar. 'It's skilfully crafted but I'd worry about those spikes after a night on the razzle. Imagine coming back the worse for wear and being impaled!'

I give him a nudge. 'Some of us know when to have an elegant sufficiency.'

'Really? I hadn't noticed,' he replies with a snort of laughter.

I give Toful a big hug and wave as he and his brother roar up the track, leaving a bemused Scotsman and Pep standing on the drive.

'Well you two, I have to get back to my kitchen. How are you getting on with unloading your bottles?'

'All stowed safely in Alan's *abajo*,' beams Pep, casting the Scotsman a furtive glance. 'I am forever indebted. Anyway, we must get on.'

They sneak off in the direction of the *abajo* before I can reply. It's at that moment that I hear my mobile phone bleating from the kitchen and catch it on the fourth ring. It's my client, Greedy George.

'So, guv, did you get my special postal package?'

'The hen door-stopper?'

'What else? It's my new brainwave. I'm going to launch a whole range.'

'Of just chickens?'

'Don't be a dope. No, they'll come first, then I'm going to design a duck, dog, cat and rabbit and I was even thinking of a dinosaur for kids' bedrooms.'

'So when do you plan on launching the hens?'

'That's just a prototype that I sent you. Can't launch them just yet as I'm refurbishing the London showroom. Bloody nightmare it is, too. Dust all over the place and Richard's getting his boxers in a twist.'

Richard is George's showroom manager and of a sensitive disposition.

'I've just had a thought,' I say.

'Steady on. You don't want to wear yourself out.'

'Witty as ever. It just so happens I've been talking with a woman named Hennie Driscoll who runs a hen sanctuary called the Chanticleer Chicken Trust in Sussex.'

'Are you having a laugh? Hennie?'

'I know. You couldn't make it up. Anyway, she's looking for commercial partners to collaborate on an event raising funds for old and abused battery hens.'

'Let me get out my hankie.'

'Less sarcasm, thank you. I was just wondering whether Havana Leather could come on board and offer a small percentage of sales on the hen doorstoppers?'

'You're not floating my boat yet. What kind of event is she planning?'

'It's called Chick-Knit and it'll be held next February in London. Hennie's going to get celebrities and volunteers to knit tiny jumpers for featherless hens.'

Greedy George erupts into uncontrolled laughter. 'You've got to be taking the…'

'I'm totally serious.'

'Well why stop at jumpers, guv? I could design her some leather capes for the poor old girls. We could call them cape-ons. Geddit?'

'Now you're just being silly.'

There's momentary silence. 'Actually, there's potential PR mileage in this. We could get one of her bald old birds modelling a mini-cape with the headline "It's a bird, it's a plane, no, it's Super Havana Hen"!'

He chortles merrily away, drowning in his own wit.

'I noticed from the label on the doorstopper you sent me that your hen is called Pertelote.'

'That was Bianca's suggestion. Don't ask me how she came up with it.'

'It's from *The Canterbury Tales*, the stories written by Chaucer in the Middle Ages.'

'Don't get all literary with me, matey.'

I ignore him. 'In *The Nun's Priest's Tale*, the favourite wife of the cockerel Chanticleer is Pertelote. Can you not see the obvious synergy of teaming up with CCT now? It could be a marriage made in heaven.'

'You could be right. I'm stunned that my missus knew about this bloke, Chaucer. Bianca's reading is strictly limited to luxury skincare-instruction leaflets and vegan diet books.'

'She may have hidden depths.'

'No, Bianca's skin deep, trust me, guv.'

'So are you interested in teaming up with Hennie?'

'You bet. Let's invite old Hennie Penny to the showroom when you're over next month. Richard's phobic about birds so it should be a good wind up. Well done. Count me in. I think this is going to be a blast!'

When he's off the line I sit and contemplate whether getting George involved with CCT is really such a good idea. After all, if it all goes belly up, I could well end up with serious egg on my face.

Three

ON THE SNAIL TRAIL

A cool sun floats just above the upper peaks of the Tramuntanas, robed in a soft mist that kisses the tips of the Aleppo pines and gnarled olive trees far below in the valley. The grasses are damp with dew and battalions of busy ants have already begun their daily travails, marching hither and thither along the cracks in the garden's old stone walls. Although we are now in May, it's a chilly morning, so I wear a long grey cardigan over my nightshirt. As usual I check the nesting compartment of the hen house, popping the four newly laid, warm brown eggs into one of my pockets. In the far corner of the corral we have erected the new boxes and I am delighted to find one of our wild hens, a black and white matron, already occupying one of them. She has a broody aspect, which makes me think that a batch of new chicks might be on the cards.

Cordelia, ever my faithful companion, pecks at my espadrilles for attention, so I bend down and pick her up, allowing her a splendid view of the grisly grey mountains beyond. She looks about her with serious eyes and makes a low, cooing sound when I stroke her feathers. Inko, our imperious, part-Siamese cat with a tail that curls bizarrely into a tight ball, regards me with some indignation from the outer perimeter, willing me to return to the kitchen to serve her breakfast. After offering my spoilt hen a handful of sunflower seeds, secreted in the other pocket of my cardigan, I gently place her on the ground and fill up the corn feeder for the rest of the mob.

No sooner has the tinkle of corn hit the feeder than ensues a veritable stampede and wild clucking as hens and cockerels appear as if from nowhere, cawing and flapping their wings as they descend on the booty. Ferdinand, aggressive as ever, begins attacking some of his harem, so I send him to the back of the queue. To my surprise he tries to peck at my sleeve. Such behaviour is bold even by naughty Ferdinand's standards. Perhaps I need to find a hen whisperer to cure him of his bad ways, should such a phenomenon exist. Cordelia stands apart from the pack, expecting exclusive treatment, unlike the cross-breeds that have found their way onto our land and spawned multiple chicks. I'm just dusting myself down when the Scotsman appears in the orchard. He frowns at me.

'Are you ready?'

'Of course. I wouldn't miss market day in Sóller. I was just communing with Cordelia.'

'But you're still in your night dress, and can I ask why you have two pink plastic clothes pegs in your hair?'

I place a hand on my head. 'Ah, that's because my fringe is so long that I can no longer see where I'm going.'

'Well, book a hair appointment with Marcos in Fornalutx, for heaven's sake.'

'Marcos is swamped. He can't squeeze me in until next Monday.'

'I could cut it for you,' he says cheerily. 'At a snip of the price!'

'Or of course I could hop on a plane to London to visit my former snippers in Hanover Square.'

He gives a snort. 'Nice try.'

I stride up the stone steps to the kitchen. Our choir of complaining cats stands in a united front at the back door. There's fat and fluffy grey Doughnut, so plump that he wheezes when he walks, twins Minky and Orlando, and regal Inko. Once fed, they sit washing their paws on the terracotta tiles of the kitchen before padding off to various warm and secret dugouts within the house, where they can slumber peacefully and undisturbed for most of the day.

Half an hour later, I am showered and dressed and looking forward to joining the throng of locals that hit the market, shops and cafés every Saturday in the town. Striding out onto the porch, I find the Scotsman and our neighbour Fernando engaged in animated conversation about snails. Fernando is standing in his lofty olive grove that overlooks our front garden and is issuing a series of *si, si, si's*, usually the preserve of the Scotsman when he has exhausted his linguistic repertoire in the Spanish language. I wave to Fernando and jump in the car with shopping bag in tow. When he has said his goodbyes, the Scotsman clambers into the driver's seat. I offer him a quizzical glance.

'Did I hear Fernando mumbling something about bowls of beer?'

'He's fed up with all the snails on his vegetable patch so I told him to give them beer.'

'Is that their favourite tipple?'

'No!' He tuts. 'It kills them.'

'That seems so cruel. Mind you, I suppose it's not a bad way to go.'

'With the snail season upon us, the blighters are everywhere. As soon as the rains come, they're like a plague.'

'I always think of good old Brian with his scarf on *The Magic Roundabout*.'

He chuckles. 'The children's TV programme? That goes back to the ark! Quite frankly the real Brians are far less appealing. Anyway, most will end up in the pot this month.'

'Poor chaps. It seems so sad that they rush to come out in the rain only to be caught and gobbled up.'

'*Es la vida*,' he sighs. 'The life of Brian.'

We set off, parking outside the town, which is just as well, as cars and people are milling in all directions. While the Scotsman heads off to buy the *Sóller*, *Veu de Sóller* and *Majorca Daily Bulletin* newspapers, I make for the market stalls. The bandstand area of the Plaça Constitució is overrun by craftspeople and huddles of teenagers vie for space, attempting to sell home-made cakes for 50 cents a slice.

'What are you raising money for?' I ask one young boy.

'We're going on a school trip to London and want some spending money,' he replies.

I pat his arm and offer him a euro. 'It's expensive. You're going to have to sell an awful lot of cakes, *mi amic*.'

As I potter about the stalls, Toful Colom, who is selling his sculptures, beckons me over.

'Come and meet Beatriz, my talented niece who is a well-known island illustrator, and also my sister Cati, the potter and artist.'

Is there no end to this family's talents? Beatriz shows me some of her beautiful illustrations, traditional Mallorcan women and girls in local historic costume and fantastical characters from some of the island's famed *rondalles*, folktales.

'I love the folktales and legends of Mallorca,' I tell Beatriz.

'Me too. Much of my work is based on them. Do you know about Maria Enganxa, the witch in the well?'

'Didn't she drown children?'

'Indeed. Legend has it that at the time of the Spanish Inquisition, she was living in Palma and because she was accused of being a witch, she was due to burn at the stake, but she escaped. The mob followed her to a field where she stood on top of an old well, promising to kill future generations of children for the crime against her. Then she threw herself into its depths.'

'A cheerful tale for children.'

'To this day it is said that any child leaning over wells and cisterns might be caught with a hook by Maria and drowned.'

'I suppose it's one way of stopping young children from misbehaving,' I reply. 'Of course the master of the *rondalles* was Antoni Maria Alcover.'

Beatriz nods enthusiastically. 'So true!'

Antoni Maria Alcover was born in the town of Manacor in 1862 and packed an incredible career into his 69 years of life. Aside from becoming a leading light in the Catholic priesthood, he created *Diccionari Alcover-Moll*, the first official Catalan etymological dictionary, with his collaborator Francesc de Borja Moll, which is now available online. He also recorded the island's many legends and fairy tales in 24 volumes, under the pseudonym Jordi d'es Racó, and wrote countless books. Somehow he also fitted in journalistic work and architectural projects.

Alan appears with the newspapers tucked under his arm and, after chatting with Toful, suggests we head to Café Paris for coffee. This well-known café on the main square used to be run by my good chum José, but when the lease expired, he decided to look for new horizons elsewhere and took up a position in a popular restaurant in the port. Meanwhile the new management tried valiantly to keep the existing loyal clientele happy. After a slightly challenging start, with some residents grumbling about the change of décor, the café began to run like clockwork and Carmelo, the head waiter, and his team successfully managed to win over both locals and expats alike. He comes up to our table, a huge smile on his face. '*Hola mis amigos*! The usual?'

I nod. 'Have all the croissants gone?'

'You're in luck. Just two left waiting for you.'

The Scotsman opens the *Veu de Sóller* and shows me images of the recent Easter parades and mouth-watering pictures of various gastronomic delights of the season. Unlike in the UK, Easter in Mallorca is not awash with chocolate eggs and bunnies, but is rather a more sober affair. All the same, most Mallorcans use the occasion to enjoy their favourite Easter bakes such as *panades*, pies stuffed with lamb and peas, or sweet half-moon shaped *robiols* and *crespells*, pastries filled with custard, angelica or chocolate. As we're tucking into our croissants and coffee, Juana, Pep's wife, bustles over, her hands weighed down with shopping. Angel, their teenage son, hovers bashfully behind. We exchange news as she has been away visiting family on the mainland for two weeks and agree to meet for supper at Es Turo restaurant in Fornalutx the following evening. Angel leans forward and asks me if Ollie will be home from the UK in time for the Moors and Christians fiesta, Sóller's most celebrated event. He looks disappointed when I explain that his half-term break isn't for another few weeks.

'But he'll also be missing the snail races and festival in San Jordi tomorrow. I'm going with my dad.'

'Can I come?' I ask.

He shrugs warily. 'If you like. I thought you didn't like snails?'

'I'm rather fond of them actually. Just don't like eating them,' I reply.

Juana is about to take her leave when she taps my arm.

'You'll be amazed to hear that Pep has given up all his ridiculous wine-making activities. As you know, I've been nagging him for some time to let me use the cellar for pickling and vegetable storage and so while I was away he got rid of everything. He was never any good at viniculture. Thank heavens he finally saw sense.'

The Scotsman looks white at the gills. 'Excellent! But where did he put all his old wine making equipment and the bottles he'd laid down?'

'All given away,' she says breezily. 'I'm sorry if he didn't think to offer you some.'

I give the Scotsman a knowing look. 'How odd that Pep should forget you.'

'Well, I'm sure it was just an oversight,' the Scotsman smiles, recovering his equilibrium. 'He's always so busy.'

'Busy doing nothing!' Juana laughs. 'Well you can take him to task when we meet for dinner.'

'I'll do just that,' he replies cheerily.

After she's left, he shakes his head. 'Another fine mess Pep has got me into!'

Back at the house, as we haul our baskets of shopping out of the car, Judas rings. To my dismay it is Manuel Ramirez, a long-standing hotelier client from Panama who owns the H Hotel Group, comprising an assortment of chic five-star properties in Europe, America and Russia. He has just purchased his second luxury hotel in Russia, this time in Moscow, which he intends to name Le Coq d'Or, the Golden Cockerel. Manuel is his usual secret squirrel self, whispering hoarsely into the receiver.

'I must be brief because my mobile is probably bugged.'

'By whom?' I ask. Manuel's paranoia knows no bounds. If it's not the FBI or CIA apparently pursuing him, then it's the Mafia, Russian mobsters and Colombian hit men. He either watched too many James Bond films as a boy or there's a grain of truth in his fantasies: hopefully not.

'The KGB or perhaps...'

'The KGB was disbanded, Manuel.'

A hollow laugh. 'That's what they want you to think. I know better. Anyway, I haven't time for this. I just wanted to advise you that the new hotel will open next March.'

'That gives us plenty of time to plan the launch.'

'Have you had any thoughts about that?'

I sit on the wall of the porch and decide to offer a tongue-in-cheek response. 'Well you could always get the Moscow Philharmonic

Orchestra to come to the hotel and perform operatic cameos from *The Golden Cockerel* by Nikolai Rimsky-Korsakov. Then, as the orchestra strikes the last note, tiny cockerels manufactured from gold foil descend from the ceilings to the delight of the gathered throng.'

Silence.

I laugh. 'Just joking, Manuel.'

He hisses animatedly into the receiver. 'An excellent idea. I will speak immediately with my contacts in Moscow but this is not a cheap option.'

I'm somewhat nonplussed that he's taken me at my word. 'The orchestra would cost a fortune to hire!'

'Leave it to me,' he says, adding mysteriously, 'I am owed a favour.'

The line goes dead. The Scotsman raises an eyebrow.

'Was that mad Manuel?'

'It was indeed. I pulled his leg about hiring the Moscow Philharmonic Orchestra to perform *The Golden Cockerel* for the launch of his new hotel and he took me seriously.'

'Actually it's a good idea,' he replies.

'When I was researching the opera on Google, I discovered that it was premiered in Moscow in 1909. You may recall that was the very same year that English fossil hunter, Dorothea Bate, discovered the remains of Myotragus, Mallorca's extinct little mouse-goat.'

'Oh don't get started on that old goat again,' he sighs. 'Anyway, I must get on. I've got to plant the aubergines.' He strides purposefully towards the orchard while I dawdle on the porch, musing about Myotragus and how important the creature was to the world of science, albeit having died out 3,000 years ago. My thoughts are interrupted by the sound of loud croaking from the pond and, to my consternation, I see that a heron has just landed on one of the rocks and is eyeing up the mass of tadpoles wriggling on the surface of the water. Clapping my hands, I rush over to the patio and watch as, with an indignant cry, the predator soars off into the blue sky.

'You took your time,' scoffs Johnny, peering out at me from behind some bushy weeds. 'We could have all been annihilated for all you care.'

I give a tut. 'Nonsense. I was on the case.'

'Next thing you know, those viperine snakes will be back in the pond, snapping and hissing at our heels.'

'I hope not. If you see one, just holler.'

He blinks. 'And about those cockerels. There's one pain in the neck that's driving us mad. He's up here all the time looking at his reflection in the water and pecking at the lilies.'

'That'll be Ferdinand. He's acting very strangely of late. I'll have to keep a close eye on him.'

Someone is calling to me from the terraced orchard above our front garden. A moment later, my neighbour, Fernando, comes into view and stares down at me as I hover by the pond.

'I told my mother Pepita about your husband's idea to feed our snails beer and just found her plying a pile of them with a bowl of it on the kitchen table. She'd even laid out cutlery and napkins for them as if they were luncheon guests.'

'Oh dear. I take it her condition's not getting any better?'

'The doctor says it's just old age. She is ninety-eight after all. He gave her some sort of medication but to be honest, a glass of red wine seems to do her more good.'

'I'm not surprised,' I reply. 'Best form of medication that I know. But given her current snail antics, don't tell her to have a quick slug, or she might take you literally and bite off more than she can chew!'

The sun is sitting high in the sky, its golden rays resting on the rich red soil and rows of olive trees and vines that are characteristic of the central area of the island. A gentle wind courses through the open window, caressing the map that I am studying, while the Scotsman concentrates on the driving. We are on the outskirts of Binissalem, famous for its wine production, but today we are en route to an establishment that has garnered my curiosity in the local press: a *cargol* or, rather, snail farm, which boasts a gastropod gastronomic restaurant.

'According to the map, we should take the next left, head under a tunnel and follow the signs.'

The Scotsman yawns. 'Shouldn't you have called first? I mean it's a bit of a cheek turning up without an appointment.'

'I always believe in the element of surprise.'

'Hm, well others may not! And to think you don't even like eating snails.'

'True, but I'm still interested to learn about Mallorcan gastropods.'

No sooner have we left the small tunnel than a sign depicting an enormous snail comes into view.

'That's it! Sa Caragolera. We're here.'

We drive into neatly maintained grounds and park in front of what appears to be a large, screened enclosure. As we stretch our legs, admiring the blissfully tranquil location of the rural idyll, a door opens and a tall and smiling man heads towards us.

'Are you lost?' he asks.

'Not at all. We rather wanted to visit your snail farm. Is that possible?'

'By all means.'

We make our introductions and shake hands. Our host informs us that he is Toni.

'Luckily my son, Miquel Angel, and I have no immediate appointments. It's nice to have English visitors. They're a rarity.'

I contemplate this fact, surmising that many Britons are probably, like me, a little coy about snail gastronomy. I've never had a penchant for the famed French *petits-gris* or the large, fleshy *Bourgognes* that have Parisians drooling. It's the same with frog legs, but that's another matter. A moment later, a handsome young blade arrives at his father's side. This, we learn, is 29-year-old Miquel Angel Salom, and the brains behind the business. Having studied economics at the local university, he came up with the idea of running a snail emporium, with the approval of his family, and four years later is reaping the benefits.

Having had their morning thrown into disarray, it is extraordinary how charming and welcoming the pair are. First we visit the hygienic cold stores where live snails, purged of any impurities and cleaned, await collection by scores of eager clients. Miquel Angel explains how important it is that the snails are kept in the right climatic conditions for freshness. Next we visit the ice-cold freezer where cleaned and prepared snails are kept for those customers who prefer to buy them frozen. And then, happily, we are out in the sunshine once more, striding towards the rectangular enclosure where the pampered snails breed in somewhat luxurious surroundings. Admittedly, they aren't provided with miniature sun loungers or deckchairs, but the main variety, *Helix aspersa maxima*, known as bovers, is free to roam in large grassy zones in which tantalising titbits of fresh beetroot, broccoli, cabbage and chard are provided. Fine water-sprayers hydrate the wards at intervals and tiny snail huts and shady retreats are provided.

'We have thousands of snails breeding and living here,' says Miquel Angel. 'They really have a happy life and only eat the very best produce.'

'It does look rather like the peaceful shires from *The Hobbit*,' I muse.

He smiles. 'I'm glad you think so. You know it takes seven to nine months for a snail to gestate, so this is a long process and as a breeder you have to have bags of patience.'

The Scotsman gives a snort. 'So it takes some time to get a return on your investment?'

'Maybe, but the snails are all at different stages, so we still manage to produce about three tonnes per year for sale. Of course this is a fraction of what is consumed annually on the island.'

'So how many snails are you talking about?' I ask.

'At least thirty tonnes. Although many of those are frozen imports from South America or Africa.'

'Are they not as good?'

'No, the taste and texture is completely different. Fresh snails are far better.'

'That's presumably why so many Mallorcans can be seen picking them along the hedgerows in May.'

Toni gives a tut. 'You know that it's not recommended or even legal to collect snails in woods and on the roadside. Some wild snails eat carrion so are contaminated. Imagine consuming a snail that had eaten some dead matter that turned out to be poisonous.'

It has been well publicised that the regional government is discouraging the gathering of snails for health and safety reasons. Fans of gastropod cuisine are instead being encouraged to purchase pure *cargols* from a legitimate source where they have been fed best-quality vegetables. Rumour has it that local police officers are even issuing a one-euro fine per snail if caught.

He leads us out into the fresh air. 'Come on, now you must see our restaurant and showroom. We are proud to be the only Mallorcan snail farm offering a snail gastronomic menu on the premises.'

We arrive in the showroom: a contemporary area with an inviting restaurant, capable of seating up to 50 guests. I study the menu. 'Oh dear, I don't think I could handle such a lavish banquet, inviting though it must be to snail connoisseurs.'

'Oh come on! It would put hairs on your chest,' opines the Scotsman with a wink.

'That's what I'm worried about,' I mumble.

'Did you know that snails are regarded as the new super food and contain protein, iron and vitamin B12? And what about *baba*?' says Miquel Angel.

I wrinkle my nose. 'Snail-slime cream? I don't find the idea of slathering my face with it very appealing.'

'Good for wrinkles,' he says with a grin.

'In that case we should invest in a few vats,' replies the Scotsman, skilfully avoiding my sideways kick.

'Tell me, do you know when snails became part of the Mallorcan diet?' I ask.

'There's historic evidence that residents as far back as the Phoenicians and Romans enjoyed them,' pipes up Toni. 'Since then, *cargols* have really become a part of our national culture. In fact, historically, Mallorcan families across the social strata would gather on special occasions to share a *caragolera*, a snail broth.'

We walk back out into the sunshine and, with Toni as guide, spend some time admiring the healthy fruit and olive orchards that surround the farm. After our leisurely tour, the Scotsman looks at his watch, reminding me that we are in danger of overstaying our welcome.

As we say our goodbyes and exchange hugs, Miquel Angel and Toni urge us to re-visit in order to sample some of their gourmet gastropods. We promise to return but it'll take some *bon courage* for me to place a snail on my fork. I might be tempted to experiment with *baba de cargol* first, purely in the interests of science, of course!

Later, as we head up the dark and winding mountain road to meet Pep and Juana for supper at Es Turo in Fornalutx, I observe many a ghostly figure caught in the headlights stowing snails, in time-honoured tradition, into plastic bags at the side of the road. It seems that the new regulations passed by the regional government are being studiously ignored.

'The road is alive with snail pickers,' I say.

The Scotsman nods. 'Snails cost ten euros per kilo, so if they can get them for nothing, who can blame them? It's the same with wild asparagus at this time of the year. It's discouraged for road safety reasons but no one gives two hoots.'

'So when are we going asparagus hunting?'

'Tomorrow?' he suggests with a mischievous smile.

Four

FEATHERING THE NEST

There's a spit of rain in the air but I keep on running, wincing as my tired feet hit the hard cobbles, one of the hallmarks of the beautiful city of Prague. This is my eighth marathon, and once again I'm wondering what on earth I thought I was doing signing up for another 26 miles of physical torture. Then I recall that I'm raising money for orphans in Sri Lanka and upbraid myself. I look at my watch: 3½ hours down, hopefully only 30 minutes to go – or less – if I get my act together. It is a beautiful mild day in May and the soft blue sky is streaked with dazzling sunlight that spills onto the leafy avenue before me. Along with my fellow sufferers I have jogged through the historic city, run alongside the magnificent Vltava River, crossed the famed Charles Bridge and am now on the home stretch, heading for the old town square. And thank heavens for that!

Crowds of well-wishers are lining the traffic-free streets, with many cheerily yelling out platitudes such as 'You can do it!' and 'Nearly there!' That might indeed be the case but to my rubbery legs, another 3 kilometres suddenly seems like an awfully long way to go. I think back to the good-luck text messages I received earlier. Greedy George had predictably written 'Break a leg!' while Ollie sent me tons of luck signing off with 'Yours from the Gulag.' As I turn a corner, I'm surprised and delighted when a small boy waving a Union Jack flag shouts out my name. It is emblazoned on the complimentary T-shirt I am wearing, which was sent to me by a friend and is proving to be a great way of connecting with spectators along the course. I give him a grateful wave and quicken my pace to show that I'm not as weak and wimpish as I might appear. Who am I kidding? In the distance now I can hear a lively band striking up and the outline of what appears to be a bank of white and red balloons comes into view.

Minutes go by and every part of me is aching. I realise that each time I do a marathon, it becomes a little bit tougher and requires more effort. Surely it's not the onset of old age? I refuse to cave in to such a notion! The poor old knees are wobbling and my calves throb but I remind myself that in order to continue eating with the enthusiasm of a truffle-hunting hog, I must continue my running regime. There's nothing else for it as diets are strictly off limits and I relish my food and wine. An elderly runner to my left looks fit to drop but doggedly pushes ahead, his feet barely lifting from the ground as he staggers on. I offer him a thumbs-up sign and point to the mirage ahead. He offers a smile and nods. The balloons are now in focus, mountains of them in different hues, and frenetic music is seeping from enormous speakers. A massive throng of people is excitedly leaning over barricades by a huge inflatable gateway that sports a digital clock. They are whistling and clapping as each exhausted runner schleps past the finishing line, relief etched on their faces. Suddenly I hear laughter: someone close by is calling my name. I turn to see the Scotsman and my good old chum, Jane, waving and pointing to the finishing line just ahead. A moment later I sprint through the arch and, with some euphoria, accept a medal and warming silver foil cape from a cheery Czech official. As I make my way through the crowds, Jane and the Scotsman rush over to greet me. Both seem extremely merry.

'We've had such a wonderful day,' enthuses Jane. 'The beer is fantastic here! We've been visiting some wonderful bars while you've been running.'

The Scotsman nods in agreement. 'Yes, we were thinking about next year's race. We'll have to choose somewhere that has decent wine or beer. I rather like the idea of Munich or Rome...'

'Or Venice perhaps?' moots Jane. 'That's my favourite option.'

'Who says I'm going to run another marathon?'

They turn to me with frowns.

'Now don't be difficult, Ans,' cautions Jane. 'It makes for such a lovely weekend and it's important that we find somewhere that suits us all.'

'Remember you've always said that you'd like to run at least ten marathons,' adds the Scotsman.

Jane smiles encouragingly. 'And look how fit it makes you. You can eat whatever you like the rest of the year. Now, about Venice...'

'But it would be a nightmare. Imagine crossing all those bridges.'

'Oh I'm sure you'd take it all in your stride,' adds the Scotsman in a placatory tone. 'Jane and I will look at flights and accommodation. You just worry about the running.'

'Did you actually see any of the race today?' I quiz.

'Of course,' replies the Scotsman vaguely. 'There were some very handy drinking dens situated at most of the key stages. We saw you whizz by on several occasions.'

As we walk away from the melee, I see a rather inviting bar. 'I don't know about you two but I could do with a nice cold beer after all that exertion.'

'We've already had a few!' giggles Jane. 'Are you sure it won't go straight to your head?'

'*My* head?!' I splutter. 'Maybe you should worry more about your own!'

'Well I suppose we could have just one more for the road,' grins the Scotsman.

'My round!' trills Jane and heads for the counter.

I pull out a chair and sit down gingerly, with a sharp intake of breath as I do so.

'You poor old thing,' remarks my husband. 'Just relax. An ice cold beer's on the way.'

A group of German runners at an adjoining table raises their glasses in our direction.

'Did you do a good time?' asks a blond-haired youth, his victory medal hanging from his neck.

'Just under four hours,' I reply.

'Well done.'

'How about you?'

He smiles bashfully. 'The thing is that we are all experienced runners so we finished in less than three hours. Your time is very good for your age. I am Moritz, by the way.'

I'm starting to go off my new friend, Moritz.

'Will you do another?' he asks.

The Scotsman butts in. 'Of course. It'll be Venice next year.'

'That's brave,' one of his chums exclaims. 'I've heard it's a tough course. Seven bridges, aren't there?'

I'm about to protest when Jane arrives back at the table, brimming over with enthusiasm.

'Fourteen actually, but they're tiny. Nothing to fret about. The marathon starts at historical Villa Pisani in a lovely country town and courses into Venice via the Liberty Bridge along the Riviera del Brenta. Just think of the magnificent views... And there are some lovely bars on the route. We're all very excited.'

I eye her suspiciously. She's certainly done her homework on the Venice marathon – or at least its drinking dens. No doubt she's been secretly mugging up on it in advance of this trip.

'So you two will also be running it?' asks one of the runners at the next table.

'Good heavens, no!' laughs Jane. 'We're not that mad. We'll be there to cheer her on.'

Indeed, from the comfort of a convivial Italian bar, no doubt.

'So you accompany your friend on all her marathon trips?' Moritz asks.

'We do our best,' replies Jane magnanimously.

The man turns to me. 'You must be thrilled to have such a wonderful support team?'

'Oh yes, they're both a tower of strength,' I mutter.

The Scotsman enjoys the moment, smiling beatifically as he raises his glass. 'Indeed, what else are friends and husbands for?'

It's Monday morning. I sit on a wall outside the country station of Amberley in West Sussex, waiting for Greedy George to arrive in his chariot, or rather his latest gas-guzzling, top-of-the-range olive-hued four-by-four. Although he had suggested that Hennie visit his showroom in London, she insisted that we first meet her *in situ* at her farm on the South Downs in order to see the charity's work in action and to meet some of her rescued hens. Somewhat moodily George agreed, offering to pick me up in Amberley, where he and his toothpick-thin wife Bianca happened to be staying with friends for the weekend. Luckily, after flying in from Prague late the night before and staying at my chum Jane's flat, I was able to catch a direct train from Victoria station first thing this morning. Hopefully this will mean that I'll only have to suffer a limited period in the car with George behind the wheel.

A cobalt-blue sky smiles down at me while puffy popcorn-shaped clouds bob on the horizon. There's the smell of freshly mown grass and the twitter of sparrows – the rural England of my childhood. I'm rudely awakened from my reverie by an urgent tooting. George has skidded to a halt outside the station and is blasting the horn.

'Stop it! You're frightening the birds,' I hiss as I clamber into the passenger seat.

'Oh don't go all *Sound of Music* on me, guv,' he guffaws. 'I see you're as fluorescent white as ever. No one would believe you lived in bleeding Spain.'

'That's because I spend too much time at my desk indoors dealing with pesky e-mails and phone calls from you.'

'You love it, really! Mind you, I like the new haircut. Very *Thoroughly Modern Millie.*'

'My lovely local hairdresser is from Brazil.'

'Isn't that where the nuts come from?' Laughing, he revs the engine and roars up the otherwise silent lane. 'So how was the marathon?'

'Painful.'

'That'll teach you. Anyway, talking of nuts, according to my satnav, Hennie's farm is only about twenty minutes from here.'

'We don't know that she's nutty yet.'

'Come on! She knits jumpers for hens, for Christ's sake. Nutty with a capital N. Now listen, I've got an important meeting with the architect and builders this afternoon in London, so I don't want to hang about.'

'Fine by me. So how is the re-design for the showroom going?'

'It's a nightmare, guv. The builders are pulling the place apart and Richard's being such a queen about the mess. Any excuse to get his feather duster out.'

'What does Bianca think about it?'

'How many times do I have to keep telling you? Bianca doesn't think. She was replaced by an alien at birth.'

'You're so mean.' I stifle a grin. Having met his rather vain and vacant wife on various occasions, it would be fair to say that the only things that really seem to float her boat are plastic surgery procedures, luxury spas and designer goods.

George rattles on. 'As long as I keep buying her branded gear from Bond Street, and she's still thin enough to fit through the eye of a needle, she's happy. I could be running a fish stall for all she cares as long as it kept her in Prada handbags.'

I'm mightily relieved that my seatbelt is fastened as George tears along the road like an unstoppable rocket. There's a sudden hysterical edge to the satnav's automatic voice as we bump violently over sleeping policemen and screech around corners. Once on empty country roads, George really puts his foot down, which elicits a series of loud and urgent-sounding bing-bings and ringing bells from the satnav. The plummy disembodied female voice develops a frantic tone, telling George to 'Reduce speed now. I repeat, reduce speed now!'

'I wish she'd put a sock in it.'

'Can't you slow down or turn her off?'

'No can do. I used to have a cool gay Aussie guy on the satnav but Bianca switched it to this dreary woman and now I can't get rid of the old bat. She gets on my nerves.'

As he increases his speed, I slip down into my seat and grab the handgrip on the passenger door.

'Chicken!' giggles George above the sound of the engine. My heart leaps when, amid the increasingly manic bings and bongs, comes the insistent blast of a submarine alarm.

'Good God, what's that?' I yell at him.

'Oh I don't know. This satnav has a mind of its own. I think that alarm goes off when you're driving at over ninety miles per hour.'

To my horror, he takes one hand off the wheel to fiddle with the satnav's controls. 'Can't find the button to turn off the sound...'

'Leave it!' I screech. 'It's fine. Just concentrate on the road.'

'Keep your hair on, guv,' he chortles as we hurtle around another sharp bend. 'I thought you were supposed to be more *mañana* since living in the sticks.'

I shut my eyes tightly and say a silent prayer to my guardian angel – and George's, too. Hopefully they haven't already bolted from the car.

Fifteen minutes later the car bounces along a muddy track that leads to a large gravel courtyard. An elegant country house in Tudor style with accompanying barns and stables appears before us. I descend the vehicle with jelly legs.

'Need a ladder?' gurgles George. 'Who'd have thought you'd just run a marathon?'

An elderly woman in country tweeds strides towards us, her grey hair partly masked by a sumptuous gold silk scarf. As she nears us I notice that it is dotted with tiny hen motifs.

'I like the scarf,' grins George wolfishly.

'A vintage Hermès,' Hennie replies in crisp tones. 'Do come in and have a coffee.'

'A double brandy might be better,' I mumble.

She turns to me. 'Prefer a brandy? No problem.'

'Oh no, thanks,' I reply with a forced chuckle. 'Just joking about George's driving.'

'Well, one can't be too careful on these roads, you know. Our local farmer lost control of his delivery van last month and all his eggs went tumbling out onto the road. One big omelette!' She roars with laughter.

'I hope he was alright,' I reply.

'Oh, fine.' She waves her hands in the air dismissively as she leads us through the house and into a cosy study. 'He broke both arms and a few ribs but nothing much else. Only concussed for a week so not much to complain about, eh?'

I offer her a weak smile as she rings a bell loudly near my ear.

'Anthea, my housekeeper, will bring the coffee and cake in a minute. First of all, meet Archie.'

Greedy George, who has settled into a comfy armchair in front of the fire, bristles when he hears a squawk from behind the sofa.

Our eyes follow the sound and widen when they alight on a large, fluffy white hen strutting towards us wearing a bright-orange jumper. Its legs and feet are covered with thick snowy hair, as is its head, which has the appearance of a white fur muffler.

'What *is* that?' exclaims George, aghast.

'This is Archie, my Silkie.'

'Silkie? Yeti, more like! Is that a Cossack's hat on its head?'

'That is his natural plumage, George. Silkies are a rare and exotic breed.'

'So what's with the jumper?' George persists. 'He's one hip dude.'

Anthea, a small, rotund woman in a pinny, bustles into the room and places a tray laden with crockery onto a mahogany table. She begins pouring coffee from a china pot. Hennie fixes her penetrating blue eyes on George.

'The reason Archie is wearing a jumper is because he has lost most of his body plumage. He was ill treated by a farmer in Somerset and was luckily rescued by an animal sanctuary and passed on to me.'

'Poor old chap,' I say. 'How long will it take for his feathers to grow back?'

'Could be months,' she replies briskly. 'You should see the state of some of the battery-farm hens we rescue.'

'Oh I can't bear battery farms. It breaks my heart to see the poor hens in those horrible conditions,' I say with passion.

George rolls his eyes and pretends to dab at non-existent tears. I scowl at him.

'Yes, it's a dreadful state of affairs. That's why we try to encourage people only to buy eggs from farms where hens are well-treated and left to roam freely.' She turns her attention to Anthea, who is dithering by the table.

'Could you pass round the cups, dear?'

Obediently her housekeeper serves up the coffee together with thick slices of fruitcake.

'So who makes all your hen sweaters?' asks George, as he shovels cake into his mouth.

'We have dozens of volunteers making jumpers for us and of course it's particularly important to have a good stock for winter when temperatures drop. So often the poor old battery hens that we rescue have no feathers at all. Bald as coots!'

'You don't provide them with cardigans and onesies, too?' giggles George.

'No, but we have recently developed an outdoor, yellow fluorescent jacket for them.'

George gulps down his cake. 'You are kidding?'

'Of course not,' she replies indignantly. 'Sometimes our inmates manage to escape through the garden gates and fly onto the track, so the fluorescent jackets are a way of alerting passing traffic to their presence.'

George stifles a guffaw and pulls an envelope out of his slipcase. 'Well, you might like a brand new concept for your hens.' He passes her a piece of cartridge paper on which there are various pencil drawings.

'Is this a cape?' asks Hennie.

'Spot on. I thought if we collaborated on your Chick-Knit gig, I could knock up a few hundred of these in leather for your old girls at the same time.'

'It's rather chic and would keep them warm in the winter. How does it fasten?'

Greedy George gives her a wink and reaches into his slipcase. 'Here's a prototype.'

He holds up a tiny, black shiny leather cape with a Velcro fastener at the neck.

In some excitement, Hennie clasps her hands together and pounces on the hapless Archie.

'Here, you can be our model.' She takes the cape from George and drapes it on the startled cockerel, fastening it around the neck.

I can't hide my amusement as the bird struts disdainfully about the room as if he's an emperor.

'I love it!' cries Hennie. 'It'll be perfect for wearing out of doors in the inclement weather.'

'Great. I'll get cracking then.' He pauses for effect. 'Thought I'd call it the Havana Cape-on.'

'Cape-on!' Hennie screeches with delight, slapping her thighs as she wipes tears of laughter from her eyes. Worryingly, this seems to be a marriage made in heaven. She and George are evidently as bonkers as each other.

She puts down her coffee cup. 'So, my friends, I think it's time to meet the gang in the orchards.'

I stand up and walk towards the door. 'How many hens and cockerels have you got?'

'About five hundred,' she replies airily.

'That's some number,' I reply.

'It certainly is and as they all have names, it's going to take some time to introduce each of them to you.' She strides out of the room. 'Come along!'

When George gives me a look of dismay I pat his shoulder sympathetically. 'It's all your own fault for egging her on.'

'Oh, the wit!' he volleys back.

I whisper in his ear. 'What you need, Caruthers, is a more *mañana* attitude because somehow I think we're going to be here for quite some time.'

Before heading back to Mallorca, I stay another night in London so that I can catch up with some journalist colleagues and friends. Rather pressingly, I have agreed to meet Ed at Waterstones bookshop in Piccadilly as he seems to be in a state about his new job. I walk into the basement café and find him brooding over a pot of tea and enormous slice of chocolate cake.

'Cheer up! It may never happen.'

He stares at me with fear-filled eyes. 'That's just the trouble. It already has.' Instinctively I see him reach for his life-saving rucksack, which I have given the acronym MEK, meaning Medical Emergency Kit. Ed has filled it with all manner of medicinal items that he believes will be of benefit in any crisis.

'What's already happened?'

'I received my first warning.'

'What? You've only been in the job five minutes.'

'I had a bit of a problem connecting up the sound equipment for a lesson and then, rather more disastrously, I forgot to go to a school assembly.'

'Does that really matter?' I ask.

'It does when you're supposed to be in charge of the music and microphones.'

'Ah.' I order a double espresso and scone from the waitress and sit back in my chair. 'Well, it could be worse. You could have set the whole school on fire.'

'For heaven's sake, don't tempt fate, Scatters.'

He pushes a tome in my direction. 'At least I can take comfort in books. I've just bought one of those creepy Swedish crime novels guaranteed to give me palpitations.'

I examine the cover. 'I wish I had a good bookshop on my doorstep in Sóller. We used to have Calabruix but when my friend Marga died quite suddenly, it had to close.'

'Couldn't anyone else have kept it going?'

'Well, her partner Margalida tried, but she was too sad to continue. It wouldn't have been the same. It's a hairdressing salon now.'

'The way of the world,' he says gloomily. 'Towns are cluttered with hairdressers, building societies and mobile phone outlets now.'

'You're right. Still, at least we have the Universal Bookshop in Portals Nous, which offers a good selection of British titles, and there's a new shop in Palma called Come In.'

'That's rather an amusing name. So, tell me, what am I going to do?'

'It's simple. Just keep your head down and work hard and try to ingratiate yourself with the boss whenever you can. Presumably you apologised for the minor cock-ups, so with any luck, the school will put it down to teething problems.'

'Hm, we'll see,' Ed muses. 'I'm not sure I suit this kind of school. It's very serious. I thought comprehensives were pleasantly laid-back but not a bit of it.'

'It seems that these days school life is all about regurgitating bite-size pieces of information for exams. Nothing else matters any more.'

He looks at me with alarm. 'Do you think I should throw in the towel?'

'Certainly not. Rela would have your guts for garters and I wouldn't blame her. She's a saint as it is putting up with you. Anyway, tell me about the wedding plans.'

He takes a glug of tea and brightens up. 'We've set the date for 25 July. Many of Rela's friends and relatives will be flying over, but we're keeping it quite low key. We don't have an enormous budget.'

'Don't worry about that. When you get to our age, it should surely just be about having a fun time with friends, not pushing the boat out?'

'If you say so. So you survived the marathon?'

'Well the legs are still a bit stiff but they won't take long to recover.'

'I hope you won't be insane enough to contemplate another one.'

'Are you joking? Jane's already hoodwinked me into doing Venice next year.'

'That's madness! It gives me heart tremors just thinking about running all those miles.'

'Still,' I say conspiratorially, 'I've had an idea to walk part of the Camino de Santiago later this year and I'm going to challenge Jane to walk it with me.'

'Is that the long hike through the northern part of Spain?'

'It certainly is. Of course we wouldn't have time to walk it all, but perhaps we could squeeze two weeks from our busy lives.'

He eyes me anxiously. 'How long is the route?'

'About seven hundred and ninety kilometres, but we'd only aim for about three hundred, I reckon, especially carrying heavy rucksacks.'

'Only?!' He fans himself with his crime novel. 'And you have to carry your own luggage? What a nightmare. If I know Jane, she'll never agree to such a thing.'

'She's a great walker, you know, and she likes a challenge. Besides, it'll be one way of getting my own back on her for hoodwinking me into running the Venice marathon.'

'But she doesn't speak any Spanish. She'll be completely at your mercy.'

'Yes,' I say with a grin. 'It's a rather delicious thought.'

Richard is pacing around the showroom with a face like thunder and whirling a feather duster about in the air in the manner of a wand, rather like a skit on the good fairy.

He thrusts it in my direction. 'I tell you, George is really pushing his luck. First he expects me to run the shop while builders are knocking down walls and drilling all day long, and then he informs me that he's going to introduce hen doorstoppers.'

'What's wrong with that?'

He puffs out his bottom lip to form a dramatic pout. 'Aside from it being an absurd idea, I am fowl-phobic.' He pauses. 'I hate hens.'

I rear back in horror. 'Why?'

'For one thing, they're smelly and noisy and they also have horrible, clawed yellow feet, tiny slitty eyes and let's not even start on their beaks!'

'But what about their wonderful plumage?'

'I can't stand feathers.'

'Oh really?' I point to his duster.

'That's different. It's an inanimate object, and I'll tell you something else. My grandmother used to say that touching a hen's drinking bowl gave you warts.'

'That's ridiculous.'

'Is it? Don't blame me when you find your hands looking like something out of a horror movie.'

I laugh. 'Come on, Richard. The Chick-Knit event will be fun and wait till you see George's leather hen capes.'

His mouth drops open. 'What are you talking about? Chick-Knit? Hen capes? I think I'm going to have a fit of the vapours.'

George has evidently chickened out of broaching the subject with him. Richard stands with his hands on his hips in defensive pose.

He fans himself with the duster. 'Well, tell me the worst.'

I take a deep breath. 'It's a long story but there's an elderly lady named Hennie…'

It's late by the time we arrive home. The Scotsman gallantly drove to Palma airport to meet my London flight and now unloads my small suitcase and rucksack from the car and carries them into the house. I dally in the courtyard, drinking in the aromatic air, the fragrance of jasmine keener than ever at this late hour. Tilting my head upwards, I admire a treacly sky brimming with white stars and, in the stillness of the night, hear the unmistakable cry of a Scops owl, the first of the season. The ghostly sound, a sharp, methodical sonar beep, is overlayered by the rasping croaks of our frogs and whispering cicadas and the occasional night-time howl of the valley's hounds. I think back to my frenetic week in Prague and London and sigh happily to be back in my beloved valley. It's always fun to travel but nothing can beat the homecoming at dusk: the smell of earth and spent wood smoke, the tranquillity and sound of tinkling sheep bells in the velvety hills. Allowing myself one last blissful glance at the magnificent dark and craggy Tramuntanas, I turn to the house and, yawning, make my way upstairs, content to be home again and back in my own comfy bed, serenaded by my incomparable musical frogs.

Five

MOORS AND MYTHS

A sliver of bright sunlight filters through the shutters, prompting me to open first one bleary eye and then the other. The Scotsman has a pillow placed over his head but I can still hear the words 'Kill the cockerel' being muttered like a mantra. It's true that from four o'clock in the morning, our dawn chorus begins. Carlos strikes up first and within a few minutes has set the pace for every cockerel in the valley. Somehow I've luckily become immune to the noise, whereas my slumbering husband seems to wake at the first squawk. He sits up in bed and rubs his eyes.

'It's seven o'clock already. Might as well get up. Cup of tea?'

He doesn't wait for a response, knowing that without my first cup of strong, black Darjeeling, I'm incapable of conducting any kind of normal conversation. This is our daily ritual, rarely interrupted, unless by a random, early visitor of human, cat, hen or amphibian kind.

No sooner has he disappeared downstairs to the kitchen than I hear the buzzer at the gate.

I wander over to the front window that overlooks the courtyard, imagining that it might be a neighbour or an early delivery – but no.

Staring through the gates is a small, serious-looking man wearing a sombre suit and tie. I watch as he speaks into the intercom. The Scotsman must have opened the gate for him. I hop back into the warm bed, resolving that I'm not going to get up for a few more luxurious minutes. My husband blunders back into the room.

'Can you believe that it's a Jehovah's Witness calling? The fellow's called Matias Sastre. I've just opened the gate for him and told him to wait until I throw on some clothes.'

'Couldn't you have just politely sent him away?'

He shakes his head. 'Better to put him out of his misery and explain that we're not interested. That way he won't keep calling.'

Moments later he emerges from the bathroom in trousers and a shirt and sets off downstairs once again. By the time I'm showered and dressed, he has returned, proffering a cup of tea.

'The man appears to have disappeared. After all that, he couldn't be bothered to wait. Honestly!'

I give him a wink. 'Maybe he got a spiritual calling elsewhere.'

With cup in hand I walk out onto the stone terrace beyond our kitchen and head towards the steps leading to the lower orchard and field. As soon as I've called, 'Morning girls!' into the cool morning air, hens appear from nowhere, flapping their wings in evident excitement at the prospect of their corn breakfast. I stop to count them all, noting that we now appear to have 32 hens and seven cockerels. I study them all, conscious that bad-tempered Ferdinand, our fiery red cockerel, is nowhere to be seen. I can only imagine he's terrorising a neighbour's hen or picking a fight with a cabbage on the Scotsman's vegetable patch. Minutes later, as I stroll back up the gravel path, I hear a desperate cry. It appears to be coming from the orchard. In some haste I deposit my empty teacup on a step and stride towards the dense rows of bushy lemon trees, wondering whether the Scotsman has had some mishap. In the long grass I hear rustling and indignant clucking and spot a red torso and several pert and glossy black tail feathers. Ferdinand is on the warpath. I step forward and see a leg dangling from a tree and then a pale face looking down at me.

'Might you be Matias Sastre?'

'I am indeed. Your cockerel attacked me while I waited in the courtyard so I fled down into the orchard and used this old ladder to climb a tree.'

I laugh. 'Ferdinand? He's a bit of a crosspatch but he'd never do you any real damage. He was probably just trying to be friendly.'

'Friendly? He went for my leg.'

Ferdinand crows loudly and begins pecking irritably at the bark of the tree.

'Do come down, Senyor Sastre. He won't touch you,' I urge.

I attempt to stroke the irascible cockerel but he shakes his head and mumbles some fowl expletives, which happily I am unable to translate.

'You see? He's harmless.'

Our visitor seems unwilling to move, grasping what appears to be a Spanish bible to his chest.

I stand guard over the ladder until he's safely down and then lead him up to the back terrace. Ferdinand struts a few paces behind, watching him with narrowed eyes and muttering darkly like a disgruntled wizard.

'He's probably putting a spell on you,' I say.

The man doesn't laugh. I offer to make him a coffee but he politely declines, explaining that he has a full agenda of house calls to make. He does, however, hand me a religious leaflet, albeit in the Catalan language. These days I can read our local newspapers written in Catalan quite effortlessly, although Spanish Castilian, which is more widely spoken on the mainland, is an easier option. Of course there's Mallorquin, too, a derivative of Catalan, but that's more of a local oral dialect.

As I accompany our guest to the front gate, the Scotsman appears on the porch and comes over to join us.

'I thought you'd gone!' he exclaims. 'I'm glad my wife found you.'

'So am I,' he puffs. 'Well, I must be off.'

The Scotsman smiles. 'I'm sorry that you've got no takers at our house but thanks for popping by. Can I at least give you a box of fresh eggs? There were twelve beauties in the nesting boxes this morning.'

'No, *gracias*. I'd best be going.'

The Scotsman turns round to find Ferdinand strutting purposefully towards us. 'Ah look, one of our cockerels has come to say adios!'

The man stumbles through the gate, an agonised look on his face and, with a hurried wave, scampers up the track.

'There's no pleasing some people,' tuts the Scotsman. 'Sometimes religious fervour blinds people and they simply can't see the woods for the trees.'

'I'd say that was certainly true in his case,' I grin. 'Perhaps he's just shy of foreigners.'

'Well then he needs to take a small leap of faith.'

'Actually, I think he's already taken one too many of those this morning. Wouldn't you agree, Ferdinand?'

The cockerel throws his head back and issues an ear-splitting crow before stomping off, in evident disgust, to the orchard below.

Having cleared my desk of all impending deadlines, I set off to meet my old friend Neus Adrillon, who lives a mere hop and skip from our *finca*. When we first moved to Sóller, I became friendly with Margalida, the elderly matriarch who resided in a cosy white bungalow at the mouth of our track. Her daughter Silvia and son-in-law Pedro, whose sprawling *finca* and land are situated directly opposite, were always amused at how we managed to communicate, especially as I spoke limited Spanish and Margalida insisted on speaking in Mallorquin dialect. Despite the linguistic hurdles, we became close chums and I was devastated when, following a short illness, she died in her nineties. Neus, a widow in her eighties with two grown-up sons, was one of her inner circle of friends who sought my help when she had problems with a troublesome British neighbour. Since then, we have often got together, catching up on news over a coffee and, occasionally, when time permits, going off on an excursion to a local attraction. In recent years, Neus and Bernat, an old-school sweetheart and widower, rekindled their relationship and got married.

Today, I have offered to take Neus to the splendid Alfabia estate, known historically as Possessió d'Alfàbia, which lies on the south side of the Sóller tunnel. Its original name was *al fabi*, meaning jar of olives, and it was once owned by a powerful Moorish nobleman named Ben Abet. Much as the Romans made a rich contribution to the island's cultural heritage, it is arguably the influence of the Islamic period that has lasting resonance. The Balearic Islands endured many a Moorish attack from as early as 707 AD, but it wasn't until 200 years later that the Emir of Cordoba finally conquered the island. For the next 300 years, Mallorca was under Moorish rule – of one kind or another – and many of the names of Mallorca's towns and villages still retain a distinctly Moorish flavour.

In my neck of the woods in the northwest of the island, the rich Islamic heritage is reflected in the steep stone terraces known as *bancales*, the brainchild of the Moorish settlers, as well as in the ingenious irrigation channels used for agricultural purposes. Sóller was originally named *Sûlyâr,* the golden valley, because of its golden olive oil, and nearby Valldemossa, *Vall d'en Mussa*, the valley belonging to the head of the Moorish Caliphates of Cordoba, Mussa. Another possible vestige of the Moorish occupation is the island's famed *ensaimada*, a spiral-shaped pastry. The word *saim*, meaning fat in Arabic, has led some academics to suggest that the Moors were the pastry's inventors. Others argue that, etymologically, the word might have hailed from Latin. Whatever the weather, it's a delicious, light and fluffy creation, regardless of how it arrived on the world's culinary stage.

As I drive up to Neus's front gate, I break into a grin, knowing that she will be spying on me through the shuttered windows of her living room. Therefore I give an exaggerated wave from the driver's window and a minute later she walks slowly along her path and takes a seat next to me in the car.

'How did you know I was watching you?'

'Because you've often told me how you love snooping unnoticed through the slats of your shutters.'

She giggles and gives me a small shove. '*Que va*!' In other words, 'no way!'

We take the main Sóller road, flanked by the craggy Tramuntanas on our left and, once through the toll tunnel, turn into the quiet parking area in front of the Alfabia estate. Neus takes her time getting out of the car, gasping when she looks up at the imposing avenue of plane trees at the entrance.

'It's years since I last visited. I'd completely forgotten how beautiful it was.' She takes my arm and, after paying the modest entrance fee, we stroll together into the shady courtyard in front of the house where Neus stops to catch her breath.

'So how did Ben Abet acquire this estate, *reina*?'

Neus often calls me queen, a Spanish term of endearment.

'As it happens, I've been mugging up on Alfabia's history for a newspaper article I've just written. Legend has it that Ben Abet was governor of Pollença, a powerful Moorish noble, who helped King Jaume I of Aragon to overthrow the Moors back in 1229. As a reward, he was given the land on which the estate was built.'

'Why would he help the enemy?'

'Apparently, before King Jaume conquered Mallorca, Ben Abet and a group of fellow Moorish noblemen had rebelled against Abu Yahya, the last Muslim ruler of Mallorca. Perhaps he was disgruntled and decided to stab old Abu in the back?'

'You mean he decided to back the right horse in battle?'

'Looks that way. At one point, when King Jaume's army had almost run out of food supplies, Ben Abet saved the day. He was rewarded handsomely for it when Jaume became ruler.'

'Bit of a turncoat, if you ask me,' sniffs Neus.

'Perhaps it was a case of expediency. All I do know is that thanks to Ben Abet we now have the glorious gardens of Alfabia right on our doorstep.'

We visit the seigniorial manor house and external buildings, our eyes drinking in the exquisite, coffered pine and oak *mudéjar* central ceiling of the gatehouse created by Almohad craftsmen. It depicts the coats of arms of various Moorish families and Ben Abet's own emblem. Inscribed on one of the friezes are the words 'Allah is great' and 'There is no other god but Allah'. I am very taken by a beautifully crafted antique Flemish chair of the fifteenth century, depicting a scene from the popular Celtic legend of Tristan and Isolde. While researching Alfabia's historic artefacts, I read about this star-crossed couple that fell in love despite the adulterous nature of their relationship. The story goes that Tristan, a Cornish knight, had been sent to escort Isolde, an Irish princess, to his Uncle Mark's home, where they would be wed. Instead, he fell in love with her himself.

When I recount the tale to Neus, she is gripped. 'What happened to them?'

'Well there are different versions of the tale but one ends with Tristan being killed at the hands of Mark.'

'These legends usually end in tears,' she says matter-of-factly. 'As you know, we have so many of our own myths and legends here on the island.'

I nod. 'I love the one about Comte Mal.'

She chuckles. 'That story used to terrify me as a child.'

Legend has it that when Ramón Burguès-Zaforteza, known as Comte Mal, the evil count, tried to impose a feudal system on the impoverished villagers of Santa Margalida, there were violent clashes and he was eventually defeated. It's said that to this day he haunts the old estate of Galatzo, riding around on his black horse and breathing fire. Sadly, I've never had the thrill of seeing the phantom whenever I've visited the impressive estate.

I look at Neus. 'What about *El Drac de na Coca*, Coch's dragon? That was one of Ollie's favourites when he was studying at school here.'

Neus claps her hands enthusiastically. 'Mine too!'

Apparently, centuries ago, a giant dragon terrorised Palma. It would slither as if from nowhere onto the streets at night and gobble up people. One night, Bartomeu Coch, a fearless knight and the governor of Alcudia, came to Palma to woo a noble woman and spied the creature on a dark lane near her mansion. He slew the dragon, demonstrating his bravery and devotion to his loved one. All the same, some historians claim that the dragon was in reality just a huge female crocodile that escaped from a merchant ship docked in Palma port and that had found its way into the city's sewers.

Neus and I marvel over a selection of beautifully preserved antique books that date from the fifteenth to the eighteenth century and some fine wooden furniture.

'And talking of myths, what about the Moor's Hand?' I say.

She nods. 'Another gem, although it's a bit grisly.'

There are different versions, but the main story goes that Ahmed, a Moorish slave in Palma, killed his master, Martí Mascort, and attempted to abscond with his valuables. He was caught and condemned to death and, as a further punishment, had the offending hand severed before he was killed. It was later placed on a wall in the master's room and it is said that on 15 November every year – the day Ahmed was condemned to death – a disembodied, bloodied hand can be heard scratching the wall.

As we dawdle by a vast tapestry, I smile. 'That story always reminds me of "Thing" from *The Addams Family*.'

'What is "Thing"?'

'It means *cosa* in Spanish, a disembodied hand that has a life of its own.'

'Those Americans have a weird sense of humour,' she says before adding, 'If you like the old *rondalles*, you should pop by the museum showing the works of the local sculptor, Pere Pujol, in the town of Arta. Much of his work was inspired by our folktales and legends. Another fun event is the Much fiesta that takes place in the town of Sineu during August. Much is a horned mythical creature that presides over the festival.'

'So much to do, so little time,' I mutter before reminding myself that my silly pun will be lost on Neus as she doesn't speak English.

We walk from one elegant room to the next, admiring the magnificent paintings and rich textiles and furnishings, which hint at Renaissance, Gothic and even baroque flourishes. At one point Neus gives a slightly critical frown as she examines an antique bookcase and desk.

'I really like the furniture and paintings in this house but they seem to be more Mallorcan than Moorish.'

'I imagine the current owners didn't have much choice. There are precious few artefacts from those times and this house has been in many different hands over the centuries.'

'So did Ben Abet build it from scratch?'

'From what I've read there was an existing Moorish homestead on the land with a flourishing spring, but it was Ben Abet who transformed the place into a magnificent home and created the wonderful, structured gardens with his artful landscaping.'

'It is a lovely old property,' she agrees.

I nod. 'I suppose what I love about Alfabia is that it is authentic and understated. I like the fact that it's a bit bruised and battered, which reflects its antiquity. I'm glad they haven't tried to modernise it or put in shiny new floors.'

'Perish the thought!' Neus adds.

After exploring the house and magnificent antique olive press and stables, we set off into the gardens: the *pièce de résistance*. Neus heads for the famed 72-columned pergola with its 24 stone hydras that spout elegant arched-water jets. She hits the button on the wall that turns the jets on and giggles.

'I could stand here all day admiring this pergola. Wouldn't it be fun to run through the dancing water?'

'I'm not sure your clothes would agree,' I laugh. 'Come and have a look at some of the other fantastic water features and then we should investigate the little nineteenth-century English garden at the rear of the house.'

We walk through the verdant grounds, a profusion of palm and citrus trees, ancient wisteria, bougainvillea, Plumbago, roses and oleander and watch the ducks gliding serenely on the pond. I am particularly happy to see several tiny green frogs basking on lily pads. As I'm telling them all out loud what handsome chaps they are, a tourist walks by with a concerned expression and gives me a wide berth.

Neus chuckles. 'That woman obviously thinks you're potty. Don't start talking to the plants, too, or we'll be thrown out.'

She sniffs the air appreciatively and stops to inspect the flow of water coursing from one of the old stone *acequias*, the irrigation channels introduced by the Moors, and turns to me. 'Are those still working?'

'It looks like it,' I reply.

After enjoying a freshly squeezed orange juice in the tranquil garden café, we head off to the orchards and livestock area and chat with the privileged goats, pigs and donkeys that enjoy unrivalled views of the magnificent Tramuntanas beyond. There's the sound of a distant toot-toot and Sóller's antique train comes into view, chugging along its mountain track, its flanks glinting in the sunlight.

'What a perfect spot this is,' sighs Neus. 'Ben Abet certainly created his own little slice of paradise.'

I think back to a nugget of information I read about a sixteenth-century royal chronicler named Antonio Flores who once visited Alfabia and wrote, 'One never knows where the gardens end and the mountains begin'. His description perfectly fits the rolling grounds of the estate today.

Once back in the car I turn left onto the Palma road.

Neus points to a large brown board at the side of the road, advertising the Sierra de Tramuntana as a UNESCO Heritage site. 'Those are springing up all over the valley. It's a shame they're so drab.'

'It probably all comes down to budget,' I reply. 'Besides, they've got to blend into the natural surroundings.'

'I suppose so.' She looks at me expectantly. 'So where are we going now?'

'I thought we'd pop by Raixa.' Raixa was once a Moorish estate called Araixa, which has recently been refurbished and re-opened.

'Are there many steps?'

'Probably, but I can carry you on my back if you like.'

She laughs. 'I might hold you to that.'

'So tell me another Mallorcan fairy tale. What's the one about the little thieves, *En Gostí Lladre*?'

Neus settles into her seat. 'Ah, now that's a long story…'

After dropping Neus off at her house, I return home to find the Scotsman busy planting aubergines in the vegetable patch. He is puffing on a large cigar and wearing his signature Rupert Bear-style checked woollen scarf.

'You're back!' he cries cheerfully. 'I was just having my very first cigar of the day.'

'I'm sure,' I say with heavy irony. 'Gosh, I need a cup of str

'Oh dear. You didn't have a good time at Alfabia?'

'As it happens, Neus and I had a magical visit b
disappointed by the refurbishment of Raixa. '

He leans on his gardening fork. 'In what way?'

'The building's exterior is still beautiful and so are the gardens but inside it's been modernised and has precious little original furniture or artefacts.'

'Perhaps you're too much of a purist.'

'You're probably right. I just don't see the point of showcasing a historical house that has been gutted and turned into an exhibition space. At least the kitchen and one or two rooms had a few vestiges of authenticity.'

'Thank heavens for small mercies, then.'

I think back to my earlier visit to the estate, which by all accounts had a turbulent past. It was once a Moorish homestead that after the conquest by King Jaume I, fell into the hands of his uncle, Nunó Sanç, and then, by the time of the fifteenth century, the Mallorcan Safortesa-Tagament family. This clan was involved in a revolt against the king and during the whole debacle, Raixa was razed to the ground. It was restored but the family eventually went bankrupt and the estate fell into the hands of the Count of Montenegro. It wasn't until it was acquired by Cardinal Don Antoni Despuig i Damento in 1797 that the property enjoyed a renaissance. It was famed for its gardens especially as, at one time, it had the largest reservoir in Mallorca. The cardinal travelled the world for sumptuous antiquities and art and employed leading Italian architects to design the grounds. The property was acquired by the state in 2002 and declared a cultural heritage site for the enjoyment of the public.

Alan turns to me. 'So it's still worth a visit?'

'For the gardens and history alone. At one time all sorts of well-
 artists and writers stayed there and it was even used for
 of that Agatha Christie thriller, *Evil under the Sun*.'

 Moorish influence?'

 of the landscaping and terracing.'

He yawns. 'We're lucky that the legacy of the Moors still lives on, even here in our own backyard. I don't know what we'd do without our *acequia*.'

Our irrigation channel that runs through our field and orchard provides us with fresh mountain-spring water all year, a particular blessing during the dry months of the summer.

'And talking of Moorish matters, one of our *bancales* has just collapsed. It must have been caused by the rains last month but good old Emilio is on the case.'

The *marjes* in Mallorquin, or *bancales* in Castilian Spanish, are the ancient stone walls that divide our land from that of our neighbours and that also support hillside terraces. Emilio, our friendly local farmer whose land backs onto ours is responsible for any supporting walls that collapse below our two fields.

'Emilio's always very amenable,' I reply.

'Very true. He's sending his Colombian gardeners to sort it out tomorrow.'

I give a yawn. 'Anyway, I'm off to put the kettle on and to get on with some work. By the way, while I was out, did you manage to replace the light bulb in my office?'

He huffs and puffs. 'Can't you see I've been flat out in the garden? I'll do it later. And don't forget that we have dinner with Pep and Juana tonight.'

'That'll be amusing given that you'll have to endorse the myth that Pep got rid of his entire supply of home-made *vino*.'

'I shall keep off the subject of his cellar at all costs.'

'A good idea. Woe betide you if Juana ever discovers that it's all been stashed away in your *abajo*.'

'I'm relying on you not to say a word.'

'What's it worth? Now about that light bulb I need replacing…'

Pep sits back in his chair in Es Turo restaurant and gives a satisfied sigh. 'You know I love this time of year when you can feast on a big plate of *arroz brut* and some succulent big snails.'

I wrinkle my nose. *Arroz brut*, literally meaning dirty rice, is one of my favourite Mallorcan dishes, a hearty rice soup, but I prefer mine without the addition of *cargols* or rather gastropods.

He throws me a smirk. 'Oh pardon me, *senyora*! I suppose you have a colony of pet snails in your garden along with your over-indulged hens and frogs.'

'Don't tempt her,' grunts the Scotsman. 'The worst of it is that she has ridiculous names for all our birds. And let's not get onto Johnny, the toad.'

'I wouldn't say Carlos or Ferdinand were absurd names for cockerels,' I say.

'I would!' giggles Pep.

The Scotsman shakes his head. 'And what about Cordelia, Hamlet or Dogberry and Verges?'

I give an impatient sigh. 'A gentle nod to Shakespeare never did any harm.'

Juana can't keep her face straight. 'Don't you call two of the hens Clytemnestra and Electra?'

'There's nothing like introducing a few classic names,' I say with as much dignity as I can muster.

Xisca wanders over with four glasses of *herbes* on ice, the local Mallorcan herbal digestif. Thanking her, I take a glug and turn to Pep.

'You know hens were considered sacred creatures in ancient times.'

'Presumably that's why the Romans fattened them up with bread soaked in milk so that they tasted sweeter.'

'Well, Mr Clever Clogs, I think you'll find that the Ancient Greeks valued them – even if they did sacrifice a few along the way.'

Juana smiles. 'Actually, I'd like to come and see your corral in action as we're thinking of getting some hens and a cockerel.'

'We are?' Pep's eyes bulge. 'I think we need to discuss this.'

'No need. I've made up my mind. What day might suit?'

'You're welcome any time.'

The Scotsman and Pep exchange anxious looks.

'As it happens, I'm in the process of clearing out my *abajo*, Juana, and as it's just by the corral, you might prefer to wait for a while.'

'Oh don't worry about that! In fact, I'm a dab hand at cleaning out storerooms. I can whip it into shape for you.'

The Scotsman gives a strangled laugh. 'There's no need for that. It's good of you but I'm better sorting out my old junk on my own.'

Juana pats his shoulder. 'Nonsense! It's no trouble. I can at least come over and supervise.'

I dive in to the conversation. 'Actually, I've remembered we're out and about early next week. How about Friday?'

'Perfect,' she replies. 'You know, perhaps it's a myth about men being untidy, after all. First Pep cleared out our cellar while I was away, and now you're spring-cleaning your *abajo*. Impressive!'

The Scotsman offers a beatific smile. 'Yes, indeed. There's nothing like a good clear out to focus the attention.'

'Here's to our new hens!' says Juana raising her glass. 'Somehow I think my visit to your corral is going to be a real eye-opener.'

'I'll drink to that,' I say with a grin, ignoring the stealthy kick Pep gives me under the table.

Six

SAINTS AND DRAGONS

A soft, pearlised sky greets me as I jog off along the track in the direction of Sóller port. It is just after seven o'clock and Rafael's hens and cockerels are littering the path ahead of me. When I reach his front door, he pops his head out, a bowl of cereal in his hands.

'*Mi amiga*! Still running. I thought you'd be taking it easy after Prague. Under four hours was a good time, you know.'

I take this as a compliment from a veteran runner who, impressively, managed to run one marathon in just under three hours. When Rafael developed a hip problem a few years ago, he swapped running for swimming and the gym instead.

'Where next?' he asks eagerly.

'It could be Venice.'

He sucks in his cheeks and waggles a spoon at me. 'Are you mad?! You know that marathon has...'

'... fourteen bridges, I know.'

'I admire that you like a big challenge. Even if it kills you!'

Little does he know that I've had virtually no choice in the matter and am shaking at the knees at the very thought.

'Just don't come back on crutches,' he says, slapping my back and bursting into a fit of inane giggles.

At the mouth of the track my neighbour Jaume, whose house sits directly opposite, is setting off in his van for work. He beckons me over.

'How are the hens?'

Generously, Jaume kept an eye on our brood of birds when we went to Prague for the weekend and enjoys popping up to our orchard for a tranquil potter about the terrain.

'Eating us out of house and home as usual.'

'I love the way they follow you wherever you go. Your hens are more like pet dogs.'

He gives me a wave and drives off in the direction of Sóller town. When I reach the main road leading to the port, I soon hear the familiar gnawing sound and pop-popping of an ancient *moto* and find Gaspar on my tail. He veers the motorbike to run alongside me.

'I'd come running with you but my doctor says I've got to lose weight. I've gained eight kilos in the last few weeks.'

'How on earth have you managed that?' I puff.

'Oh it's easy. Chocolate, *ensaimadas,* Easter *rubiols*, bread, sausages...'

'But you told me you were on a new high-protein diet.'

'I tried it for a few days but it was so boring.'

Well, you've just got to be more disciplined, Gaspar. I'm a bit of a chocoholic myself, so I just avoid buying it.'

He gives a sniff and shifts his ample buttocks to stop the bike listing. 'The problem is that I still live at home and my mother gives me lots of treats.'

'That's no excuse. You've just got to tell her to stop.'

He lets out a howl of a laugh. 'You haven't met my mother or you wouldn't suggest that! She's a bit of a dragon.'

'And a brilliant cook, no doubt.'

'*Exacto*!'

'I'm turning off towards Can Repic beach now,' I shout to Gaspar above the noise of his engine.

He nods. 'Don't forget the town's orange festival starts on Saturday. They usually sell my favourite orange chocolate and sponge cake.'

'Great for diets,' I reply.

He throws me a guilty smile. 'There's always tomorrow!'

I laugh and run along the tranquil lane towards Can Repic beach. On my left are elegant rustic terraces of hand-hewn stone where once the rundown Rocomar Hotel used to stand. This veteran of the days of mass tourism and package holidays was demolished recently and nature has thankfully been allowed to run its course. I pass Toful's sculpture park on my left, its wrought-iron works covered in dew and, on the right, the wonderful vegetable garden nurtured by local Agapanto restaurant. At the small estuary where the river flows into the sea on Can Repic beach, I stop to catch my breath. Paddling happily in the swirling water are mallards, baby egrets and Muscovy ducks. I hear a sharp cry and spot two geese heading along the sandy embankment to join the party. How this motley crew all ended up together here I can't say, but would hazard that some were at one time domestic pets that did a runner.

On the pedestrianised area in front of the sea-facing hotels, tourists are tucking into al fresco breakfasts and freshly squeezed orange juice while a few valiant souls appear to be braving an early-morning dip in the briny waves. I give an involuntary shiver and, making a loop, head towards the port. A small huddle of elderly neighbours who take an habitual walk together every morning offer me an 'Hola!' as I chug past. Tolo, who runs the car-hire shop yawns and gives a cursory wave, evidently needing his first strong coffee of the day. I pass Sara, owner of the port's popular Pizzeria del Puerto restaurant, walking one of her dogs and tell her that I'll be back with the Scotsman soon for supper.

It's then, as I reach the very end of the port, that I see a strange item cast aside in the gutter. Curiosity gets the better of me and I bend down to inspect it. The discarded item is a figurine of a man in a flowing brown cassock. He is bearded and sports a halo about his head while wearing a benign expression on his face. Between his hands appear to be five doves in flight and a cat is curled at his feet. It can be no other than St Francis of Assisi, the Roman friar and preacher who loved all creatures great and small. As saints go, Francis was a particularly good egg and I don't say that just because he would have approved of my chickens. As an animal lover, he apparently spent his life caring for wounded creatures that crossed his path and once persuaded a disgruntled wolf to stop gobbling up the citizens of a nearby village. The reason why St Francis has always topped my list of saints is because he, too, spoke to animals as a matter of course and yet no one considered him potty. I can't very well leave my hero languishing in the gutter so I decide to carry him back to the house.

Once home, I take St Francis and give him a good scrub in the sink before placing him on my desk. Downstairs I find Cordelia waiting at the kitchen door for some sunflower seeds, her morning treat and, behind her, our most senior cockerel, Carlos I. He seems distinctly out of sorts and when I approach him, limps off behind the rosemary bush. He's evidently hurt his leg, just as I remember our poor old cockerel Salvador had, before him. I prepare him a special snack of chopped-up salad bits and bread soaked in warm water, which he demolishes with gusto. The Scotsman walks into the kitchen and surveys the scene on the outside patio in some dismay.

'What are you doing feeding those two here? It'll only encourage the others.'

'Ah, but they're pensioners so they deserve special treatment. Besides, Carlos appears to have hurt his leg.'

'That's all we need,' he sighs.

I tell him about my find in the port but before he has a chance to comment, a terrible caterwauling rends the air and beyond the kitchen window a tree shakes violently. I dash outside and espy a fluffy grey cat that is neither Doughnut nor Orlando, wedged uncomfortably in the midst of the branches of our Celtis tree. It lets out a pitiful yowl as it attempts to free itself from its leafy prison. The Scotsman offers to fetch a ladder but I decide that a kitchen chair might do the job. Somehow the unfortunate feline must have tumbled into the tree from the orchard above our back terrace. I climb onto the chair and reach up into the mass of branches. A claw extends and grazes my arm.

'Ouch!'

The Scotsman tuts. 'That's gratitude for you.'

'Poor little thing is scared. I'll just have to go for it.' I feel the soft grey swishing tail that dangles in my face and, ignoring the alternating snarling and plaintive mewling, quickly grasp the creature between my hands. The chair wobbles and before the Scotsman can react, my furry ward and I have tumbled to the ground. In its terror it has sunk its claws into my neck and stares at me in horror when I emit a shriek.

'Good God! Are you OK?' asks my husband, as he helps me to my feet. 'I hope it's grateful.'

I examine the scratches on my arms and neck while the grey cat begins weaving seductively around my legs, purring happily. It doesn't sport a collar but I note that it is female.

The Scotsman grimaces. 'Your neck looks as though it's been ravaged by Dracula.'

'Thanks. Now what do we do with her? She might be a stray.'

He offers a resigned smile. 'I'll get her some food.'

I leave him fussing over our latest arrival and pop upstairs to have a shower. Sometime later, on reaching the top landing, I hear a persistent scratching sound coming from the television room. Now what? The noise seems to be emanating from our large airing cupboard. In some trepidation I slowly open the door and am relieved to see nothing but sheets and towels. I listen for a few seconds and am on the point of closing it again when a black and white ball of fur comes hurtling towards me from the back of the cupboard, leaps onto the wooden floor boards and vanishes.

The Scotsman calls up at me from the bottom of the staircase. 'Why are you screaming?'

'Did you see a stray cat just now?' I call down at him.

'No. One is enough for today.'

'But it just jumped out of the airing cupboard,' I protest.

'How could it have got in there?' he asks, mystified.

In truth, I haven't got a clue but I imagine that it must have slunk in there one day and got trapped when one of us inadvertently closed the door.

I plod off to my office and, sitting down at my desk, look beseechingly at Saint Francis.

'Now, come on, spill the beans. Did you just plant those cats there for a jolly good wheeze?'

He stares blankly back at me but when I look closer, I'm sure I can see the hint of a grin on his painted lips.

I am sitting in my office listening to Greedy George – literally – spitting chips down the phone line.

'You see, the thing is, guv,' he manages to say in between mouthfuls of what he reliably informs me are hamburger and fries, 'old Hennie isn't quite as barmy as she might at first appear.'

'What do you mean exactly?'

'Well she's not as dragon-like as the MIL, but she can be fierce if she doesn't get her way.'

The MIL is George's mother-in-law, a woman with the apparent girth of a Sumo wrestler and the charm of Lady Macbeth.

'Hennie insists that to be chief sponsor of her Chick-Knit event, Havana Leather pays for all the wool for her volunteers, donates all the leather cape-ons I've designed and offers a ten per cent donation on every Pertelote doorstopper sold.'

'Sounds fair enough to me.'

'Whose team are you on?'

'The one that wins, of course.'

After George has eventually got off the line, I work at my desk for another hour, listening to the soothing quack-cum-croak of my frogs below my window. The distant cockerels are singing in unison and, as I listen, I have a sudden thought. The Scotsman strides into my office, tapping his watch.

'We've got to leave for Dragonera soon so I hope you're ready.'

The Scotsman and I have arranged to meet some friends in Sant Elm from where we'll all make the brief sail across to Dragonera Island, a local national park.

I beckon him over to the window. 'Listen to the cockerels. What do you think they're saying?'

'Bugger all. Cock-a-doodle-do, I suppose.'

I shake my head. 'If you listen carefully, they're actually saying "happy birthday".'

He gives a hearty guffaw. 'How can you possibly have deduced that?'

We stand in silence for a few moments while the cockerels crow. The Scotsman suddenly frowns. 'It does sound as if they're saying happy birthday. Why didn't I notice that before?'

'There! You see how history and literature have misled people? Cock-a-doodle-do is a figment of people's imagination.'

'That's as may be but we have to be at Sant Elm in one and a half hours to meet Cristina and Ignacio and the gang so get a move on.'

'Do I need walking shoes?'

He casts me a despairing glance. 'Of course you'll need them. We're walking around Dragonera National Park. Mallorcan slippers will simply not do.'

'Last time I went walking with Cristina and Ignacio, my boots fell apart. Do you remember?'

'On the way to Lluc Monastery? How could I forget? That rubber bug is a real menace. Let's hope your other boots haven't been infected.'

As we head for the door, I hear the ping of a new e-mail being delivered to my inbox. I turn to him with a groan.

'Oh no. It's from Dannie Popescu-Miller.'

Daniella Popescu-Miller is the owner of Miller Magic Interiors, which has offices in New York, Paris, St Petersburg and Moscow and whose Moscow office happens to be a mere hop and skip from Manuel Ramirez's soon-to-open Le Coq d'Or hotel. Dannie claims to be of Rumanian origin and a direct descendant of Vlad the Impaler, much to Greedy George's amusement. The Scotsman directs me away from the computer. 'I don't care whether your client Dannie is a direct descendant of Vlad the Impaler or not, but for once she can jolly well wait in her vault until your return.'

There is a sharp smell of ozone on the breeze as we all get ready to board the little ferry at Mollet de na Caragola in Sant Elm that will take us to Dragonera. As its name suggests, the slate-hued bijoux island that stretches out ahead of us has the silhouette of a slumbering lizard and is a natural prolongation of the Tramuntana mountain range. Although only 4 kilometres in length and barely a kilometre wide, its rugged terrain is home to 361 plant varieties, five species of bat and many birds, such as Eleanora's falcons, Shearwaters, Audouin gulls, Balearic warblers, barn owls and kingfishers.

Since 1995, the uninhabited isle at the extreme southwest tip of Mallorca has enjoyed national park status and is a popular destination for environmentalists, ornithologists, day trippers and those seeking a bracing hike in a wholly natural environment. Similarly to Cabrera, Mallorca's other island-turned-nature reserve, there are no gimmicky tourist shops or eateries and the best entertainment for children can be found in the antics of the endangered sludgy-green Lilford's wall lizard, a native of Mallorca and Menorca, that scampers all over the rocky terrain and is game enough to sit in one's hand.

It is some time since we planned this excursion with our good friends from Sóller, Cristina and Ignacio, and Joan and Tiffany who live in Cala Major, and all of us are champing at the bit to reach our destination. After exchanging greetings, we board the small vessel that will ferry us across to Dragonera and discuss the day ahead.

The 20-minute boat trip affords breathtaking views over the glinting sea as we course by the tiny islets of Es Pantaleu and Mitjana, observed by red-billed Audouin gulls that swoop low, performing an elegant mid-air acrobatic display by the bow. Ignacio, a practical naval architect with a deep interest in Spanish history, inspects my trainers.

'I think they'll be OK. If the worst comes to the worst, Alan can always give you a piggy back.'

'I'd like to see him attempt that going uphill,' laughs Tiffany.

'Poor Alan,' chimes in Cristina with a grin. 'He needs his hands free to light and smoke his *puro*.'

The Scotsman laughs and holds up his prized cigar, primed and ready for the walk. Meanwhile, Tiffany's partner, whose Mallorcan name, Joan, is the equivalent of Juan in Castilian Spanish, walks along the deck and chats with the captain. He is an experienced guide and geographer and always enjoys sharing his expert knowledge of the island with his friends. As we head in to land, we are preceded by a flock of Balearic shearwaters that skim the frothy waves, cawing excitedly. We dock in the tiny natural port of Cala Lladó and make our way to the visitor hut where a simple map offers us the choice of four walking routes across the island. Joan and Ignacio, who have gallantly taken on the role of tour guides, suggest that we take the central prong up to Far Vell, the dilapidated old lighthouse, which stands 352 m above sea level. According to the map, the round trip should take no more than 4 hours, leading us through the island's fauna and flora, up to the lighthouse, from where we can enjoy spectacular views out to sea. From there we will be able to enjoy a cliff walk before making our descent to the port. We set off up the steep hillside, enjoying watching the curious Lilford's wall lizards as they dart about the rocks and scuttle confidently across our hiking boots. While Tiffany, Cristina and I catch up on news, the Scotsman stops at intervals to inspect the various trees and shrubs on the rugged path, consulting with Joan and Ignacio at every turn. With delight he identifies a patch of St John's wort and the greeny flowers of the bushy Euphorbia shrub. High above us a graceful Eleonora's falcon catches the breeze and, after performing a showy loop-the-loop, dives low in pursuit of hidden prey. Halfway to the summit, the Scotsman yawns and settles on a rock to study his ornithological guide.

'You can all go ahead,' he says magnanimously. 'Enjoy the vistas.'

I know his little game. As we wave adios, I see out of the corner of my eye that he has drawn a *puro* from his pocket and is evidently looking forward to puffing away in relative peace.

Although it is a warm day in June, as we climb higher, the air becomes cooler and a light mist settles on the craggy outcrops of rock and shrub that hug the hillside. My breath is white and ghostly and a strong breeze rustles the leaves on the small clusters of tamarisk and olive trees that huddle on the steep, stony slopes nearby. At the summit of Puig de Na Pòpia are the crumbling remains of Far Vell, the grand old lighthouse built in 1850 on the spot where 300 years previously an ancient watchtower stood. It was one of two historic defence towers installed on the island to forewarn the small garrison stationed in Sant Elm of imminent attacks by Barbary pirates.

After an hour and a half of walking, Cristina, Tiffany and I are relieved to reach the summit and stop to admire the clear vistas out to sea and the spectacular views over to Cabrera and, in the far distance, Ibiza. Moments later, soft cloud descends on the carcass of the old lighthouse as we explore its damaged shell, obscuring our vision. As it happens, building this lighthouse here wasn't such a good idea. The constructors hadn't taken into account that low cloud often descended on the Puig, obscuring views out to sea. So in 1907, the lighthouse of Far de Tramuntana was built in the north and, in 1910, Far de Llebeig, in the south of the island.

We explore the carcass of Far Vell, now just a hollow shell surrounded by huge grey boulders and mounds of rock. A slice of sunshine illuminates one of the grey walls and in that instant I can almost imagine how splendid the building must have been in better times.

'Time for a break!' yells Tiffany, flinging herself on a small patch of wild pampas grass and unfastening her rucksack. She pulls out some nuts and passes them round.

As we all sit swigging at our bottles of water, Joan scrapes off a piece of the smoky-grey lichen, otherwise known as *roccella phycopsis*, that spreads across the cliff faces close to the lighthouse.

He passes it to me. 'This is *orxella* or orchill, a highly prized purple dye. It was used in the old dye houses of Palma to stain the tunics, known as *grammales*, of magistrates and other nobility.'

'You're like a walking encyclopedia,' I tease.

Joan shrugs. 'It's my job to be.'

Tiffany groans. 'Try living with him! Every day is like a non-stop history lesson.'

'Well, I'm fascinated, Joan, so carry on,' I say encouragingly, with a complicit wink to Tiffany.

He points towards the steep cliffs that stretch along the rocky coastline. 'I was just going to add that orchill tends to grow on north-facing cliffs by the sea and thrives on the humidity and mineral salts that are usually found there.'

During the Middle Ages, locals would gather lichen and bring it over to the mainland, often risking their necks climbing the steep cliffs to reach it. Despite the care with which experienced collectors scaled the dizzying heights, a historic document from 1334 records how a local collector plummeted to his death in the pursuit. Locals who succeeded in gathering their quarry would sell the lichen in powder form to dyers or offer it directly to merchants who would export it to Barcelona, Valencia, Nice and Genoa. One of the disadvantages of orchill production was that urine was used in the process of fermentation. In fact, the smell emanating from the dye houses was so bad that in 1381 an order was passed that the *tintorers,* the dyers, had to ply their trade beyond the city walls.

While orchill collectors clambered up the lofty cliff faces, they would also take baby falcons from their nests for use by King Jaume I, as falconry was a popular pursuit for the nobility. Another popular industry at the time was the making of baskets with palm leaves, which grew copiously on Dragonera. Other local trades would have included olives, with the wood being burnt to make charcoal.

Ignacio gets up and throws his rucksack over his shoulder once more. 'Shall we continue along the path, otherwise Alan will get bored waiting for us?'

Joan nods and leads us along the cliff face towards a rugged point that affords magnificent panoramic views of Mallorca, the Tramuntanas and all the outlying small islets.

Along the way, Cristina pulls a piece of lichen off a rock and crumbles it between her fingers. 'Would orchill dye have been very expensive to buy?'

'You bet,' grins Joan. 'That's why it was only used by the nobility and the ecclesiastical orders.'

Ignacio turns to him along the track. 'Wasn't this island a stopping off place for Jaume I when he invaded Mallorca?'

'It certainly was,' says Joan and stops to point to a small island that is visible between us and the bay of Sant Elm. 'Jaume and his troops apparently pitched their tents on Panteleu, that tiny islet, and came over here for water supplies.'

Legend has it that Barbary pirates also frequented Dragonera in search of water, discovering a fresh water source deep underground. The famed Barbarossa, popularly known as Red Beard, was believed to have hidden in deep caves near Cala Lladó on the island.

An inquisitive lizard scampers over Ignacio's foot when he stops to drink some water. He laughs. 'Aren't they tame?'

I nod. 'It's a pity the geckos around our house aren't quite so bold, but maybe they're right to be nervous with all our felines stalking about.'

The Lilford's wall lizard used to be found all over Mallorca and Menorca but the population was decimated by predators such as cats, weasels and other species of lizard introduced to Mallorca over the years. It now only really exists on Dragonera and in the national park of Cabrera.

Ignacio takes a bite of an energy bar from his rucksack and stretches. 'I read that a lot of smuggling used to go on here. Wasn't contraband stored here during the Spanish Civil War and even later?'

'That's very likely,' Joan replies, then looks at his watch. 'Come on, let's head back and find Alan. Then I can show you all the entrance to the well and caves that Barbarossa supposedly used.'

Tiffany gives a yawn. 'I don't know about the rest of you but I could do with a coffee or maybe something stronger!'

'Good thinking,' I reply and, patting Joan on the back, say, 'Lead on Macduff!'

Walking downhill to Cala Lladó is much less arduous and we return to the waterfront in under an hour. We find the Scotsman there, studying a map.

'You'll never believe what happened to me when you were gone. I was attacked by a Yellow-legged gull.'

Tiffany, Cristina and I get the giggles.

'What happened?' asks Ignacio, trying not to laugh.

'I was sitting on a rock minding my own business, when the wretched bird dive-bombed me. I had to shoo it away with my map and in the end had to flee to the visitor hut. I discovered I'd been sitting right next to a shrub where it had hidden its nest.'

'Trust you!' I say. 'I suppose it was one way to get you moving.'

'Poor Alan,' says Joan sympathetically. 'You women are so mean.'

'Maybe it didn't approve of your brand of *puro*,' retorts Cristina.

'Very funny,' puffs the Scotsman. 'Now, Joan, any chance of showing me where the Mediterranean monk seals once lived?'

Joan points to a small cave to the right of the landing pier. 'There used to be a colony here but not now. They are also on the endangered list.'

'Are there any Moorish remains on the island?' I ask.

'Yes, and even from the Talayotic and Roman periods. There used to be a Roman necropolis here at Cala Lladró.'

Cristina turns to Joan. 'Do you know when Dragonera was bought by the regional government?'

He shrugs. 'About thirty years ago.'

Dragonera was in private hands for many decades. Various people took ownership, such as Juan March, the famed founder of Banca March, the island's own private bank, and a speculator named Juan Flexas. However, in 1974 it was sold to a Spanish consortium that wanted to turn it into a major tourism resort with hotels and attractions. Following an outcry by locals and fierce campaigning by environmentalists, the scheme was finally blocked. The Consell de Mallorca, the Council of Mallorca, acquired it in 1987.

Cristina fixes her gaze on the crystal clear, turquoise waters. 'This really is such a natural paradise.'

Tiffany nods. 'I wouldn't mind a week's holiday here.'

I laugh. 'Me too. It's so unspoilt and serene.'

Joan pops into the visitor centre and, with the guide, a good chum, beckons us to follow them along a rough track. We soon arrive at the dark and gaping mouth of the famed cave, now barred from the public.

He addresses us all. 'This is where Barbarossa would have come for water supplies. The caves below here are a real warren.'

'I'd love to have a snoop down there,' I say.

The Scotsman gives a grunt. 'With your sense of direction, you'd be down there for some years.'

Tiffany laughs. 'Not great for claustrophobics either.'

We head back to the landing stage just as the ferry arrives to deliver us back to Sant Elm.

'Perfect timing,' says Ignacio. 'We all deserve a good lunch after that walk.'

'And it's the best thing for shock following a bird attack,' Cristina says wryly to the Scotsman.

'Indeed,' he replies, taking her arm as we step onto the awaiting boat. 'But the best cure of all, of course, is a large glass of *vino tinto*.'

Joan gives an encouraging nod. 'Definitely what the doctor ordered.'

The engine shudders into life and we're off. We stand on the deck looking out over the rippling waves, a gentle sun smiling down at us as the ferry slowly turns towards Mallorca's coastline. At that moment a Yellow-legged gull swoops low over the Scotsman's head and gives him an imperious look, before flitting back up into the deep blue sky, its loud cackling, like helpless laughter, floating on the breeze.

It's past midnight and a shimmering sickle-shaped moon peeps out at us from the tips of the inky-black Tramuntanas. We are full of sun, sea air, good food and wine. Following our Dragonera adventure, we enjoyed a hearty paella lunch at Na Caragola restaurant in Sant Elm and later retired to Ignacio and Cristina's rambling and tranquil *finca* on the outskirts of Sóller for an al fresco supper. We were joined by their friends Salud, a brilliant Mallorcan oceanographer, and Mimo, her waggish Italian husband, a yacht captain. The Scotsman and I emerge from the car and stand in the shadowy courtyard inspecting the dazzling white stars. The air is heavy with the scent of jasmine and fretful cicadas rustle in the long grasses, their rhythmic clicking exaggerated in the stillness of the night.

'Joan's home-made *patxaran* liqueur was so moreish,' I sigh. 'I probably shouldn't have had that extra glass after dessert. And Mimo's home-made *herbes* was heavenly if rather potent.'

He yawns. 'They were both delicious. We'll sleep well tonight.'

Suddenly we hear the familiar shriek of a barn owl followed shortly by that of the Scops owl.

'Imagine that, two wise owls on the prowl,' I say.

The Scotsman laughs when I start imitating a dog bark. 'What on earth are you doing?'

'I was thinking back to our conversation tonight about the sounds given to animals in different countries. Remember that Ignacio said *woof, woof* was wrong and that the Spanish *guau, guau* was how a dog barked.'

'But Mimo claimed that the Italians had nailed it with *bau-bau*.'

'I liked Cristina saying that the Spanish sound for a bird was *pio-pio* and *béeee* for a sheep!'

We stand in the darkness, baying to the moon until, sleepily, the Scotsman opens the front door and heads for the kitchen. I dither on the porch trying out one last loud *pio-pio* when a throaty voice cuts through the silent night. 'Give it a rest, will you? Jeez! Me and the boys are trying to get a bit of kip. The only kinda bird you are is a crazy one.'

I lean over the pond's edge. 'Johnny, where are you?'

'Up here, deaf ears! And before you mention it, frogs and toads don't go croak-croak or ribbit-ribbit.'

I look up at him, amazed to find him sitting aloft the pond's wall. 'In his play *The Frogs*, Aristophanes wrote that the sound made was more like *brekekekèx-koàx-koàx*.'

'What a load of frogspawn! And anyway, since you're so ignorant you should know that only male frogs make a sound. Even if we had a couple of females in the pond they wouldn't say a peep.'

'What kind of sound do you make, then?'

'Give me a break!' His eyes bulge in indignation. 'We talk, lady. Just like you. We talk.'

A moment later he flies through the air and lands with a huge plop into the treacly black waters of the pond. I whisper 'goodnight' into the still air and, retracing my steps to the courtyard, look up at the last sliver of silvery moon and yell at the top of my voice, *brekekèx brekekèx brekekèx koàx koàx koàx*!

Seven

TYING THE KNOT

I stand on the dazzling jetty in Sóller port, giggling inanely as the Scotsman attempts to board the small, white sailing boat while holding a heavy bag of home-grown lemons, a gift for our hostess. Buffeted by frisky waves, the boat creaks and rocks as he hovers on the short gangplank.

'Oh for heaven's sake, man. Stop dithering!' booms Victoria Duvall from the bow.

'I'm coming!' he puffs and is suddenly jet-propelled onto the deck as the boat lurches forward. He grabs the side rail for support, flinching at the heat it radiates under the relentless rays of the sun. He turns to me. 'You're a fat lot of help. Now let's see how you fare.'

Wiping my eyes, I head shakily up the gangplank and jump ungracefully onto the deck. 'Piece of cake!'

Victoria appears with hands on hips. 'Well let's see if you find undoing the fenders quite so simple. Now, how are you with knots?'

'Knots? I can tie a shoelace,' I reply. 'What's a fender, again?'

With an impatient tut, she bustles past, her devoted little Jack Russell, Chelsea, at her heels. A moment later she pulls up an oblong white float hanging over the side of the boat. 'This is a fender. Didn't you both go on a sailing course a few years ago with Pep and Juana?'

I raise an eyebrow. 'Ah, yes, that little sortie is best forgotten. It was a miracle that we didn't end up in Davy Jones's locker.'

'You might today if you don't pull your weight,' she intones crisply. Victoria was for many years a leading British film director in Hollywood, coordinating the crews and sets for many a film. Despite retiring from the business, she hasn't lost her edge and keeps all of us expat residents in the valley on our toes. She peers into the bag Alan has brought and, softening, offers him a bright smile. 'Your wonderful lemons! Thank you.'

'In my youth I used to be a bit of a dab hand with knots, Victoria,' asserts the Scotsman. 'I learnt how to do a reef and a bowline when I was a Boy Scout in Scotland. Mind you, whether I can remember how to do them now is questionable.'

Victoria throws him a few loose ropes. 'Well, you can practise on the way. Now, where is Rachel? At least she's a woman who does know her clove from her cleat hitch.'

The sun is beating down on the deck and beads of sweat break out on my forehead. I pull a small bottle of lukewarm water from my rucksack and take a glug while Victoria sorts out her food supplies in the galley below. A moment later I hear someone calling and see Rachel walking purposefully towards us along the jetty in blue skirt and peach T-shirt. She tucks her short dark hair behind her ears and, swinging her pannier over her shoulder, effortlessly steps onto the boat and makes her way over to us.

'What a morning! I'm so frantic with work this month. It's nice to have a day off.'

Rachel provides catering services to local hoteliers, residents and holidaymakers and naturally the summer is her busiest season. Before moving permanently to Mallorca, she was a chef in Ireland. Victoria's head pops up from the galley below. 'I'm afraid you can't quite put your feet up yet, Rachel. I need your help with the fenders. Do show them the ropes.'

Rachel takes this all in her stride, instructing us on the untying of knots while doing most of the work herself. The engine hums as Victoria stands at the helm under a bright blue awning and slowly reverses out of the mooring, while the Scotsman keeps an eye on the boat's inflatable dinghy attached to a rope at its rear. The sea is a mirror image of the sky, a rich and vibrant blue, as we head for the mouth of the bay and cut a path through the rocky cliffs, passing sleek yachts and smaller fishing crafts on our way. Before us unfurls a turquoise expanse of water, glinting under a hot lemon sun. Victoria, bronzed and clad in shorts and a T-shirt, stands at the wheel with Chelsea at her side, gently guiding the boat south-west in the direction of Deia and Valldemossa beyond.

Today we are heading for lunch at a cosy restaurant nestled into a cliff side overlooking Sa Foradada, the scrubby finger of land between Deia and Valldemossa, that is punctured by a 10-metre diameter hole. This rocky point – a particularly bewitching sight at sunset – juts out into the sea and faces the magnificent 400-year-old estate of San Marroig, once owned by Archduke Luis Salvador. It is said that when asked why he had purchased the estate for a sizeable sum in the late-nineteenth century, the good duke replied that it was worth every penny just to have ownership of Sa Foradada. Although one can take a pleasant walk along the rocky ridge with its outcrops of pines, cypresses and juniper shrubs, legend cautions against entering the wide hole itself as doing so is supposed to change one's sex. So far on hikes to the famed spot I have skirted around the edges but next time I might put the legend to the test, volunteering the Scotsman as bait.

We head into the breeze, boisterous and foamy waves licking the sides of the boat as it gathers speed. Rachel has stripped down to her swimming costume and sarong and is sitting on the deck admiring the views while the Scotsman curses over his knots. Occasionally Rachel leans forward to offer some kindly advice, in between undoing some of his less seafaring efforts. Sometime later, Sa Foradada, or 'the hole' in Mallorquin, comes into view. From a distance it resembles an enormous grey elephant, its rocky trunk reaching out to the waves above the cavity. Minutes later, Victoria parks our boat amid several smart yachts and smaller vessels and drops anchor. So crystal clear is the water that I am able to count the rocks and small fish darting around below the surface.

'Who fancies a swim before lunch?' Victoria challenges.

We have all come prepared and are soon in our swimming gear and clambering down the wooden ladder with an excitable, tail-wagging Chelsea in tow. Just as we jump into the cool briny water, a sharp-eyed Yellow-legged gull flits overhead, causing the Scotsman a moment's unease before it soars up into the sky.

'I hope that blighter hasn't followed me all the way from Dragonera,' he complains. 'It seems to have buzzed off.'

'Don't be gulled into a false sense of security,' I reply, and he groans and shakes his head. As we splash about, Rachel strikes out away from the boat, returning at double-quick speed when she spots a jellyfish.

'A jellyfish?' barks Victoria. 'Surely not?'

We scour the rocks and tendrils of floating seaweed, cautiously checking the water as we glide through the lapping waves. Jellyfish, or *medusas*, have become an increasing nuisance in the azure waters off the coast of Mallorca, and so it is left to the heroic sea turtles to gobble up as many as they can. That is also why holidaymakers are urged not to leave plastic bags on the beach as many end up in the water and are mistaken for jellyfish by hungry turtles, many of whom don't live to tell the tale.

'I must have imagined it,' shrugs Rachel. 'Come on, let's get back in the boat and have a quick snifter before lunch.'

'I've a bottle of chilled *rosado* waiting for us,' tempts Victoria.

'I'll be up in a minute,' calls the Scotsman as we all head up the ladder.

I watch as he luxuriates in the water, floating on his back and enjoying the warm sun on his face and the stillness of the air. As Rachel, Victoria and I clink glasses on deck and Chelsea shakes the water from her fur, I suddenly see a bloom of jellyfish skimming the water's surface. Ominously, they appear to have the Scotsman in their sights, their translucent balletic tentacles outstretched towards him in deadly greeting. Without a moment to lose, I plunge into the water like a human bomb, sinking the Scotsman and causing so many waves that the *medusas* are flung far out into the bay.

His head appears above the waves and, after a heavy choking fit, he eyes me in alarm.

'Are you trying to kill me, woman?'

'Not today. Didn't you see all those jellyfish?'

The others are laughing too much to come to my defence.

'Jellyfish?' says Rachel with a wink. 'I think it was just the light playing on the water.'

'Not true! There were loads of the blighters,' I protest.

The Scotsman eyes the serene and clear waters around him. 'Yes, I can see battalions!'

He swims after me towards the ladder, greatly cheered when Victoria waves a bottle of wine in our direction.

'I could do with a drink after such an ordeal. As for my dear wife, I think an eye test is in order.'

We stand dripping on the deck with towels wrapped around us and glasses of cool *rosado* in hand.

'*Medusas*, my eye!' scoffs the Scotsman, ignoring my protests. 'Just one of your warped little practical jokes.'

Across the bay, the alluring upper terrace of Sa Foradada restaurant beckons like a siren and we all agree that seafood paella cooked on the restaurant's traditional wooden stove is the order of the day. We finish our drinks and get dressed hurriedly, keen not to lose our table reservation at such a busy time of the summer.

'It's only a short ride in the dinghy to the jetty,' says Victoria cheerily, striding towards the stern of the boat.

'You take the ladder,' she says commandingly to the Scotsman.

We follow behind and stop dead in our tracks when Victoria points towards the water. 'What's up?' asks Rachel.

'A few unanticipated luncheon guests,' she replies wryly.

We lean over the side of the boat and see the tethered dinghy bobbing happily on the waves, a fan of ghostly jellyfish dancing about it. The Scotsman eyes me ruefully.

'OK,' says Victoria with a mischievous smile. 'Who's first to walk the plank?'

Later that day, Ollie and I stand on the little bridge near the tramline, watching the busy ducks as they scratch around the arid base of the *torrente*, the river that wriggles down from the Tramuntana mountains, through Binaraix village, Sóller and the port to the sea. The walk from our *finca*, through a series of tranquil and shady winding alleys, culminating in a tiny pedestrian bridge and, beyond, tram tracks, is one of my favourites. Today the ducks and geese pad around the dry stones and furrowed mud, quacking wildly in their forlorn and futile search for water. At this time of year, the river simply dries up, its bed a mass of withered weeds and bulrushes, boulders and rocks. One side is flanked by a wall of tall rushes and long grasses and also some brambles, which Ollie raids for berries. We follow the tram tracks towards the town, hopping onto the wooden edges of the sleepers to avoid walking on the rough, grey stones. Soon we reach the stables on the left of the rails where Toni, founder of famed Frau Bakery in town, keeps his horses. Today a foal peeps out at us as well as one of Toni's handsome colts. We stroke their noses and turn when we hear him call over to us.

'Fancy a turn in my carriage?' he asks with a grin. He is sitting in his horse-drawn cart on a strip of turf.

'Sadly, time doesn't permit,' I reply. 'We've been out all day on a boat and I need to get to the supermarket.'

He slackens the reins and offers a wave. 'Well, another time.'

We watch as his horse clip-clops out of the yard.

'Wouldn't that be fun?' I say cheerfully.

Ollie raises an eyebrow. 'I think you've had enough excursions for one day. Besides you'd better get something for that sunburn.'

'What sunburn?'

'Evidently you haven't seen your face.'

'Is it sun-kissed?'

'That's one way of describing it,' he says with a sardonic twang.

At Eroski, our local supermarket, the aisles are full of happy and carefree holidaymakers stocking up on supplies for their rented villas, with many congregating, sensibly in my opinion, around the tempting wine section. As we push the trolley into the store, we almost collide with Antonia, who, with her American husband Albert, used to run Hibit, the main computer shop in the town. Albert now offers a local consultancy service instead. She casts me an anxious gaze. 'Wow, what happened to you? You look as if you've been caught in a fire!'

Ollie stifles a guffaw.

'Is it that bad? I've been out on Victoria Duvall's boat all day.'

'Maybe sun cream's a good idea next time. Especially with skin as white as yours.'

'But it's July. I'm as tanned as can be!'

She gives me a pitiful look. 'Really? Well that's too bad.'

I remember that the Scotsman is having problems with his computer. 'I suppose Albert wouldn't have time to take a look at Alan's computer?'

'Of course. What's wrong with it?'

'The computer's fine,' interjects Ollie. 'It's the user that's the problem.'

She laughs and heads for the exit. 'I'll get him to call Alan.'

As we wave goodbye she turns back. 'Put some aloe vera on your face!'

We are strolling around the vegetable section when Teresa from Colmado Sa Lluna, our beloved deli in the town, calls over to us.

'*Hombre*! You've caught the sun. Next time, wear a hat!'

The expression, *hombre*, meaning man, is often used to express surprise in Spanish.

'Is it that bad?' I hiss at Ollie as we steer the trolley along the aisles.

He stares at me. 'Well, mother, it could be a lot worse.'

'Really?'

He studies me for a few seconds with a warped grin. 'Actually, on second thoughts, no. It really is as bad as it gets.'

It's early morning and yet the heat is already palpitating. The Scotsman strides around the orchard, plucking fat yellow lemons from the branches of a nearby tree, which he carefully loads into a wicker basket. By his side is a straw pannier groaning with aubergines, tomatoes, potatoes and lettuces. I stand yawning in the corral, having arrived back from London in the early hours of the morning. Cordelia pecks at my slippers while the rest of the flock hungrily descends on the corn that I've scattered about. I carry a bowl of food to the far side of the field where Carlos I is sitting under a shady tree on his tod. He has recovered from his temporary leg injury but is still keeping apart from the others, perhaps to avoid being taunted by our younger, boisterous and macho cockerels and the perennially bad-tempered Ferdinand. The Scotsman appears at my side.

'I see Cordelia's in fine fettle. She's a tough old bird,' he remarks.

'It's a bit sad that she seems to have abandoned Carlos I. As soon as he got his leg injury, it was as though he'd never existed,' I reply.

'That's females for you. He's looked after her all these years and when the poor old stick is ill and needs the loving feathered wings of his partner around him, she's off. Fickle, if you ask me.'

'Perhaps it's a stark warning for the male species in general,' I reply with a grin.

He gives me a frown. 'You're probably right. You'd throw us all to the lions for a designer handbag.'

'As long as it was the right brand.'

There's the growl of an engine and the sound of tyres crunching on gravel.

I pat him on the shoulder. 'Be warned. Another mad female is on the loose.'

Doors slam and a loud '*Hola*!' rents the air. Catalina has arrived.

I walk up through the orchard and greet her in the courtyard.

'Still in your nightdress?' she scolds. 'How was Ed and Rela's wedding?'

'I caught the late flight from Gatwick, which was delayed, so didn't get to bed until three this morning.'

'I'll let you off then,' she grins. 'I'm on my own today. Miquela has a dental appointment in Palma.'

I follow her into the kitchen where we both sit at the table enjoying hot coffees and home-made chocolate muffins. She is keen to know about Ed and Rela's wedding celebrations in London.

'Rela looked beautiful all in white with a stunning pearl headdress and train and Ed had really smartened up for the event.'

'Did he bring his MEK with him?' she giggles.

Catalina has often heard me joke about Ed's famed Medical Emergency Kit.

'Of course, MEK had pride of place next to them at the top table with a white ribbon tied to its handle,' I joke.

'And how was your speech?'

'I think it went off alright, although I was quite jittery. Being the last speaker means you're always on tenterhooks and can't have a drink until it's over.'

'I think a drink might have helped,' she replies.

'On second thoughts you're probably right. It was wonderful to see Ed and Rela looking so happy. If he can just find the right job, his life will be on course.'

'Is the school job still not working out?'

'I'm afraid not. I think he may have to throw in the towel.'

'Talking of which, can you help me sort these?'

She gets up and starts raking through the towels and sheets in the wash basket before holding up a clump of Ollie's tops. 'How many T-shirts does that boy have?'

'Don't go there! I'm convinced they're like amoebas and self-multiply.'

Catalina and I gather up the freshly laundered towels and sheets and together we shake them out and fold them on the patio. In the distance we can see a new foal galloping around one of Emilio's fields.

'I'd love a foal to add to the menagerie one day,' I say.

Back in the kitchen, Catalina switches on the iron and sets to work on the pile of crumpled clothes in the basket. 'Talking of which, where are Minny and Della?'

I begin clearing away the plates and cups on the table. 'They're staying with Jacinto on his farm in the Tramuntanas for the summer. It's much cooler for them up there.'

Jacinto reared our donkeys and his farm is a second home to our docile mother-and-daughter team, Minny and Della.

She pauses, iron in hand, the wispy steam curling about her fingers. 'I think you've got more than enough creatures crawling about this place,' she tuts. 'What with the hens, cats and frogs and…' she points to the wall where a fat gecko blinks down at us, 'reptiles!'

'Well I should let you know that we're planning on getting some lambs.'

'Why am I not surprised?' she tuts.

I load the plates and cups into the dishwasher, reminding myself what a luxury this is. Until recently, we did all our washing up by hand because there simply wasn't room to accommodate a dishwasher in the kitchen. And then one day our plumber had a brainwave and suggested installing the washing machine in our outside bathroom while plumbing in a dishwasher in the kitchen.

The Scotsman labours up the stone steps from the lower orchard and holds out his prize, a basket full to the brim with freshly picked vegetables and fruit.

'What do you make of that lot?' he beams.

'A good crop. Your tomatoes will make a perfect *trampo*,' Catalina replies, as she inserts a hanger inside a newly ironed shirt.

The local *trampo* salad, consisting of finely chopped tomatoes, green peppers, sweet white onions and garlic with a good splash of red wine or apple cider vinegar and virgin olive oil, has become part of our summer diet.

The Scotsman looks across at Catalina. 'We're off to the museum tonight to hear the *glosadors* sing.'

Carolina Constantino, the enthusiastic curator of the Museu Balear Ciències Naturals, the Balearic natural science museum based in Sóller, which was opened in 1992, works tirelessly to raise funds to keep it on its feet as it receives precious little state funding. She has in recent years taken to devising all sorts of fundraising events that attract hundreds of locals. The latest is an evening with three well-known local *glosadors*, who create improvised songs, rather like those quick-witted souls who can create humorous limericks out of the air, and the funnier and bawdier, the better. The oral tradition of *gloses* is an important part of the island's cultural heritage and an association of these songsters-cum-poets has a thriving community with members travelling the world, performing their art. As members of the museum, we try to support Carolina's events.

Catalina clicks her teeth. 'Lucky you! I'd love to come and hear the *glosadors* but I have some clients arriving on a late flight from London and I need to give them the keys to their rented property. Is there a dinner as well?'

'They're serving *pa amb oli* and wines. The perfect summer menu,' I reply.

'It's such a simple and delicious dish, too,' opines the Scotsman. 'A slice of bread rubbed with garlic and smeared with olive oil and tomato.'

I give a tut as I use a soapy sponge to clear away crumbs on the table. 'But it isn't just any bread. It's got to be *pa de pages*, bread of the peasant farmer, preferably sliced with a sharp *trinxet*, my favourite Mallorcan kitchen knife.'

'And the tomatoes must be *ramellets*, the long-lasting variety that are rusty-hued,' cuts in Catalina. 'Of course, it's important to serve it with good cheese, such as Manchego, and Serrano ham and home-cured olives.'

'So, in other words it's not so simple after all,' I say with a wink. 'Anyway, I'm sure the museum will get it spot on.'

The Scotsman sits down at the kitchen table and removes his gardening boots while Catalina eyes him critically.

'Take those boots out of the house now!' she orders.

'Give me a minute,' he blusters. 'I never get any peace in this house.'

He does her bidding and deposits them on the doorstep.

I eye them thoughtfully. 'At Ed's wedding, Jane and I were discussing our idea of walking part of the Camino de Santiago. The important thing is to have comfortable hiking boots.'

'I've always wanted to do that walk,' sighs Catalina as she flattens a sheet with the hissing iron. 'It's all a question of time. When are you two planning it?'

'We thought October would be a good month when most tourists will be off the trail.'

The Scotsman smiles. 'Excellent thought and I can enjoy two weeks of uninterrupted peace.'

'With the donkeys, hens, cockerels and cats of course,' adds Catalina.

'Indeed,' he grunts. 'Our ever faithful entourage.'

'And will you carry your own luggage?' she asks.

I lean against the kitchen table and dry my hands with a tea towel. 'That was the idea although Jane's found a cheap carrier service and thinks it would be easier to walk rucksack-free.'

She gives me a cheeky wink. 'Makes sense, especially at your ages.'

When Catalina finishes her ironing and sets to work on the oven with rubber gloves firmly in place, I head upstairs for a shower and to finish a newspaper article in the office. An hour later I stretch my arms and lean out of the window, basking in the rays of the sun that touch my face. Down in the pond the frogs are in full throttle, sitting on the dark green lilypads and lapping up the sunshine until a heron suddenly swoops down and hovers over the water. There's a series of loud plops and all disappear in a flash. I clap my hands loudly in the heron's direction and, with a haughty cry, it soars back up into the sky. Silence reigns. It seems that my frogs are taking no chances. As I'm peering out of the window, Judas whines from the desk. It's mad Manuel Ramirez sounding paranoid as usual.

'I will be brief. You never know who is monitoring this phone call.'

I play along. 'Well, the frogs are probably eavesdropping, too, Manuel. You can never be too careful.'

'The French secret service? Why do you think this?'

'I'm talking about the frogs in my pond.' Sometimes I wish Manuel would lighten up.

He gives an impatient cough. 'Listen carefully. I have managed to secure the Moscow Philharmonic Orchestra for the launch of Le Coq d'Or. Please do not ask me how.'

'Go on, Manuel. Spill the beans!'

He laughs manically. 'If I told you, I'd have to shoot you.'

Given that he keeps a solid gold Kalashnikov on display in his office in Panama, I decide not to push the point.

'That's great news. The launch will be phenomenal.'

He rattles on. 'I have also commissioned one of Russia's leading sculptors to create a giant golden cockerel that will form the centrepiece in the lobby of the hotel.'

'Wonderful, and you can give replica pin brooches to all your guests on the night.'

'I will do that. A good idea. Keep in touch but do not use this mobile number.'

'Why ever not?'

'From now onwards I am using only disposable mobiles. Better safe than sorry.'

The line goes dead. It's good to know that some things never change.

The frogs appear to have come out of hiding for their chatter is louder than ever. In fact, it sounds as though they're chortling with laughter. Maybe they listened in on Manuel's call after all.

The vast terrace of the beautiful seigniorial property that houses Museu Balear de Ciències Naturals has been transformed into an outside dining area with trestle tables placed cheek by jowl in order to accommodate the huge swell of guests. Tiny lights hang from the rafters and, in the pulsating heat, comes the rhythmic clicking of the cicadas and the odd belch from one of the portly frogs in the pond. In front of us, cloaked in darkness, is Sóller's famed botanical garden, home to 350 indigenous species of Mallorcan plants and a special collection of 200 plants and trees native to the Canary Islands. We have all enjoyed a delicious *pa amb oli* supper with lashings of red wine and now sit – at nearly eleven o'clock – waiting for the performers to begin. Our friend Cristina Alcover and her partner Rafa wave across at us from a nearby table as we buy a book of raffle tickets.

'Fingers crossed you might win a prize,' smiles one of the helpers.

I laugh. 'I never win anything but this is for an excellent cause, which is all that matters.'

Another guest at our table nods her head. 'It's just the same for me. I never win *El Gordo*, either.' *El Gordo*, meaning the 'fat one', is Spain's famed big Christmas lottery.

I turn to the woman. 'Will the *glosadors* perform with the *ximbomba* tonight?'

The *ximbomba* is a rudimentary instrument formed from a stick and a drum that creates a bizarre sound, rather like a groaning cow. It is normally used to accompany the *gloses*.

She smiles. 'Not tonight. The three performers will sing without accompaniment.'

Carolina, host of the event, pops by our table.

'I do hope you enjoy the songs, but don't worry if you can't understand everything. The *glosadors* speak rapidly in Mallorquin and even we find it hard to follow them sometimes!'

'We'll do our best but we're just here to drink up the atmosphere and to see friends.'

She smiles and rushes off in the direction of the makeshift stage area.

Cristina now grabs me by the hand. 'Come and meet Jaume Servera, Sóller's new mayor, and Mateu Matas, one of the *glosadors*. He's won many awards for his entertaining *gloses*.'

We walk through the melee and I enjoy a pleasant chat with both men before stopping to catch up with some other Mallorcan chums. As we sit chatting with guests at our table, Caroline grabs the microphone and announces that the raffle will be held before the *glosadors* take to the floor. The first number is called out and there is an excited bubble of chatter followed by silence as everyone examines their tickets. The Scotsman smiles genially at a *senyora* sitting alongside him, not bothering to look at the jumble of tickets before him. No one claims the prize and there is minor uproar. Surely someone present must have the winning ticket! And then all of a sudden heads turn. Could it be the only foreigners at the event? People at our table grab our tickets.

'Maybe you have the winning number,' they cry excitedly.

'Oh no!' laughs the Scotsman. 'We never win anything.'

'But you have!' says the lady sitting next to him, holding up the winning ticket. 'Quickly, go to the stage.'

In some embarrassment the Scotsman rises and modestly ambles over to Carolina to collect his prize, an enormous decorative plate. Everyone claps and he returns to his seat, congratulated by those around us.

'Can you believe that?' he hisses at me.

'I'm glad you went up,' I reply. 'I'm always too shy about that sort of thing.'

He shows me the plate and we smile happily and in some relief when another number is called, but there is silence yet again. Once more, heads turn. 'It has to be the English!' someone shouts excitedly. There's whistling, laughter and clapping. I pray that we haven't hit the jackpot again but, to our embarrassment, we discover that indeed we are the winners. Politely we decline the gift of a necklace but the crowds of diners insist that we claim our prize. The Scotsman bravely stands and bows and, to much laughter and merriment, collects the gift. My cheeks are burning. Please God, these things don't happen in threes like buses arriving all at once. When the third number is called, everyone looks towards us. We refuse even to peep at our pile of paper numbers but Cristina, almost weeping with laughter crouches between us and triumphantly flags up the winning ticket. 'Three times in a row!' she shouts. 'That's some record.'

As more whistling and clapping ensues, we shake our heads and flatly refuse any more gifts. Instead, we hand the entire cache of tickets over to the laughing Cristina and others at her table. This is particularly fortunate as our third prize would have been a huge, cream-filled *ensaimada* pastry for twelve people.

'We could always have shared it with the cats and hens,' hisses the Scotsman in an attempt at levity.

By the time the *glosadors* start to sing, following our comic contribution to the raffle, it is getting on for midnight.

'Phew, well now we can just relax,' I whisper to the Scotsman.

'Too right, but we'll never live this down.'

Looking around at the guests, I see many familiar and friendly faces still trying to catch our attention as they giggle openly, overcome with mirth.

But our ordeal is not yet over. As my ears strain to catch the words of the first humorous song, I give a small groan as more laughter erupts from the floor. Mateu Matas, one of the *glosadors*, turns to us while his two companions look on, with grins on their faces.

'What are they saying?' hisses the Scotsman.

'Well, he is saying something to the effect that the only foreigners at the feast manage to take all the prizes!'

'Oh dear. We're the butt of the jokes now.'

'It's all in jest but I'd rather we weren't the centre of attention,' I mumble.

'Best laid plans,' he says stoically, sharing smiles with those around us. Cristina and Rafa are still incapable of looking at us without erupting with laughter while Carolina casts us a sympathetic glance. And so the night continues but luckily, after our 15 minutes of uncomfortable fame, the songs move on to cover other, more interesting topical issues of the day.

At one-thirty in the morning, after a final, splendid encore, the singers Mateu, Maribel and Rafa take their bows and the lively throng rises to its feet and heads for the exit. We catch up with others on the way, deciding that being good sports at such an event isn't such a bad thing. At least we have given everyone a good laugh.

'That's the last time we'll ever buy raffle tickets,' I say decisively as we stroll along the dark Sóller road, waving goodbye to fellow revellers on the way.

'We did get a nice plate though,' the Scotsman replies.

'And a lovely necklace,' I concede.

'All in all it was a magical evening,' he grins. 'And a real hoot.'

As if in agreement comes the ghostly call of a barn owl as we turn right and head along the shadowy lane leading towards our home. The sky is teeming with stars and a runway of tiny glow-worms lights up a nearby orchard.

As we reach our track, I turn to him and laugh. 'What a strange night! Next time, let's skip the raffle and just make a donation.'

'It must have been a fluke. We'll never win a raffle ever again.'

'You could be right,' I laugh. 'But don't count on it!'

Eight

FIRE AND ICE

The air is dry and cool and soft tendrils of mist curl mysteriously about the lower peaks of the mountains and woods of holm oak and pine, far below. The Puig de Maçanella, the second highest peak in the Tramuntana mountain range, is at such an early hour completely devoid of human life. A black vulture stains the marbled sky; its huge jet wings extended elegantly either side like a ballet dancer in flight. I capture it through my binoculars and pass them to Ollie.

'Isn't it beautiful?'

He shifts his sunglasses to the top of his head and holds the binoculars to his eyes, muttering, 'It's a bird, it's a plane, it's Superman!'

I give him a shove. 'Will you stop playing the fool!'

Agustin laughs and turns to Ollie. 'I know that expression. It's from the Hollywood film, right?'

He nods and gives a yawn. 'So where do we go now, Agustin?'

The spectacled young man before us passes a hand through his dark curly locks and consults his map. 'We just need to walk for another five minutes or so and we'll arrive at the snow houses. It will have been worth the long walk. You realise that we're now at a height of just over one thousand three hundred metres?'

Agustin is the son of our plumber and is in the second year of training to be a mountain guide. When I expressed an interest in visiting some good examples of historic snow houses and charcoal burners' huts, he volunteered to act as our guide, hoping to practise his English and to put his knowledge to the test. When he qualifies for the job in a year's time, he will need to have a good command of our language and be able to demonstrate a thorough understanding of the fauna and flora of the island as well as its history and geography. He passes Ollie a flask with two small cups.

'Brandy, I hope,' quips my son.

'Strong black coffee,' he replies with a huge grin. 'I'll buy you a beer when we get back to Sóller.'

'Deal.'

Ollie passes me a cup of the steaming brew and, balancing it on a rock, I pull out a bag of nuts and blueberry muffins from my rucksack and pass them round. We sit enjoying our snack, watching the sun hovering sleepily on the horizon and listening to the distant tinkle of sheep bells. It is only 8:30 in the morning and we have already walked for nearly 2 hours from the reservoir of Gorg Blau, where Agustin parked his car. Ollie gives another hearty yawn.

'I suppose you're not used to such early starts?' says Agustin.

He gives a cynical snort. 'You must be kidding. I have to get up at the crack of dawn at school. I'm tired because I was out with friends until late. I rarely go to sleep before two in the morning when I'm on holiday.'

Agustin shakes his head. 'I'm twenty-four but I couldn't do that any more. It's so different when you're working. I take out groups with a senior guide throughout the year and every day we have to get up at five-thirty, just like today.'

I examine the scrubby vegetation around me and reach towards a nearby clump of pungent thyme and rub the leaves between my fingertips, breathing in the delicious aroma. All around the heavy boulders and rocks are patches of wild rosemary, juniper and stubby lentisc trees. My eye catches the profusion of box covering a pile of rocks.

'You know, that was one of the favourite foods of Myotragus, the extinct mouse-goat that once roamed these parts,' I say.

Ollie rolls his eyes. 'Don't get her started on the old goat, Agustin, or we'll be here all night.'

He laughs. 'I reckon Myotragus would have enjoyed your home-made muffins, too. They're delicious!'

He gets up from the rock he's been sitting on and brushes the crumbs from his shorts. 'OK, shall we finish our excursion?'

We pack up and head up the steep, rocky incline for another few minutes, soon arriving at an outcrop of small, dilapidated dry-stone structures.

Agustin addresses us. 'These remains offer some idea of how snow houses of the seventeenth century would have looked. You know, a lot of people don't quite understand that the Tramuntanas were awarded UNESCO status for their interaction between nature and humans.'

'I remember Tomeu Deya, the local UNESCO project leader, telling me that. He said the status celebrated the way inhabitants adapted to the mountainous environment and worked and lived in synergy with nature.'

'*Exacto*,' he replies. 'Did you also know that there are nineteen municipalities in the Tramuntana region and that as much as ninety-five per cent of the land here is privately owned?'

'And are there any ice houses or charcoal furnaces on private estates here?'

'Of course. In fact, of the eleven ice houses that exist in the northwest, four are on private land.'

'So how did the ice houses work?' asks Ollie.

Agustin beckons us over to one of the buildings, now a shadow of its former self, with its roof open to the elements and its stone walls crumbling.

'Allow me to give you a quick, potted history. Snow houses, known as *casas de neu*, already had a long history in the Middle East and India before they were introduced in Mallorca. They were used in Mesopotamia in 2000 BC and in Ancient Greece. In fact, the Romans also created artificial tanks for collecting snow, which they compacted into ice.'

Ollie listens attentively as he examines one of the roughly hewn stone walls. 'I never realised ice was so common back then.'

He nods. 'I know, it's quite surprising, isn't it? As far as Mallorca's concerned, ice grew in popularity during the sixteenth century. It was used for gastronomic and medicinal purposes and was in huge demand, so much so that the industry had to be regulated by law with the introduction of the Capítol de l'Obligat de la Neu in 1656. Its aim was to create fair standards for the letting of snow houses and prices and taxation.'

'And so the houses were built underground?' I ask.

'That's right. They were rectangular buildings dug into the ground, with cobbled floors and walls fabricated from dry stone, what we call *pedra en sec*. They rose about two metres above the ground and were tiled over or had reed roofs.'

'It must have been chilly working in the ice trade,' Ollie grins.

Agustin nods. 'It was certainly tough work. The *nevaters*, the snow gatherers, used a series of interconnected paths to transport the blocks of ice down the mountain. Come winter, they'd shovel up the snow for hours on end before carting their cargo to the snow houses where it would be covered with layers of bracken until the spring.'

'How did they get the ice down the mountains?' I enquire.

'One of the best methods was to wrap the blocks in padded bundles strapped to the back of a donkey. They also used wooden pallets and cloth backpacks. You have to remember that it paid well because ice was always in demand. All the same, it was gruelling and back-breaking work in the bitter cold.'

'Not for the faint-hearted,' I say.

'Indeed. There's a nice little traditional *glose* in Mallorquin that goes: "*Pitgen sa neu, pitgen sa neu, i tots estan dins ses cases; peguen potades, peguen potades, en Toni, en Xisco, en Joan i n'Andreu*".'

'Toni, Xisco, Joan and Andreu tread the snow, tread the snow, striking away, striking away, inside the snow houses,' translates Ollie. 'That's a cheerful little ditty.'

Agustin laughs. 'Maybe not your cup of tea. Anyway, the whole trade tailed off in the 1800s when a more industrialised system of making ice came into being.'

He looks around him. 'So, now we'll walk a little further, down towards Tossals Verds, which you probably know is the third highest peak in the Tramuntanas. Puig Major is the loftiest at one thousand four hundred and forty five metres.'

'You're a mine of information,' I say.

He smiles at me. 'I do my best.'

As we head along the rocky mountain-paths, Agustin identifies falcons, ospreys and a majestic eagle that circles above our heads before diving on some distant prey. We soon arrive at a huddle of decimated dry-stone dwellings.

'These are the huts that the charcoal burners, known as *sitgers*, would have lived in. As you can see, they were round and would have had conical-shaped roofs with a wooden frame covered in reeds. The beds would have been made from stone and covered in straw.'

'At least they kept warm,' I say.

He laughs. 'Actually, it was a difficult existence, living a solitary life in the hills, earning very little and having to suffer the effects of smoke inhalation.'

'So possibly worse than being a snow gatherer?' suggests Ollie.

He shrugs. 'I'd say so. The creation of charcoal goes back to Egyptian, Greek and Roman times but I'm not sure when it arrived here in Mallorca. Although coal mining was introduced in Mallorca in the nineteenth century, carbonated wood would have been a cheaper option and used for heating, cooking and construction.'

'I always remember the wonderful account about charcoal burners in the travel memoir, *Jogging Round Majorca* by Gordon West,' I say.

'I don't know this title. Can I buy it?' he asks.

I give a nod. 'Well, it was published in 1929 and out of print but Leonard Pearcy, a broadcaster friend of mine who used to own a home in Deia, managed to get it re-published.'

He listens carefully. 'So what happened with the charcoal burners?'

'The author tells how he and his wife got caught in a storm and ended up having to camp with a bunch of charcoal burners in the Tramuntanas, sleeping overnight in a primitive hut on stone beds covered with straw. It certainly illustrated how grim life in the hills was back then.'

'It's funny you should say that. Today holidaymakers walk in the Tramuntanas and see it as a natural paradise, which it is, of course, but it has a dark history. Aside from the manual labourers who toiled away in the lonely hills, such as charcoal and ice workers, during the seventeenth century there were highwaymen, known as *bandolers*, who formed marauding gangs. They kept huge hounds known as *alanos*. I think you call them mastiffs.'

'Who did they target?' Ollie suddenly livens up.

'Anyone really. You'd have been mad to walk into the mountains alone, especially at night. They'd rob and kill anybody. These gangs were in their element a century earlier during the violent clashes between two rival noble clans in Mallorca, the Canamunts and Canavalls. Enemy *bandoler* factions were apparently employed by both families to protect their households.'

'It sounds a bit like Shakespeare's Montagues and Capulets,' I muse.

'Very similar,' he replies. 'Anyway, I want you to look at this remnant of a charcoal furnace.'

He points to a pile of tumbled stones around a cobbled base. 'Similarly to the charcoal burners' huts, they were circular with a conical roof over-layered with branches and earth. The workers would have burned pine and holm-oak wood, which is still plentiful in these parts.'

'So whole families lived up here?'

He turns to me. 'Yes, and all were involved because wood needed chopping and the fire tended to constantly, maybe for up to ten days before the wood became carbonised. Afterwards, the families would take the charcoal to the villages by cart for sale, earning a measly thirty pesetas per week for their efforts.'

'And would they then return to the mountains?' Ollie asks.

'Where else? It was their only pitiful livelihood. And when any area had been sufficiently mined of trees, they'd move on to a green-field site and start again. It was a nomadic existence.'

I survey the humble remains of the *sitger* village. 'It's strange to think that such a profession existed when you consider how pyromaniacs are a constant threat in the Tramuntanas at this time of year.'

Agustin tuts. 'I know, and charcoal burning these days is considered to be one of the primary causes of deforestation in the developing world, so it's just as well it died out here.'

We walk on through the rugged terrain, enjoying the crisp air and spectacular forest and mountain views until Agustin suddenly looks at his watch.

'It's already ten o'clock, time perhaps to head back to the car and to Sóller for a cool beer and a *bocadillo*?'

Ollie gives him a satisfied smile. 'I'd second that.'

Despite it being early August, a cool breeze blows in the higher echelons of the mountains and I fasten up my jacket. 'I was thinking…'

'Oh no,' sighs Ollie. 'That always spells disaster.'

I ignore him. '… that it's not surprising that Gordon West described Mallorcan charcoal burners as "strange, lonely people… shut off from mankind".'

Ollie grins. 'That pretty much sums you up, mother, when you're writing in your study. Mind you, at least the charcoal burners had something useful to show for their efforts.'

I turn to a laughing Agustin. 'Remind me of the benefits of having teenage children?'

He smiles, 'Because they always bring you down to earth?'

Ollie ruffles my hair good-naturedly and, taking my arm, as if he were guiding an ailing geriatric, sets off down the hill.

A golden sun gazes down at us as we sit under a cool cream parasol in Café Paris. Agustin joined us for lunch but had to depart for a meeting in Palma, leaving Ollie and me to sit back in our chairs, enjoying the comings and goings of visitors in the square. As we observe the busy scene before us, the antique tram clatters slowly through the *plaça* and, with a stirring toot, chugs off in the direction of the port. A moment later, Antonia, the wife of my computer consultant, Albert, bustles over to us.

'What do you think of this heat? It's like the ten plagues of Egypt in our house, what with the ants and wasps and flies…'

'But do you have snakes and scorpions?' I say with a grin.

'Not yet. Don't tell me you have?'

'We've had two grass snakes in our *entrada* this week and a scorpion scuttled out of Alan's *abajo* yesterday, but can you blame it? The poor creature was probably stifled by his *puro* fumes.'

'Oh my gosh, that's terrible.' She fumbles in her handbag and pulls out a cigarette.

I shake my head disapprovingly.

'Come on, give me a break! I'm only having the odd one. It's good for stress. You ask Alan! How is his computer by the way? Did Albert fix it?'

'He did a great job but I fear he'll need to return to help with our Wi-Fi relay system.'

Antonia laughs. 'He likes getting out of the house. Don't worry.' She lights her cigarette. 'By the way, a new clothes shop has just opened near the post office called Ca Na Luca. It's got some nice T-shirts and dresses.'

'Don't tempt her. She's got more than enough clothes,' says Ollie.

'Women never have enough!' she counters with a wink. 'Anyway, I have to go and pick up my grandson, so I'll catch you later.'

She gives a wave and steps quickly into the busy square. Meanwhile, Carmelo dashes from table to table, taking orders from the many tourists who have sought shelter from the fiery rays of the sun. Carrying trays groaning with fizzy drinks, cool beers, iced coffees and ice creams, he looks fit to drop. He blots the sweat from his face with his sleeve and picks up the note and coins we have left on the table.

'What heat! I just want to pour ice-cold water over my head.'

I think of the hard grafting snow gatherers of the Tramuntanas and how these days we all take ice for granted, given that it is so freely available.

'Have you nearly finished your shift?' Ollie asks Carmelo.

'Another hour, *mi amic*.'

Ollie casts him a sympathetic look and pats his arm as we take our leave. We walk along Calle Sa Lluna and wave at Javier, who is closing the shutters on his deli, Colmado Sa Lluna, for the afternoon. I'm tempted to pop by Ainere, a new café and takeaway situated further along the street, to buy some of its delicious home-made *croquetas*, savoury croquettes, but decide that it can wait until tomorrow. It is already 1:30 and most of the town's folk have retired indoors for lunch followed by siestas. As we head down Carrer de la Victoria, Ollie suddenly stops, a puzzled smile on his lips. Ahead of us an elderly woman with a cigarette placed firmly between her lips and wearing a nylon overall and flip-flops is vacuuming her front doorstep and the pavement in front of it. We watch in disbelief.

'Now that's a memorable sight,' I snigger.

'It's comforting to know that there are people in this town more unhinged than you are,' he counters.

I give him a mock clip around the ear and, giggling, we walk past, pretending not to notice the eccentric activity taking place. Unable to resist, I steal a glance backwards and see the woman smiling up at the sun, her arms folded, while the unattended vacuum cleaner happily sucks at the ground as if it had a mind all of its own.

By the time I return home, my legs are feeling stiff and creaky.

'Have you stopped going to your Saturday Pilates classes in Deia?' Ollie chides.

'Of course not! I wouldn't miss them for the world. It's a wonderful excuse to do exercise and then gorge myself silly on croissants and coffees straight afterwards with the girls.'

He throws me a despairing look. 'That's not the attitude, mother. Talking of your friends, when I was having a drink with Angel the other night, he told me that Juana is desperate to come over and see our chickens but that Alan keeps putting her off.'

'Ha! You know why? He is storing a whole load of Pep's lethal home-made wine in his *abajo*, which Juana thinks was thrown out or given away. She'd be furious with Pep for lying to her.'

'So what's the plan?'

'Well Pep and your father are planning on hiding it around the house before she visits. Once she's gone, they'll replace it all in the *abajo*. I want nothing to do with it.'

'Maybe they should just drink the lot? Some mates and I could help.'

'Nice try.'

He gives a shrug. 'Well, I don't know about you, but I'm off for a kip. I only had about three hours sleep last night since you insisted on dragging me up a mountain this morning.'

'It was fun though.'

'Hm. It was certainly interesting. Agustin obviously mugged up on his notes.'

'I'm sure he'll make a great guide. There were things he told us that I hadn't known before.'

He gives me a wink. 'Well now, that is a revelation.'

Sleepily he enters his bedroom with his beloved cat Orlando tucked under his arm. For some moments I hear him bustling around in his room, getting ready for bed and then, quite suddenly, all is still.

It is early evening and we are sitting in the aromatic and tranquil gardens of Can Prunera, the modernist art museum in Calle de Sa Lluna, in the centre of the town. The magnificent property was once owned by merchant Joan Magraner and his wife, Margalida Vicens, who, similarly to many Mallorcans at the time, emigrated to France in the late-nineteenth century in the hope of making a fortune or at least a handsome living selling Mallorcan delicacies. Having made a huge success of their grocery business, the Magraners returned home to Sóller at the turn of the century and built Can Prunera, meaning plum tree, a likely reference to their trade in the fruit. Now a public museum, the building has been tastefully restored, retaining its art nouveau flourishes and, aside from offering an excellent exhibition space, is an aesthetic venue for cultural events.

Tonight we have been invited to attend a *son et lumière* performance to celebrate the creation of WOW, an acronym for Walking on Words. This new initiative by Fundació Casa Museu, the foundation of house-museums in Mallorca, and the

Council of Mallorca will highlight seven literary walking routes across the island in areas where historic writers, both local and international, have either lived or visited. As we sit in the shady garden illuminated by tiny twinkling lights, the Scotsman and I wait in anticipation for the performance to begin. Suddenly a searing spotlight hits the stage and hovers on what appears to be a bright red beach hut with a curtain drawn across its facade. A second later, a head pokes through and well-known journalist, Carlos Garrido, erupts onto the stage. Clearly he is master of ceremonies as he skilfully and colourfully guides the audience through Mallorca's literary epochs. He pauses at each historic period to allow his co-performers, singer Mariona Forteza and actor Xim Vidal, to emerge from the curtained hut to take central stage. They deliver haunting songs and spellbinding readings, taken from the works of both local and international writers who sought their inspiration in Mallorca. We are sad when, after an hour, the magical performance finally comes to an end. Afterwards, as guests mingle at the reception, enjoying glasses of delicious local wine from the cellars of Anima Negre, Mesquida Mora, Mortitx and Jaume de Puntiró, we get chatting with Carme Castells, the director of Walking on Words, and her colleague Carlotta. They are both hugely enthusiastic about the project.

Carme shows me a beautiful pictorial tome, which outlines the whole scheme.

'The walks will cover Palma and the island's coastal and mountain towns and villages where authors and poets left their mark. Some of our walks will also feature museums or places with literary significance.'

'So how many authors will you feature?' the Scotsman asks.

'Forty-nine authors and poets in total. Of course we have our own Mallorcan writers with the likes of Blai Bonet, Rafel Ginard, Llorenç Villalonga or, for example, Miquel Costa i Llobera. But there are many international authors and poets as well, such as

Albert Camus, Robert Graves, Gertrude Stein or, say, Agatha Christie.'

'Didn't she write *Problem at Pollensa Bay* while holidaying in Mallorca?'

She turns to me. '*Exacto*! She used to stay at the atmospheric Illa d'Or Hotel in Pollença port and must have found inspiration there.'

'Wise woman. It's in an idyllic location and still hugely popular with British holidaymakers,' says the Scotsman.

'We're likely to hold our official launch there in October. I hope you'll come.'

I laugh. 'Wild hens wouldn't stop me.'

The Scotsman gives me a nudge and whispers, 'Steady.'

I pick up the little WOW guide map that will be available for visitors. 'So is the idea that people will guide themselves along these literary routes using your map?'

Carlotta takes over. 'The beauty of WOW is that visitors to the island can use a free app on their mobiles to source the map and to learn about all the authors and the various locations.'

Carmel nods. 'And at each literary spot, we will have a sign with information about the writer together with a literary quote. There will be seventy-two altogether.'

'Actually, I'm also interested to learn more about the house museums that your foundation runs on the island,' I reply.

'Good! You must visit. We will arrange a grand-island tour for you,' smiles Carlotta.

All the other guests have now dispersed, a reminder to us that we have agreed to meet Ollie for a late supper in the port and must get going. Out in the street, the light is fading as the waning sun, like a flirty *senyorita* hiding behind her fan, dips low behind the tips of the Tramuntanas.

I turn to the Scotsman. 'Wouldn't it be fun to explore the foundation's properties around Mallorca?'

'Indeed,' he says wryly. 'I feel that I am about to reprise my chauffeur role shortly, whether willingly or not.'

'Surely it's too hot for gardening now, anyway?' I protest.

'True,' he replies with an arch smile. 'But remember that it's never too hot for watering.'

After a delicious supper at Pizzeria del Puerto in Sóller port, we amble along the dark sandy beach, espadrilles in hand, drinking in the pungent saline air and marvelling at the tiny golden lights dotted across the port like falling stars. It is a balmy night and the smell of sizzling calamaris, fragrant rosemary and pungent garlic merge tantalisingly to tease the senses. As we stroll past carefree locals and holidaymakers, enjoying the sensation of warm sand between our toes, we decide to stop for a nightcap of *herbes* liqueur before making our way home. Minutes later, ensconced at a local bar, with the black treacly sea stretching out before us, Ollie and I recall our earlier mountain adventure and try to remember the words to a beloved poem by American poet, Robert Frost.

'Some say the world will end in fire, / Some say in ice,' mutters Ollie.

He pauses as I scrunch up my nose, unable to recall the next line. Then, out of nowhere, we hear a disembodied voice. 'From what I've tasted of desire / I hold with those who favour fire.'

We all turn and find a man smiling at us.

'Forgive me, but it is one of my favourite poems, too. Such a powerful few lines and yet written so simply.'

'Funnily enough, we have just been to a literary event at our local art museum and it has got us in the mood for poetry,' replies the Scotsman.

Soon we get chatting and join our new German friend, Hans, and his wife, Laura, at their table. They tell us that they have been touring the island in a camper van and, although German, live in

Switzerland. Some time later, as we finally take our leave, Hans stands on the pavement and calls after us. 'Here's one for the road. I'll leave you with a line from a little masterpiece by Robert Frost. "When a friend calls to me from the road / and slows his horse to a meaning walk, / I don't stand still and look around..."'

I smile and turn to him. 'It's from "A Time to Talk". One of my favourites.'

He laughs. 'Spot on. Nice knowing you. Let's hope we all meet again one day. *Buenas noches*!'

We wend our way home along the esplanade with the opal sea, swathed in moonlight, accompanying us as far as Can Repic beach, where we strike forth along the jet-black Sóller road, laughing and ineptly reciting our favourite poems as we go.

Nine

ART OF THE CRAFT

Strolling on to the back terrace with a tray of coffee cups, I listen to the hullabaloo coming from the orchard below. Something has got my hens all of a dither. Despite the din, I pause on the patio to inspect the clusters of fat, ruby grapes hanging low from the iron rungs of the pergola, almost ripe for the picking. In just another week's time they will sport a rich, purple hue and taste as sweet as honey. Sprawled out in front of the pool I survey our various pieces of outdoor furniture, noting that the tatty old covers on the chairs and loungers are now in desperate need of replacement. I know just the place to go for bright new covers; that's if I can lure the Scotsman to join me on the expedition. As I descend the stone steps to the orchard, the sound of indignant squawks rents the air. I can see Juana stalking around the corral inspecting every nook and cranny, with Pep and the Scotsman hot on her heels. Hens are fluttering around them in evident panic while Carlos I and Cordelia sit calmly on a pile of hay in the hen house, observing the scene in some bemusement. I arrive just as Juana is admonishing the two men.

'What is wrong with you both? You're sticking to me like a plaster. Haven't you got anything better to do?'

Pep offers an unctuous smile. 'I'm just excited about the prospect of us having our own little flock of hens. It's fascinating to see the workings of a corral.'

She frowns. 'Are you feeling the effects of the sun, Pep?'

The Scotsman takes her arm. 'Let me show you our new nesting boxes and our corn feeder. It's all quite simple to use.'

I hand out coffees. 'Why don't you two go and play and I'll give Juana the grand tour.'

Juana looks relieved. 'A great idea. Afterwards I can come and assess your *abajo* for you, Alan. We can have a good look at what needs clearing out.'

'Oh, don't worry about that,' he blusters. 'It's all under control. Pep has promised to give me a hand when the time comes.'

When they are out of earshot, Juana narrows her eyes. 'OK, spill the beans. What's going on with those two? They're up to something. I can sniff it a mile away.'

I shrug. 'Who knows? They've always got some nefarious scheme up their sleeves. Probably plotting to make some new noxious brew, no doubt.'

'Hm. I think something's amiss in Alan's *abajo*. I shall give it a good inspection.'

'Good luck. I try to avoid it like the plague. It's the same with Ollie's bedroom, otherwise known as the bear pit. You enter at your peril.'

We stroll around the field and orchard, followed by my troupe of faithful hens, whom I introduce to Juana one by one. She humours me when I reel off all their individual names, assuring me that her new brood will be nameless and, in some cases, headless when it comes to their time for the pot. Ferdinand tails her but, to my surprise, stands sweetly at her side when she stops to admire the view and even allows her to feed him a handful of corn.

'By Jove, you're a marvel!'

She laughs. 'Am I?'

I stare in wonderment at my malevolent cockerel. 'Ferdinand is a terror and yet you've literally got him eating out of your hand.'

'I rather like him,' she replies.

'That's fantastic! I will gift him to you as long as you don't do away with him.'

'Are you sure? How wonderful. All I need are five hens now.'

'Do take Delilah, his paramour. She'll be bereft without him.'

I feel a little sad to be giving Ferdinand away, but we have more than our fair share of cockerels and I could do without his increasingly aggressive behaviour directed at the others and at us.

Juana takes a sip of her coffee. 'Our corral is being erected this week so I should be able to collect them next weekend if that's OK?'

'Perfect, but remember that neither must end up in a hot pot.'

'Scout's honour!' She pauses and, with a glint in her eye, says, 'Let's keep this a secret for now. I'll come over on Saturday to collect the birds in order to house them in my new corral before Pep returns from his morning football practice.'

'Fine by me. Is Pep still playing in the local team?'

'It's what I call Team Geriatric,' she says dismissively. 'A group of ageing men tottering about the pitch, and all old enough to know better.'

As we arrive at the *abajo*, Pep and the Scotsman smile genially from the open doorway. Quite to their joint surprise, Juana steps in, surveys the organised chaos and smiles sweetly. 'This all looks in order, Alan, so I'll leave you to it. I've taken a note of the equipment we need for our corral and it all seems quite straightforward so Pep and I should probably head off. We don't want to overstay our welcome.'

'No, indeed,' Pep chimes in. With some relief he joins her in the hot sunshine. 'Ah, another beautiful summer's day, my *chérie*!'

Juana offers a broad smile. 'Yes, it's certainly hotting up.'

'Getting warmer all the time!' I trill.

She gives the Scotsman a searing look. 'What's that expression in English? If you can't stand the heat, get out of the fire.'

The Scotsman furrows his brow. 'It's kitchen, not fire. Besides, that's less about the weather and more about people who can't cope under pressure.'

'Really?' she beams. 'I must remember that.'

Minutes later, Pep and Juana say their goodbyes and roar up the precarious track in their old van, observed by the Scotsman who stands pensively in the courtyard, hugging a basket of lemons to his chest.

'Juana was acting a bit oddly, don't you think?'

'Not particularly,' I reply. 'She's got a lot to think about with the corral and her new hens.'

'I suppose so,' he laughs. 'Anyway, Pep and I couldn't believe our luck when she opted to leave my *abajo* alone. Now she's inspected it, we're going to move all the hooch and Pep's wine-making equipment back.'

'I'd wait, if I were you.'

'What for? We'd rather have it all in one safe place. Besides, we have a few plans in hand.'

Now it's my turn to narrow my eyes. 'What sort of plans?'

He cheerfully passes me his basket loaded with ripe tomatoes and lemons and bends to pick up a gardening tool by the well.

'Nothing important,' he replies. 'I'll fill you in, all in good time.' And with a roguish grin, he disappears with his spade down into the orchard.

The languid rural town of Santa Maria sits on the edge of the wine-producing district, a hop and a skip from neighbouring Binissalem, famous for its viticulture. Although some might argue that the town, though picturesque, has little to recommend it, I would care to differ. For one thing, Santa Maria's lively Sunday market is a delight and a treat for the senses, with its stalls brimming with aromatic, locally produced fruit and vegetables. There are egg, meat and cheese sellers in abundance, and ironmongers and olive producers happily tout their wares, but perhaps best of all is the livestock section. For it is here that we purchase our hens and cockerels and, if I had my way, a lot more besides if the Scotsman were more accommodating. But aside from the glorious market, there is one culturally important – yet often overlooked – landmark in Santa Maria that sits on the main road to Palma: Artesanía Tèxtil Bujosa. Indeed, it is easy to glide past this historic emporium with its modest frontage and understated sign crafted from white, handmade tiles. But rather like a Tardis, there is more to this narrow terraced property than meets the eye. Established by Guillermo Bujosa Rosselló in 1949, Artesanía Tèxtil Bujosa specialises in Mallorca's famed *robes de llengües*, fabric of flames, the vibrantly coloured cotton and linen cloth that has a distinctive flame-shaped motif.

Once upon a time, there were many such textile workshops and factories on the island, employing thousands of locals, but all that came to an end with the arrival of synthetic fabrics and the tourism boom in the sixties. Today, only three other artisan producers of *robes de llengües* exist, Teixits Vicens in Pollença, which began life in 1854; Teixits Riera, established originally in the village of Biniera in 1896 and now in the hands of the same family in Lloseta; and José Cañameras, who renovated an old workshop that had closed in 1918 in Establiments.

As it's a relaxed Saturday morning, I have finally cajoled the Scotsman and Ollie to pop by the shop to order some covers for our battered old loungers. As we enter the shop, a little bell tinkles from above the door and Maribel, who now runs the business with her brother, Guillermo, bustles out from behind the counter to greet us. From the back of the showroom comes the familiar clattering and chuntering of the old nineteenth-century mechanical looms as they magically transform simple cotton thread into pieces of brightly coloured cloth. Ollie asks to take a peek at them and so Maribel ushers us all into the vast, draughty backroom with its simple stone walls, lofty concrete beams and strip-lighting. Standing at one of the fast-moving machines, one of Maribel's colleagues skilfully monitors the fast, automated weaving of the many-coloured threads as they are rapidly converted into cloth of the highest quality.

'You know, we still hand-dye all the threads in batches and dry them on traditional wood burners as in the old days,' she remarks, above the loud clanking of the loom. 'That's why, when the fabric is woven, there are small differences in the colour and detail. It means that they are all unique.'

'And who creates the designs?' Ollie asks.

Maribel beckons for us to move to a quiet corner of the room. 'We create many designs from scratch in-house, and they take at least a month to complete, but we also revive old patterns and colourways from the past.'

'That sounds like a lot of work,' he grunts.

She laughs. 'It certainly is and needs patience and care.'

'Evidently not a profession for you,' I whisper in his ear.

We have a grand tour of the various mechanical looms, marvelling at the giant wooden reels of brightly dyed thread, the ancient bobbins and fusty old historic machinery. Back in the showroom, Maribel pulls roll upon roll of cloth from the shelves and spreads each out on a large table for us to inspect. I notice that some fabrics are verging on gaudy in colour, while others in the familiar geometric design are fairly muted and mostly in hues of blue.

'That is because we have been able to experiment with more modern colours than was possible historically. The original *robes de llengües* were mostly in the blue spectrum,' Maribel explains.

'And is it true that it was inspired by ancient oriental ikat cloth?' Alan asks.

She nods. 'One of the theories is that Mallorca was a staging route for merchants on the Silk Route crossing between Asia and Europe and that they introduced ikat to the island.'

'Perhaps it arrived with the Moors in the ninth century and they trained locals to make their own version?' I add.

'Maybe,' she smiles. 'We know that countries such as Malaysia and Indonesia were producing ikat or batik designs hundreds of years ago. Some historians believe that the art began in the Bronze Age. There are also versions of ikat in Afghanistan, Iraq and even Japan.'

'Fascinating,' I enthuse.

'Of course, one has to remember that before the eighteenth century, *robes de llengües* were created from silk and would only have been available to the wealthy classes. When cotton and linen were substituted, more of the population could afford it,' she says.

I pinch a piece of smooth cloth between my fingers. 'And you use a mixture today?'

'That's right. We combine linen and cotton, also sometimes with silk.'

'It still seems to be very popular today here on the island,' says Alan.

'It is but it's a specialist cloth. As you probably know, very few artisans still continue the tradition and most of us work for the love of our art. It isn't a huge commercial operation.'

I lean on the shop's counter. 'I read somewhere that during the eighteenth century, up to sixty per cent of the workforce in Mallorca was dedicated to textile manufacture.'

Ollie gives a guffaw. 'Why the heck would you know something like that?'

'Because I find it interesting.'

He shakes his head. 'You really should get out more.'

Maribel laughs. 'But your mother's right.'

The textile industry was once very important in Mallorca, with Palma and Sóller being the main centres. In 1830, there were 120 workshops in Sóller alone, producing mainly cotton, linen and wool, and some silks and hemp. In Bunyola, there was the vast Rullan y Compañia factory, which was taken over by a company called Cruells i Rovira. In fact, Guillem Bujosa Rosselló, the founder of Artesanía Tèxtil Bujosa, worked there as an apprentice.

'Ah, those were the good old days,' yawns the Scotsman. 'While we're on the subject of Sóller, can we please choose some durable material for the covers of our old pool chairs?'

Maribel claps her hands together and faces the yards of colourful cotton fabrics before her. 'Now let me see. As it happens I think I have just what you're looking for.'

On the drive back to Sóller, Ollie looks out of the car window at the rich green pastureland and gives a sigh.

'Much as I like that blue design we chose, I do wonder what all the fuss is about. At the end of the day, they're just pool loungers.'

'True enough, but it's important to cover them in hardy cloth that actually looks good and supports local businesses at the same time.'

He smirks. 'Very worthy of you, mother.'

'Actually, you might both be interested to know that Mallorca is the only country in Europe still producing the flame-motif cloth,' I say.

'I think it looks more water-stained than flame-shaped,' Ollie opines.

'I agree,' drawls Alan as he heads along the quiet country road in the direction of Bunyola village. 'What I find fascinating is that it's become such an emblem for the identity of the island.'

'Can we stop talking about textiles now? It's all wearing a bit thin,' replies my son dryly.

'Oh you're so witty,' I retort.

He grins back at me in the driver's mirror. 'I know. Now, talking of craftsmanship, have either of you seen the new work of art in the car park at Plaça Teixidors in Sóller?'

The Scotsman nods. 'I'd hardly call it art. It's a graffiti of a snake.'

'It's supposed to be a political statement about the state of tourism in the Baleares,' Ollie argues. 'The snake is symbolic of tourism gobbling up the island.'

'Do you agree with it?' I ask.

He shrugs at me from the backseat. 'If you want to make money from tourism, you have to accept what comes with it. That's life.'

'I can think of more positive images I'd have chosen to put there,' I reply.

'Orange, olive and lemon trees and fluffy chickens under blue skies?' he teases.

I laugh. 'Exactly!'

Some time later we arrive back at our track, only to find a band of renegade hens staring at us belligerently outside the front gate.

'They must have escaped onto the track when we opened the gate earlier. It looks as if they haven't been able to get back into the courtyard, silly things!'

Ollie gets out of the car and shoos them all out of the way. Ferdinand gives him a filthy look and marches off into the orchard below, chortling as he goes.

The Scotsman stands in the courtyard and stretches his arms. 'Well, I don't know about you lot but I've got to water and sort out my vegetables before we go out tonight.'

Ollie picks up Inko, who is standing patiently on the front porch. 'I'm off out with Angel later. Where are you two going?'

'The Nit de l'Art, of course,' I reply.

The annual Night of Art in Sóller, when artists display their works in shops and on Calle Sa Lluna, the town's main shopping street, is one of the highlights of the social calendar. Bands play and cafés and restaurants in the *plaça* are besieged by locals and visitors.

'Don't you and Angel want to join us?' I ask Ollie. 'We're meeting Juana and Pep at Café Sóller for a drink at eight-thirty.'

He stands at the front door, evidently sizing up the offer. 'Yeah, we'll meet you for a beer and then head off to see some friends in Deia.'

No sooner has he slipped into the *entrada* than I hear Johnny coughing from his dark bunker in the rocks by the pond. 'All on your tod?'

'Yes, a bit of peace for a while.'

'That boy's growing up fast. All of mine were independent, too. Hopping out of the pond as soon as they found their little webbed feet. Of course, in my time I've heard the patter of several thousand tiny webbed feet and it's never ending. Never free of the pests, squirming around in their spawn come the spring.'

'I imagine parenthood must be quite demanding.'

'You have no idea. Just ask the frogs. Same for them, too.'

I'm about to reply when I hear an urgent buzzing at the gate. It is Juana, who – I suddenly recall – was coming to pick up Ferdinand and Delilah. I watch as her car swerves inelegantly into the courtyard. She hops out, looking svelte as ever in cropped black linen trousers and a white T-shirt. 'So, how was your trip to Bujosa?'

'Fantastic. Hopefully we'll have more presentable lounger covers soon. Can I get you a cool drink?'

She shakes her head and pushes her hand through her henna-tinted locks. 'I can't be long because I want to have Ferdinand and his sweetheart *in situ* before Pep returns home. It'll be a lovely surprise!'

As I head down to the corral I see the Scotsman standing outside his *abajo*, puffing happily on a *puro*. He does a double take when he sees Juana and hastily closes the door of his lair, a look of undisguised panic on his face.

'Ah, Juana! How lovely to see you, but I thought we were all meeting tonight?'

'Indeed we are, but your generous wife offered to donate me one of your cockerels and a hen, so here I am. Pep doesn't know anything about it. It's going to be a big surprise.'

He smiles genially and waves her towards the corral. In the hen house, I have two large cardboard boxes filled with straw, awaiting Ferdinand and Delilah's departure. They'll only suffer the indignity of being confined inside for the brief car journey to Juana's home.

'Catching Ferdinand isn't going to be easy – I'll use my heavy gardening gloves,' mutters Alan. He turns to me. 'I'll leave Delilah to you.'

As he plods off in search of my least favourite cockerel, I pull the boxes into the corral and make air holes in the lids. Juana wanders off while I am busy at my task and when Alan returns with an indignant Ferdinand clamped between his hands, I am easily able to catch Delilah who devotedly trails her imprisoned partner. When both are firmly secured in their respective boxes, the Scotsman and I carry them out of the corral and call to Juana. It is at that moment that I see her emerging from the *abajo* with a steely look on her face. The Scotsman curses silently and casts me a helpless glance.

'Don't tell me that you put all the hooch back in there?' I hiss.

He nods. 'Oh dear. Pep and I are undone.'

I give a tut. 'You're telling me, but you only have yourselves to blame.'

He exhales deeply. 'Thanks for the show of support. Tonight's going to be jolly.'

'There's only one thing for it. You're just going to have to face the music and beg forgiveness.'

He watches as Juana strides menacingly towards us and offers her his most charming of smiles. 'Now, Juana, I can explain everything…'

The night sky is still oyster-hued as we sit in Café Sóller in the town's bustling *plaça*, supping on glasses of robust red wine. All about us are laughing locals and holidaymakers enjoying the festive atmosphere, pulsating heat, and the entertainment unfolding on the lofty stage in front of the town hall. Tonight, practically every local artist, sculptor and artisan worth their salt has taken to the street to display their skills and craftsmanship, and I am champing at the bit to view the works. A band strikes up and Ollie and Angel pick up their beer glasses and head over to the stage to get a better view. Pep has already gulped down his first glass of wine and is being uncharacteristically solicitous to Juana, having apparently been given an earful about his duplicitous ways. In an earlier phone call to the Scotsman he recounted how his wife had returned home and demanded that he dispose of all his crates of home-made wine secreted in the *abajo* before the week was out. To crown it all, Ferdinand had given him a sharp peck on the leg, much to Juana's delight. I turn the conversation to the safe subject of poultry.

'So have Ferdinand and Delilah settled happily into your corral?'

'Perfectly,' purrs Juana. 'They can't believe how much space they have all to themselves but next week, they'll be joined by some pullets from Santa Maria market. Pep is getting up especially early to get the pick of the crop.'

He grimaces. 'For you, anything, my dear.'

'In that case, you might pick me up a Cartier watch on the way home, too,' she says with a lean smile.

Pep offers a good-natured guffaw and is about to ask the waiter for another glass of red wine when Juana fixes him with a stony expression.

'Remember that you're driving,' she cautions.

A surreptitious smile passes between him and the Scotsman.

'How about we go for a stroll to look at the stalls and have another drink later, perhaps with some *tapas*?' suggests my husband.

'An excellent idea,' replies Pep.

Some time later we find ourselves in lively Calle Sa Lluna, along with hordes of others. Progress is particularly slow as we stop every few minutes to chat with friends and neighbours and to study the works of local artists. At basket emporium Ca's

Sarrier, Cristina Alcover's partner Rafa wants to show us the T-shirts he has designed under the brand name Rupit, meaning robin in Mallorquin. Handily, his sister, Gracia, owns the shop and sells his wares alongside her beautifully crafted baskets and traditional sandals from the island of Menorca. At estate agent Casas Mallorca, we are treated to glasses of cava by owners Gerhard and wife Regina and invited to view a wonderful collection of art and hanging lamps by up-and-coming local artist, Mónica Abad.

Next door, Juana and I are enthralled by a selection of handmade lamps crafted from driftwood and leaves by an artisan named Nicolas. The Scotsman takes his card and assures me that this isn't the moment to be carrying an awkwardly shaped standard lamp along the street. Pep stops to admire some fish sculptures by my chum Toful Colom, while the Scotsman is most enamoured by a series of book sculptures by local Argentinean artist, Ricardo Sacco. We all head for Can Prunera museum, where we hope to explore a new exhibition of works by former Deia-based American artists, Bob and Dorothy Bradbury. I have long been a fan of their art and regret that they slipped out of our world before I ever had a chance to meet either of them. However, their talented daughter Suzanne, a celebrated classical pianist locally, kindly ensures that our piano is tuned each year by visiting experts from Germany.

As we are about to step into the museum, I bump into Uta Carlsson, a good friend and interiors specialist who lives a hop and a skip from our own home.

She gives me a hug. 'Goodness, have you ever seen such crowds?'

Juana and I laugh.

'It's sheer madness,' I reply. 'And where is that mischievous Swedish husband of yours?'

'Hakan? Oh he's gone to get the car. We are quite worn out but it's been a magical evening. Before you head off, don't forget to visit the exhibition by Eyle Reinhold. It's just next door to Can Prunera.'

'Of course,' Juana enthuses. 'We have plenty of time.'

Pep gives a snort and turns to the Scotsman. 'We're never going to sup our second glass of wine at this rate.'

'Or sit down to *tapas*,' laments the Scotsman.

Uta smiles. 'Ah, but the night is but young.'

Juana nods. 'Indeed, we can all wait. Culture first, food and wine later. Don't you agree?'

Pep and the Scotsman offer each other despairing looks, but not wanting to slide further in Juana's bad books, smile cordially and, with an exaggerated bounce in their step, follow us both into Can Prunera museum, sharing a complicit wink on the way.

Ten

FIGS AND PIGS

Under a canopy of azure sky, I sit munching *tostados*, fresh, brown bread smeared with tomato and garlic, outside a café in the charming village of Sencelles. It is a mellow morning and a warm sun massages my back as I set about a hearty breakfast. Today we are visiting Son Mut Nou, an experimental fig farm in Llucmajor in the south of Es Pla, the agricultural central region of the island, but have decided to take a short pit stop en route. The Scotsman's black coffee idles by his plate, awaiting its owner's return, but he could be some time. No sooner had we placed our order with the chirpy waitress than his mobile phone rang and, in some excitement, he got up and wandered up the road, away from café noise and chatter. Who can be calling, I wonder, to have animated my husband in such a way? I don't wait long for an answer as he returns to his chair with a spring in his step and takes a glug of coffee.

'Guess who that was?'

'Angelina Jolie?'

'The actress? Why on earth would she be calling me?'

'Father Christmas taking advance orders?'

He shakes his head. 'Now you're just being silly. Actually it was the casting director of Focus Films. They said that I've been chosen out of fifty candidates for that German advert.'

I giggle. 'The one where you've got to tuck into a plate of German wurst and sauerkraut?'

'The same. It's going to involve two days of filming in Palma in a fortnight's time.'

'Congratulations, but don't you have to be able to speak German?'

'Of course not! There's a voice-over and I just sit gorging myself on food. Not a bad way to earn some bucks. I might treat myself to a new rotavator for the garden.'

Some years ago, the Scotsman signed up for auditions at Focus Films in Palma and has since participated in a steady stream of adverts shot on the island, mainly because of its all-year temperate climate. He has played a butler in a French lottery television commercial and appeared in print publicity for banks and insurance companies. Aside from receiving a fee for his endeavours, he thoroughly enjoys the experience, chatting with film crews and generally having an enjoyable day's excursion. However, promoting sausages seems a bit of a step down from some of his more ritzy shoots.

He tucks into his *tostados* and waves his fork in the air. 'Do you think they might give me some free supplies of wurst?'

'I do hope not,' I reply. 'I'd prefer sauerkraut.'

'I'm not mad on the stuff, myself. There's nothing to beat a good sausage, though.'

We finish our breakfast and head for the car, which is parked on a shady side street close to the village's old church of Sant Pere. A statue of Francinaina Cirer i Carbonell, arguably Sencelles' most famed historic resident, graces the front of the church. She lived between 1781 and 1855 and was beatified by Pope John Paul II in 1989. Her life was apparently devoted to selfless acts, helping the poor and teaching children, despite the fact that she went against the wishes of her parents. Probably, according to the traditions of the time, they would have preferred her to have married prosperously or spent her life as a spinster looking after them. Women didn't have a lot of choice at that time.

I give a yawn and tap the Scotsman's arm. 'I read that Francinaina had quite a reputation in her day. Many Catholics came from all over the island to see her, believing that she could perform miracles. She became Mother Superior of the local convent.'

We return to the car and study the map.

The Scotsman turns to me. 'How about we take a look at one of the famed archaeological sites around here?'

Ruta Arqueológica is an archaeological route comprising four talaiot sites that run between Sencelles and Costitx village. The two villages used to be linked but, due to constant squabbling, they split in 1855. Poor old Sencelles had a hard time of it in the latter part of that century when the phylloxera plague struck and destroyed all the vines.

'A great idea,' I reply. 'It wouldn't take too long.'

The Scotsman studies the sign ahead. 'So we'll take the road for Llucmajor?'

'Wait a tick. Could we just pop by the site of the shrine of Son Corró, it's not too much of a diversion. It's just a few kilometres along the road.'

He sighs. 'If we keep being diverted we'll never get there. Let's make it quick.'

A few minutes later we veer off the main road to Costitx and park up on a rough piece of ground at the side of a field full of wild, yellow grasses and thistles. There isn't a car or soul in sight on this most perfect of days. Rolling hills surround us and pockets of fig, olive and almond trees can be seen in small agricultural enclaves close to weathered old *fincas*. The tinkle of sheep bells carries on the warm breeze and the sharp tang of freshly cut grass mingles with the rich odour of wood smoke.

I stand on a small mound of grass and look out at the scene before me. 'This is so beautiful. It's just how I imagine Homer's Elysian plain.'

'Indeed,' the Scotsman replies. 'It's a shame more visitors don't come to this part of the island. It's so magical.'

'And unspoilt.'

He winks. 'Much cheaper, too! You can get a *menú del día* for half the price of Palma.'

'Always a Scot at heart,' I quip.

At the brow of the hill, we find a fig tree laden with fruit, and so we give in to temptation and gorge ourselves on the ripe, black crop. We munch on our spoils as we explore the wide circle of roughly hewn dove-grey pillars of the Santuari de Son Corró, originally discovered in the nineteenth century. The post-talaiot site, which dates to between the fifth and second century BC, was reconstructed into its current format in 1995, much to the chagrin of some purists who felt it should have been left as was.

I place a hand on the warm stone. 'You know, three decorative bronze bulls' heads were discovered on the site but they were carted off to the National Archaeological Museum of Madrid. The locals are still trying to get them back.'

'Just like the Greeks with the Elgin Marbles,' he muses.

'A smaller scale rumpus but I do have sympathy with the locals. They should be returned, don't you think?'

'It does make sense.' He looks at his watch. 'Come on. We don't want to be late.'

The experimental fig farm of Son Mut Nou is tucked away along a quiet rural track close to the sea, surrounded by fields of rich, red soil and towering pine trees. The air is dry and fragrant and, as we roll up to the one-storey *finca* surrounded by 18 hectares of cultivated *figueres*, fig trees, our bearded host, the smiling and charismatic Montserrat Pons i Boscana, is waiting to greet us. As a lover of figs, I have always had a yearning to visit this much-heralded farm, the largest of its kind in the world. Montserrat and I have spoken by telephone and finally set on today for a visit. No sooner have we exchanged greetings than he ushers us into his jeep and off we go for a whirlwind tour of the terrain.

'You should know that we have three hundred and sixty-seven varieties of figs growing here and one thousand two hundred and eighty-seven fig trees. There are also sixty-five foreign fig varieties from places you wouldn't even imagine!'

Dust flies all around as the vehicle bumps up and down along the muddy and furrowed tracks that lead into the heart of the fig orchards. We follow the sharp twists and bends until we arrive on the edge of a wide field of coppery soil. Before us are row upon row of leafy trees, their branches drooping with fruit. We jump out of the car and follow Montserrat as he strides purposefully across the arid terrain. He points to a clump of trees, each sporting figs of varying hues and varieties.

'These are all from different countries – South Africa, Chile, Bolivia, Syria, Iraq, and over here, for example, we have varieties from Turkey, Israel and Japan.'

The Scotsman examines a fat green fig plucked by his host and nods approvingly. 'This is a very healthy specimen.'

'The current conditions are perfect for figs. We have little rain and the saline air suits them. All the same, I have quite a complex irrigation system underground, which is essential at this time of the year.'

I almost swoon with delight when I taste the sweet fig, a native Abaldufada Rimada, which Montserrat passes me. The skin is apple-green in hue, with fine, yellow stripes running vertically from its tip. Next we sample Coll de Dama Blanca, a beetroot-coloured fig with a rich, aromatic fragrance. Montserrat smiles enthusiastically as he leads us across his land, pointing out the different varieties of trees as he goes.

'You might find it odd that I practised as a pharmacist for many years in Llucmajor before creating my fig haven, but since childhood I have always loved figs and had a passion for botany. We planted our first specimens here in 1995 and now produce about five hundred tonnes of fruit annually. The main season runs from May until September.'

'What on earth do you do with so many figs?' I ask.

He shrugs. 'Well, we sell a fair few, but my wife Hortensia masterminds all sorts of uses for them. We have created fig beer and liqueur as well as aromatic vinegar, jams and *pan de higo*, fig cake, and dried figs. I'll let you try some when we return to the house.'

Soon we are back in the car and hurtling around the farm's rugged tracks, en route to the walled nursery where Montserrat cultivates many a sapling. Outside the gate, there are rows of tawny-skinned figs drying in the sun.

'When were figs first cultivated in Mallorca?'

He throws out his arms expansively. 'They've been a stalwart of the Mallorcan diet for hundreds of years and of course, during Moorish and Roman times, they were cultivated. It's said that humans have been eating *figues* for the last seven thousand years, and why not? It is such a delicious and nutritious fruit.'

Unfortunately, production has diminished over the years. In the forties, there were 22,000 hectares of land devoted to fig growing, but today only about 800 hectares are used. Of course, the other problem is that many figs are imported to the island. It's a shame more residents don't opt for home-grown figs.

I pull a dark purple fig apart and admire the bright red fruit within. 'Don't farmers need them for their livestock, too?'

'That's a good point. In the past, figs were essential for the diet of pigs, especially the Mallorcan black pig, which is highly prized. But agriculture isn't what it once was here on the island. There are far fewer people in the industry.'

'It's so sad. We have our own fig trees so only need to supplement every so often but surely locals should be supporting Mallorcan varieties?' I reply.

'I can't agree more,' he sighs. 'One of my other goals here is to revive old varieties and protect all of the different species that we grow. It's also important to nurture specimens from war-torn countries, such as Syria, to ensure that they will always have a place in the horticultural world, come what may.'

We drive back to the main *finca* where Montserrat shows us images taken of him with other international specialists at some of the many fig conferences that are held around the globe. He is regarded as a world expert and often jumps on a plane to impart his knowledge to others at global seminars. I study the antique collection of wooden sticks that he keeps on one of the old rustic walls in his courtyard.

'You'll see that they're forked at the tip to enable you to pull down a branch more easily,' he chuckles. 'It's useful if you're not tall.'

He taps my arm. 'Of course you'll know that Juniper Serra from the town of Petra sailed with fig specimens to America and look at how many are now cultivated in California, all thanks to him – a son of Mallorca. The story goes that during the voyage, the crew got fed up with all his specimens on deck and threatened to throw them overboard.'

The Scotsman laughs. 'He must have taken a huge amount of supplies on board in his work as a missionary, so that probably included fig saplings.'

We sit at his old pine table out in the sunshine, eating dried figs and olive oil biscuits with cheese and *sobrasada,* washed down with some of his delicious fig liqueur. Montserrat proudly shows us his work of art, *Les Figueres a les Illes de Balears*, a huge pictorial tome of 450 pages that painstakingly lists every fig variety throughout the Balearic Islands. It has obviously been a labour of love and must prove a veritable goldmine for Mediterranean gardeners and fig aficionados.

FIGS AND PIGS

After pigging out on so many fig products, we leave with a clutch of bottles and jars and, with windows down, take the country road for the town of Algaida. The warm breeze whips through the car, rustling the map and newspaper that sit on my lap.

The Scotsman yells over the moaning wind and loud classical music playing on the radio. 'It's interesting that black pigs feed on bacon and pigs. I suppose that explains why they're so special. The island's poor old pink pigs probably just survive on shallots.'

I look at him in some wonderment. 'Have you completely lost your marbles or is this Scottish humour? To the best of my knowledge, black pigs don't eat bacon and pigs! And where on earth did you get the idea that pink pigs eat shallots?'

He looks at me from the wheel. 'What did you say? Black pigs eat bacon and pigs? Are you being funny?'

I turn the music off. 'You said black pigs ate bacon and pigs!'

'No I didn't, you silly goose,' he blasts good-naturedly. 'I said ACORNS and FIGS!'

'And what about pink pigs eating shallots, then?'

'Are you going deaf? I said SLOPS!' he shouts.

I close the windows and switch the air conditioning onto the lowest setting. 'Well, that's a relief. I really thought the sun was getting to you.'

'So where are we going now?' he says with a grin.

'I thought on the way home we could pop by the village of San Joan to visit the Pare Ginard museum.'

'Is that the literary museum?'

'Yes, remember it's one of the stopping points on the Walking on Words route. We need to see the other museums, too.'

He pushes down the sun visor against the searing rays of the sun. 'Not today, thank you! Don't forget we promised to pop by to see Toni Frau at La Luna *sobrasada* factory later.'

'There are so many surprising little gems tucked away on the island,' I say with a smile. 'Isn't that the joy of Mallorca, though? We've been here all these years and every day we learn something new.'

In the tranquil and bijoux village of San Joan, with its lean and shady streets, we find the unobtrusive doorway of an ancient terraced stone house, the erstwhile home of Father Rafel Ginard I Bauçà, the priest, folklorist and author whose mission in life was to keep the island's oral traditions alive. He lived from 1899 until 1976 and is most famed for compiling a book of 15,000 popular island folk songs, entitled *Cançoner Popular de Mallorca*. We are met by Joana, the curator who works for Fundació Casa Museu, who shows us around the simple, whitewashed rooms and exhibits of photos, letters and works by the revered priest.

I follow her through the hallway. 'Do many visitors come here?'

She smiles. 'We would love more British to pop by. We're a bit off the tourist map here but there's so much to do in the area.'

'There's the Calderers estate just up the road, which is worth a look,' agrees the Scotsman. 'And the Juniper Serra museum in Petra.'

'True. Es Pla is a goldmine for visitors but most never venture beyond the popular areas.'

Joana leads us into the tiny kitchen, barely big enough for two adults to move about.

'This is where the family would have dined and tried to keep warm. They were very poor, rural people and so ate from one bowl and with just one spoon.'

After showing us a variety of Pare Ginard's tomes, we walk into the small inner courtyard that served as a garden and where an enclosure remains, once used for hens and livestock. 'Even the eggs the family produced were immediately sold in the market,' Joana says. 'They survived on meagre rations.'

I examine the old stone bread-oven, cistern and latrine. 'So how did the family afford to send Rafel to school?'

'Luckily children from poor rural homes such as Rafel were often given an education by the Catholic Church, which is why he started ecclesiastic studies at thirteen in Arta and entered into the priesthood in 1924. All the same, he was fervent about the oral traditions and songs, the *gloses,* of the island and spent much of his life recording them in several volumes for posterity.'

'It's hard to imagine how harsh life was at that time for rural folk,' Alan says.

Back in the house, Joana shows us a photo of the young Rafel looking reserved and shy. 'It's a sad fact that the children didn't receive a single gift at Christmas, although it wasn't all gloom. They sang together and chatted around the fire. It was the normal way of life at the time.'

'And how did rural women fare?'

She frowns. 'Well in truth, if you weren't married by thirty, you were on the shelf and destined for a life of poverty and hard work.'

After our visit, the Scotsman and I are in contemplative mood back in the car.

'What an incredible visit that was,' he says.

I smile. 'Indeed, but I wouldn't have fancied being a woman back then. All work and no play.'

'Think of the poor chaps, sweating away in the fields all day or working in stone quarries.'

'At least they could go for a beer after the day was done. The women just went home from the fields and carried on with domestic work!'

He grins. 'Talking of beer, perhaps we've got time for a quick bite and a glass of *vino* before we head back to Sóller. What do you say?'

'A splendid idea,' I concur. 'And as the menus in Es Pla are so cheap, you won't even moan about the cost all the way home!'

With a dismissive grunt he starts the car and, in cheerful anticipation, we head off along the sunny lane.

As the Scotsman and I stride along Avinguda d'Asturias, en route to Embutidos Aguiló, better known by its commercial brand name of La Luna, meaning the moon, Judas rings. I fumble for the mobile in my voluminous pannier. It's Greedy George.

'Hi guv, doing anything exciting?'

'On my way to an artisanal factory that produces *sobrasada,* if you must know.'

'What the heck's *sobrasada*?'

'One of the most emblematic food products of Mallorca. It's a paprika-cured pork sausage.'

'Sounds good. Stocking up, are you?' he asks.

'Actually, I'm writing an article about it for a magazine, so Toni, one of the owners, kindly invited me to revisit. It's the oldest manufacturer of the stuff in Mallorca.'

He gives a yawn. 'You have all the fun, guv. Bring one back for me, will you?'

'So what do you want?'

'Full of charm as ever! I just wanted you to know that we're running our first production of the cape-ons for Hennie's mangy old chickens. She's swooning over the final design and so she should be. I've sent you one by post.'

It'll be fun opening that little package when Jorge next pops by with the mail.

'Good-oh. Actually, Hennie called me just the other day to say that she should have more than a hundred volunteers for the Chick-Knit next February. She's already contacted Guinness World Records about creating a new record category.'

He guffaws. 'That woman is as crazy as a bag of frogs...'

'There's nothing crazy about my frogs!'

'Coming from you, that's rich. By the way, Dannie Popescu-Miller has agreed to take an exclusive supply of my Pertelote doorstops to sell in her Miller Magic stores in Russia and New York. She's going to touch base with you about publicising our collaboration.'

'Super, can't wait.'

He giggles. 'Less of the sarcasm, guv. Anyway, must dash, got to take Bianca to her embalmer, sorry, her Botox doctor. Don't forget my sausage!'

'What was all that about?' enquires the Scotsman as we reach the courtyard of Embutidos Aguiló.

'You really wouldn't want to know.'

On the far side of the wide stone patio is La Luna, the factory shop, where all sorts of local products are sold, most noticeably *sobrasada* and pâté made in the factory. Its purple façade, with the familiar moon logo at its centre, has a 1920s feel about it. Shop manager Ana greets us enthusiastically at the door.

'Isn't it a beautiful day? I love it at this time of the year when we head into autumn. It's so tranquil and the heat is so much less intense. I'll let Toni know you're here.'

As a child, Ana and her family used to live on our track in the house now owned by our German neighbours, Helge and Wolfgang, and she remembers playing on our land when it was a smallholding, given over to vegetable growing on a large scale, and where pigs and hens were sold or slaughtered for market. Her mother used to do housework for Silvia and Pedro at the far end of the track.

A few moments later, Toni appears. He is slightly built with bright, intelligent eyes and a winning smile. A marine biologist by training, he and his economist brother Juan recently took over the reins of the family firm when their father decided to retire. It's evident from his enthusiastic demeanour that he loves his job. Inside one of the storerooms we find Juan, who is checking various packages of sausages being sent to restaurants and grocery stores across the island.

He comes forward to greet us. 'We distribute our products overseas as well and, believe it or not, the UK!'

Toni laughs. 'There are a good few Spanish restaurants in London now and *sobrasada* is in demand.'

Alan sniffs appreciatively at the outer wrapping of a u-shaped *llonganissa* sausage. 'Where else do you have markets?'

'All over the place. In Spain we supply to most regions, particularly Catalonia, Valencia, Madrid, Murcia and Andalucia, and we take orders from countries such as France and Denmark.'

Toni leads us into an internal courtyard where heavy, antique wrought-iron mincing and grinding machines are on display. They look rather like instruments of torture so probably best left as museum pieces. Two wonderfully evocative historic images catch my eye from the wall. They are reproductions of old black-and-white prints of factory workers, including young children, preparing *sobrasada*. Toni points to one of them.

'That was taken in 1934 at the time when José Aguiló owned the company. He founded it in 1900 but had no heirs and so my father took it over during the eighties. As a family, we have kept it small and artisanal, ensuring that we produce sausage and pâté of the highest quality. There are only seven of us working here.'

He shows us a large, blue bucket full of long, dark pine poles. I notice that each is numbered.

'We hang the *sobrasadas* on these poles during the maturing process and number each one, so that we can keep a record of the dates and batches. It's a simple but effective system,' he tells us.

The Scotsman examines one of the sticks. 'How does the maturing process actually work?'

'Our highest-quality sausage is made from one-year-old black pigs from Felanitx in Es Pla region.'

Mallorca's prized black indigenous pig, *cerdo negro Mallorquín*, was the only swine bred on the island until the early part of the twentieth century. It has distinctive floppy ears, thick black hair and a double chin. Up until the mid-1800s, it used to be so in demand that about 20,000 black pigs were transported annually to Barcelona for

12190114

commercial purposes. Even the French writer George Sand referred to it in her revered tome, *A Winter in Mallorca*. The famed black pig's reputation was further enhanced when Mallorcan *sobrasada* was given the official 'designation of origin' status that protects the name and manufacturing destination of a traditional quality product.

I turn to the Scotsman. 'They're the ones fed on figs and acorns.'

He groans. 'Oh let's not start that one again!'

'And what about the less refined *sobrasada*?' I persist.

'Well that's a mixture of meat from both the black and normal variety of pig. We get about a hundred and fifty kilos of meat from one pig and produce about fifteen hundred kilos of *sobrasada* each week. The ratio is about fifty per cent meat to fat in each sausage. As you know, we also make pâtés and other varieties, such as the thinner *llonganissa*, which only takes two weeks to mature. Then there are *blanquets*, made with pork, eggs, spices, salt and cinnamon and *camaiot*, the fat round sausage, and *botiffaron*, which contains blood.'

We enter the factory's atmospheric museum, which displays historic, handwritten account ledgers, penned in ink, old order books, letters, ancient weighing scales, ladles and pots and pans and, my favourite item, the iconic La Luna tin, which is bright yellow with its red La Luna logo superimposed on a blue background framed by red flowers.

'I'd love one of those tins, Toni,' I say.

He cocks an eyebrow. 'Join the club! Everyone asks for them. The samples on display are all historic but we're seriously considering re-producing them as gift boxes.'

'I'll be your first customer,' I enthuse.

In the two cold stores, which have a slightly yeasty, hoppy odour, we find row upon row of sausages hanging from wooden poles, all at different stages in the curing cycle.

'It takes about two months to cure a *sobrasada*,' Toni says. 'We mix the raw pork with paprika and salt and, once stuffed into intestinal skins, we hang the sausages on these poles. Some clients like the mixture matured longer, often up to six months. Both taste good.'

It is believed that *sobrasada* came into its own during the sixteenth century as the cured sausage could be preserved for long periods. Apparently the name originated in Sicily where it was known as *sopresa*, meaning 'pressed', a method used for stuffing sausages.

'So when did Mallorcans start adding paprika?' the Scotsman asks.

'Paprika became popular after it was brought back from the New World, of course. It seems that islanders began adding it to *sobrasada* from the eighteenth century. Before that time, the sausage wouldn't have had its familiar red colour. By the nineteenth century it was very popular, and during the industrial period of the twentieth century, *sobrasada* sausage was transported far and wide.'

The Scotsman smiles. 'So no good era in which to be born a black pig?'

'No, it's never been a good time to be a black pig here. There are at least six hundred specialist breeders on Mallorca and they even have their own association. *Sobrasada* is a serious business.'

We come to the end of our tour and are accompanied back to the shop by Toni. With a bag full of goodies to enjoy at home, we say our farewells to Toni and the factory crew and walk back up the quiet street to our car.

'I wonder how long the black pig has existed here,' the Scotsman muses as he gets into the car and starts the ignition.

I settle myself in my seat. 'Hundreds of years, according to one tome I read on the subject. They were certainly around at the time of the Romans who probably brought the commonplace pink pig here, too. The black pig apparently thrived during Moorish times and was bred and eaten by the non-Islamic community.'

'I read that the Mallorcan black pig was an Iberian and Celtic crossbreed,' he says.

I laugh. 'True. A recipe for disaster, you'd imagine.'

The Scotsman suddenly gives a loud tut.

'What's up?'

'It's gone five o'clock and we were supposed to have collected our vegetables from Va de Bio half an hour ago. I hope one of the others picked up our box for us.'

The terrain where we go to pick up our weekly Va de Bio order is owned by our friends, Cristina and Ignacio, who kindly loan it to locals who don't have gardens in which to grow produce. It includes a ready water supply from their own *acequia* and a hut for storing produce. Meanwhile, Manel and Teo of Va de Bio also are permitted to use the field to deliver orders from their island-wide delivery service of eco fruit and vegetables.

'Perhaps we can drive down to the field now?' I suggest. 'Manel or one of the others might still be there.'

My mobile rings. It is our friend Natalie from our eco group, telling me that she has picked up our box and will pop round to the house with it later.

'Good old Natalie. Saved by the bell!' smiles the Scotsman.

'Or, you could say, Natalie saved our bacon,' I say inanely.

He levers himself into the driver's seat. 'There's only one thing to say to that – oink-oink!'

Eleven

PRICKLY MATTERS

A hazy sun, hovering above a forest of shaggy pines in the upper tiers of the Tramuntanas, smiles down at me as I drive into the courtyard. Lingering on the driveway with car keys in hand, I marvel at the cloudless azure sky, as intense as a meadow of bluebells. A wisp of ghostly wood smoke rises up from a distant orchard while an eagle, with vast silvery wings outspread, glides elegantly past, caught on the softest of breezes. The cares of the world never seem quite so acute when one contemplates the sheer beauty and magnificence of Sóller at the break of day. My reverie is rudely interrupted by the sound of the front door opening. Standing on the porch is Catalina armed with a sweeping brush. My eyes catch the glint of her blue car parked just a few yards from my own. How hadn't I noticed it before? I walk up the front steps and show her the fruits of my labour, a new resident's tram pass, collected earlier from the railway office in Sóller. This useful card entitles me to discounted fares when travelling on the atmospheric historic tram that runs between the town and the port. She hands it back to me.

'So I hear from Alan that you're off to buy some new hens today?'

'Did he tell you about the breeder?'

Catalina gives the porch a cursory sweep. 'He told me that the man lives outside Manacor and sells exotic breeds. Haven't you got enough hens as it is?'

'But the chickens that Nacho Pons sells are very special. He's got fluffy white Silkies, Peking Bantams and all sorts. Just imagine how wonderful they'd look strutting around the orchard. I only want to buy a pair at this stage.'

'Well don't get any more cockerels. There are far too many already. I think a few should go in the pot.'

I follow her into the kitchen and put the kettle on. She opens the muffin tin.

'No cakes?'

I open the fridge door and show her some freshly baked chocolate and pecan muffins whose icing is just setting.

'Fancy one?'

She grins. 'No. I want two!'

Cradling cups of tea at the table, with the warm sun pouring in through the open kitchen door, we sit, enjoying our muffins and discussing the hens we might be tempted to purchase.

'By the way,' I say. 'Where is the Scotsman hiding?'

She raises her eyebrows. 'In his *abajo* with Pep. Earlier, I saw them transferring crates of empty bottles and several heavy bags from Pep's van down there.'

'Oh no. He got into big trouble with Juana when she discovered Pep had hidden all his old hooch in the *abajo*. She made Pep give it all away. If she hears that they're up to some new mischief, she will not be pleased.'

'Best not to get involved,' she opines. 'Boys will be boys.'

'Talking of boys, I'm going to spruce up Ollie's room before Christmas, sand down and paint the furniture matt grey and turn it into more of a cool teen room. Hopefully it'll be a nice surprise for him.'

Catalina nods. 'Good idea. I think he's outgrown bunk beds and football posters. Haven't you got a spare double bed in the *abajo* that you had in your London flat?'

'Well remembered.'

'When you clear out Ollie's room, remember to give any old clothes of his to the Red Cross.'

'Of course. They were very grateful for my last offerings a few months ago.'

She cocks her head towards the back door. 'I like your new pool covers from Bujosa, by the way. I discovered them in the airing cupboard upstairs.'

I laugh. 'Trust you not to miss a trick! I put them there for safety until we replace the old ones next spring.'

She suddenly breaks into a grin. 'I hear that you have a new TV star in the household.'

'I take it you're referring to the Scotsman's leading role in the German wurst advert last week?'

She nods. 'He was very proud to tell me all about it. Apparently they even got a chauffeur to collect him.'

'That amused Rafael no end. He happened to be standing on the track when the limo passed by. We'll never hear the end of it!'

While we're chatting, Miquela appears from the *entrada* and comes over to greet me.

'Am I the only one working today?' she winks.

'Here, come and join us and have a muffin,' I reply.

She shakes her head. 'I'd rather finish upstairs, but can I take a few home with me for my sons? They'll go mad for them.'

'Of course,' I reply. 'And you can take some lemons if you like.'

Unlike Catalina, Miquela lives in a flat in the town and so doesn't have her own fruit trees. She wanders happily back upstairs with a duster tucked under her arm while Catalina sets off with a pail of water and mop to the lower bathroom. I am just clearing away the dishes when I hear snuffling and turn to see Horatio, once a baby, now a fully fledged hedgehog, tucking into the remains of grain in one of the cat bowls. He carefully skirts the water dish and, without further ado, scuttles behind the fridge, his favourite hidey-hole.

In the absence of excuses not to get on with my work, I slope upstairs and answer a mountain of e-mails that have collected in my inbox, after which I polish off one of my regular blogs for the expat section of *The Daily Telegraph*. The frogs are quacking merrily in the pond below and the sound of clicking cicadas is almost deafening as I sit working on an article. Absorbed in my work, I almost jump out of my skin when the telephone rings. It is Dannie Popescu-Miller.

'Darling, how are you? George and I were only talking about you the other day. I hope your ears were burning!'

I laugh. 'Oh yes, burning away. He told me that you'll soon be selling his Pertelote doorstops at Miller Magic outlets in Russia and New York.'

Her honeyed tones fill the air waves. 'That's precisely why I'm ringing. We'll have the stock in three months' time, and I'd like your wonderful help in promoting the story to the media.'

'Of course.'

She titters. 'Wonderful, darling. Now, tell me, was George joking or do you really keep chickens on your land?'

'We have many.'

'Oh my! That's so quaint. You do love the peasant life, I must say. It's so charming, like something out of a Constable painting,' she ploughs on. 'You'd never know that you lived such a humble lifestyle from the way you dress in London.'

'Ah, yes, I usually leave my wooden clogs and cheesecloth smocks back in the corral.'

'Really? That's so authentic. Anyway, I must dash. I have my Botox doctor arriving any moment. Toodle-pip, darling!'

Once the line goes dead I lean out of the window and take a deep breath. Between Hennie and Dannie, any last vestiges of sanity might soon desert me. The door to my office opens and the Scotsman and Pep blunder in. I eye them sternly.

'Whatever you two are up to now, please keep it to yourselves.'

Pep offers me an effusive hug. 'That's a trifle difficult as we need the kitchen.'

'For what?'

The Scotsman beams. 'We decided to spring a lovely surprise on Juana this Christmas. We're making *patxaran*.'

Patxaran is a very special liqueur from the Navarra area of Spain with one of its most famous brands being Zoco from the Basque region. It was very popular in the Middle Ages and was used by Queen Blanche I of Navarra to cure stomach upsets. Blanche I lived from 1387 to 1441 and had a rather monstrous husband by all accounts. When Blanche's eldest daughter – also called Blanche – had a failed marriage, her father and conniving sister, Eleanor, locked her up and eventually poisoned her. Originally, they had tried unsuccessfully to marry her off to someone she didn't like and when she demurred, Eleanor hatched the plan to dispatch her in order to inherit the kingdom when their father died.

'As in the oxblood-coloured, sloe-flavoured liqueur?' I say in some alarm.

'The same,' says Pep encouragingly. 'It just so happens that I came across several *aranyoners*, blackthorn bushes, near the Torrent d'Orient, and they were heavy with juicy purple berries. I got badly scratched in my quest, but you should see my haul!'

'So why don't you just buy a bottle in the shop?' I ask.

They look affronted.

'But home-made brews are always so much better,' says Pep, hastily adding, 'True, my wine-making hasn't always been a success but this is foolproof.'

The Scotsman gives a frustrated sigh. 'What has any of this got to do with our making *patxaran*?'

'Nothing at all but if you use my kitchen, you can jolly well humour me. And now we've got to head off to Manacor or we're going to be late for our appointment with Nacho Pons.'

'Is it OK if I get cracking with the *patxaran* while you're out?' asks Pep.

'Not really. The last time you made wine in my kitchen, it was a disaster!'

'This is different. The whole process is so simple. I just add anisette liqueur to sloe berries with a few cinnamon sticks and coffee beans and Bob's your aunt.'

'Uncle! When will you get your English idioms right?' I tut.

'What if he's a cross-dresser?'

'Stop being ridiculous, Pep. Look, if I leave you here all day, I don't want to come home to a mess. Understand?'

'I promise it will all be perfect,' he replies solemnly. 'It will only take a couple of hours to prepare a batch. Alan's given me the spare house key.'

Urgent footsteps can be heard from the passageway and Catalina suddenly pokes her head round the door. 'Miquela and I are going.' She stares at me. 'Don't buy too many strange-looking hens and as for you, Pep, if you mess up the kitchen, I'll be after you with a rolling pin.'

The Scotsman shakes his head in frustration. 'What can possibly go wrong?'

'Everything!' replies Catalina with an indignant sniff. 'Where you and Pep are concerned, everything.'

And on that warning note, she marches out of the room.

We are standing on a broad patch of bald, dry land in the wilds of rural Manacor, in the east of the island. The car is parked on the verge of a narrow lane by an unobtrusive wooden sign that reads: NACHO PONS. CRIADOR DE GALLINAS. In other words, Nacho Pons, the hen breeder. As I cast my gaze around us, the only reprieve on the parched landscape is the occasional tuft of limp, yellowing grass and struggling weeds. Elderly Nacho Pons, his tanned and wizened skin shiny under the fierce heat of the sun, stares out at the soft hills before us and shakes his head.

'We need rain.' He gives a hearty cough and stamps his foot on a crack in the soil that runs like a black vein across the pasture. Ants are congregating along its borders and now run every which way to avoid sudden extinction.

He gives a throaty cough. 'Once the rains come, I'm going to turn this into a verdant paradise so that I can expand my little enterprise. I'm keen to get my hands on some buttercups.'

'Oh, I love them too,' I enthuse. 'They grow all over the place in rural England.'

He eyes me in some amusement. 'I'm talking about Buttercup hens. It's a breed.'

'Ah, I see.'

The Scotsman stifles a grin. 'Well I have to say that you have a beautiful situation here.'

Nacho beckons to us to follow. 'Just leave your car there. It'll be safe. Now I will take you to see my children. They are keen to meet you.'

We follow dutifully behind, the Scotsman offering me a puzzled frown. 'Why are we going to meet his kids?'

'I've no idea,' I whisper. 'He's rather loopy.'

'You should know,' he sniggers.

After a brisk, 10-minute walk, we arrive in a small glade beyond which is a vast verdant plain sporting several corrals. Each has a wooden hen hut at its heart and a garden and is segregated from the next by wooden fencing. In each corral are different varieties of hen. I gasp when I reach the first. Hopping cheerfully around the garden are the oddest hens I have ever seen. They seem to have sprouted pom-poms instead of heads and have a wild and fluffy crest.

'Polish,' he shouts enthusiastically, 'and over there are my Turkish Sultans.'

We peer into the corral where several fluffy snowballs with massively hairy feet peck about the grass. Next he points to a corral full of Favorelles with puffy beards and long whiskers.

'They've got five toes,' he proffers. 'And here are my docile Silkies. Aren't they handsome?'

'What are those gorgeous bluey-black birds?' I ask.

'They're my Andalusian blues and the grey-marbled hens are Cuckoo Marins.'

'I've never seen so many different kinds of hen. I'd love them all.'

The Scotsman takes a sharp intake of breath. 'In your dreams. We're getting two at most as they'll no doubt cost an arm and a leg.'

Nacho strides over to the corral full of Turkish Sultans. '*Venga*! My children are full of anticipation. Come and let me introduce you to them.'

The Scotsman follows him into the swarm of inquisitive birds and watches as the small man leans down to stroke his wards.

'See how tame they are? You try.'

The Scotsman reluctantly extends his hand towards one of the feathered brethren and receives a sharp peck for his pains. 'Ouch!'

The old man clicks his teeth and laughs. 'Never approach them like that. They think you're offering food.'

I throw the Scotsman a sympathetic look as he sucks on his bloodied finger.

'We're not going for one of those brutes,' he hisses in my ear.

As we visit the long-tailed Sumatras that cluck about the last enclosure, I turn to Nacho. 'I think we'd like a couple of Silkies to start with. They've got such lovely faces and plumages.'

'And they're so mild tempered,' he agrees. 'They're very spiritual Buddhist birds from South East Asia.'

The Scotsman gives a snort of derision. 'Do they meditate each morning?'

He taps his chin. 'An interesting question. They certainly seem very calm and contemplative. You could be right.'

As I open the gate to the corral and crouch down by one of the pure, white hens, she comes over and gives my leg a nudge.

'See, she likes you,' smiles Nacho. 'That's Aye Thin Zar.'

'Gosh, that's an intriguing name. Isn't she lovely?' I say to the Scotsman who is already perusing his watch and yawning.

'Can we buy her? And what about a female companion?'

He picks up a huge fluffy white hen. Her feet are hard to see under the mass of feathers. 'They are from the same nest. This is Cudabhiksuni.'

The Scotsman can hardly contain himself. 'Cuda-what? What kind of a name is that for a hen?'

'It's Buddhist,' Nacho replies solemnly, pushing a hand through his bushy white hair.

I shoot a warning grimace at my husband. 'I think the names are perfect. Why don't we take Aye thingamajig and Cudabeeksunny and call it a day?' I say.

We tell Nacho that we'll be back later to collect them.

'Perfect. I will have everything prepared for you, including the bill,' he says brightly.

Back in the car, the Scotsman holds up his finger. 'I'm probably going to get septicaemia after that nip.'

'Oh don't be silly. It was only a little peck. Far less severe than the time that goose bit your backside in Suffolk.'

He winces at the memory. 'Well, all I can say is that I'll be giving a wide berth to those white poodle hens when we get them home. More dog than hen if you ask me. And look at the cost of them! Forty euros a piece.'

'Money well spent.'

He starts up the car. 'Well, after that ordeal, the least you can do is let me have a horticultural moment at Botanicactus. I've been yearning to pop by.'

'I've always found cacti very uninspiring,' I reply.

'Me too, but Tomeu at the Tramuntana nursery told me it was well worth a visit.'

I peruse the map. 'Actually we can pop into Ses Salines for a potter. It's such a lovely little town and we can stock up with some flavoured sea salt from the Flor de Sal shop.'

'Better still, we could stop for a bite at Casa Manolo, one of my favourite fishy haunts.'

'I couldn't have come up with a better plan myself,' I say with gusto. 'Lead on, Macduff!'

Having glutted ourselves on seafood salad, baby calamari and cool white Albariño wine in Ses Salines, we arrive at the grand driveway of Botanicactus in need of an invigorating stroll. We are greeted by a comical sign showing a cheery green cactus man wearing a sombrero. I pull a face.

'I hope this isn't going to be some kind of awful children's theme park. That sign's very off-putting,' I moan.

'Don't be such a snob,' he replies. 'Give it a chance.'

We course up the impressive driveway flanked by mature palm trees and are pleasantly surprised to find a wide, leafy car park and tranquil reception hut. We pay our modest entry fee and set off into the wilderness. And wilderness it is. Beyond the confines of the small shop and café area we shortly find ourselves in a paradise never imagined possible from the main road.

'This is spectacular,' I gasp.

'First impressions can be very deceptive.'

We consult the little plan accompanying our tickets.

There are three designated zones all interlinked by paths, with the first two being a 50,000-sq-mile wetland area beside the lake and a semi-arid, desert-like section of cacti and other succulents.

The third area is devoted to natural flora of Mallorca with a wealth of Mediterranean specimens.

In total peace, we follow the simple soil pathways to the enormous artificial lake – the largest in the Balearic Islands at 10,000 sq miles. Dominated by bulrushes and towering reeds, the cries of wandering peacocks, coots and long-legged stilts merge harmoniously with the gentle hissing of cicadas. As far as the eye can see, a vast prairie of wild pampas grass rises up, dotted with tall mature palms interspersed with tropical vegetation, like a scene from *The Lost World* by Arthur Conan Doyle. On the serene lake, with its majestic fountain and profusion of lily pads, attracting an abundance of iridescent dragon flies, we spy two cultivated islands, one home to ducks and the other accessible by way of a contemporary metal bridge.

'This is like something out of a film,' I say. 'It's so dramatic.'

'A veritable Garden of Eden,' he replies in some wonderment. 'Look at all these mature cacti and indigenous plants. They must be a haven for local bird and insect life.'

We wander on to a vast area where succulents and cacti thrive. There are countless examples of *opuntia*, 'prickly pears', which are a favourite here on the island, both for their use as animal fodder and also as fruit. We wander on along the earthy pathways bordered by limestone rocks and reach the heart of the cacti kingdom.

The Scotsman looks about him in admiration. 'Apparently there are more than four hundred species and twelve thousand plants here. There are specimens from the Arizona Desert, Mexico and all over the Americas.'

On a gentle slope, giant shaggy *yuccas*, sporting pretty white flowers on their tips, vie for attention alongside enormous stout cacti and squat *cycas*, with their verdant feathery fan-like protrusions. In amongst craggy outcrops are more towering prickly pears with their characteristic red-ish fruit and yellow flowers, and succulents, such as aloe and agave, and samples of slender and elegant green-grey silver-torch cacti.

I point to a lofty cactus. 'You always see those in westerns,' I laugh.

The Scotsman nods. 'I'll have you know that's an Arizonian saguaro.'

'Show off!'

We head back along a leafy path in the direction of the entrance and suddenly find ourselves in a paradise of Mediterranean plants and flowers – bougainvillea, box, agapanthus, passion flowers, hibiscus and broom. More thrillingly for me is that I spy cockerels and hens in a large enclosure in a shady zone.

'Look at that!' I yell at the Scotsman. 'They've got Silkies!'

He looks through the cage and laughs. 'Can't get away from the beasties.'

A man in beige shorts and with sleeves rolled up is working hard on the land and stops to chat.

'You don't know who owns this wonderful park, do you?' I enquire in Spanish.

He smiles. 'Actually I do. As you can see I am both owner and worker!'

We get chatting and he tells us that his name is Jean Marc Maccario and that with his Italian father, Oswald, he created the concept of Botanicactus 25 years earlier. It was a long-held dream and they worked hard to make it a reality, against the odds. So charming and engaging is our host that I don't have the heart to tell him that I'm no fan of his little green man on the front gate.

The Scotsman throws out his hands expansively. 'But tell me, Marco, surely this has to be one of the largest botanical gardens in Europe?'

Marco pushes a bronzed hand through his wiry brown hair and smiles. 'Well, we have sixteen hundred species and fifteen thousand plants so there can't be many gardens to rival us.'

Enthusiastically, I draw his attention to the chuntering white Silkies in the run before us.

'Do you know much about rearing Silkies?' I ask.
'Of course,' he smiles pleasantly. 'What do you want to know?'

After a cross-country drive back to Sóller, we arrive at the house to find Pep's white van still installed in our courtyard. It is gone eight o'clock and the house is flooded with light.

'Oh no, I wonder what he's been up to!' I say.

The Scotsman feigns nonchalance. 'Everything is fine. He probably fell asleep watching the football on TV or maybe he had a few complications during his *patxaran* making...'

I march into the house and find Pep in the *entrada*, stretched out on the cream sofa by the fire, snoring profusely. His shoes rest on the rug and his black-socked feet hang over a raised cushion. In front of him, on the glass table, is an empty tumbler with what appears to be the residue of an amber liquid. The Scotsman gives an embarrassed tut behind me and strides into the kitchen where row upon row of glass bottles are lined up on the old oak table, their bellies filled with a pinky-red liquid. Various bits of paraphernalia, sieves, measuring jugs, weighing scales and spoons sit piled high in the sink, while white sugar grains and purple juice, evidently from sloe berries, stain the marble work surfaces and terracotta floor tiles.

'What on earth has he been doing?' I exclaim. 'I thought making *patxaran* was supposed to be foolproof?'

'So did I,' the Scotsman adds, looking ruefully at the unruly scene before us. He holds up an empty bottle of Scotch. 'I think perhaps Pep got a little distracted during his mission.'

I look at my watch. Heaven knows what Juana will think has happened to her husband. He had told her that he was coming round to help the Scotsman with digging up the vegetable patch. I reach for the mobile phone and stop.

'Perhaps because I've had such a lovely day, I'm going to save Pep's bacon and call Juana and say that he was helping you in the garden and lost track of time. I'll say that he inadvertently left the mobile in his car.'

The Scotsman grins in relief. 'That would be kind. What can I do in return?'

'Simple,' I reply with meaning. 'First of all, you can clear up the mess in my kitchen and, secondly, take all those bottles of hooch down to your *abajo*.'

He smiles genially. 'Of course. Anything else?'

I take my mobile phone and head up the stairs. 'Yes, I suggest you sober up your *amic* with some coffee before driving him home. And before that, pour me a very large glass of *vino tinto*!'

Twelve

MYSTICS AND MUSES

It's an uncharacteristically rainy day in Palma and so Ollie and I stand sheltering in the shady medieval cloisters of the Monastery of Sant Francesc, contemplating how we will spend the rest of the morning. Neither of us has brought an umbrella and, as usual, Ollie is wearing his threadbare, grubby white espadrilles, shorts and a thin T-shirt. He looks up at the scowling grey sky and yawns.

'I reckon we should do a spin of the church and then head off for a bite to eat as soon as the rain tails off.'

'It looks as if it's in for the day and you haven't even got a jacket on!'

He shrugs. 'Stop fussing, mother. It's not cold.'

'What about popping by the exhibition that William Graves recommended? It's being held at the municipal archives not far from here.'

Ollie rubs his hands together. 'Fine by me. What's it about?'

'It's called *The Muse and the Sea* and features works by English-speaking writers and artists who visited or lived in Mallorca between 1900 and 1965.' I look around us. 'Isn't this church a wonder? And just look at the Gothic arches. It's incredible to think that work began on this building in 1281 and that it took one hundred years to complete.'

'Fascinating,' he replies listlessly.

'And then the Franciscan monks who lived here for centuries were unceremoniously booted out when the property was put to civilian use. Mind you, the Franciscan order returned and set up a school in the fifties.'

As if on cue, a bell sounds and the pitter-patter of little feet echoes around the walls. Soon young children swarm into the cloisters, dressed in blue sports kit.

'Good luck to them in this weather,' mutters Ollie as we quickly step into the cavernous basilica in order to avoid the scrum. It takes some time to adjust to the sudden gloom of the interior, but even in the dim light the sheer scale of the towering nave with its elegant, arched stone ribs is spectacular. It is like walking inside the body of an enormous beast. Aside from a young woman praying in the first pew, we are the sole visitors and so my footsteps echo as we walk the length of the church, exploring the ornate side chapels on either side.

Ollie hisses at me. 'I'd just like to point out that if you were wearing espadrilles, you wouldn't be making such a din.'

'Touché.'

The *pièce de résistance*, and the real reason we are here, lies at the head of the basilica. It is the sepulchre of Ramon Llull, Mallorca's beloved son: the mystic, philosopher and scholar who lived from 1232 until 1315. The 700th anniversary of his death is almost upon us. I tap Ollie's arm.

'You know that during the Middle Ages, Palma's noblest and richest families would do anything to secure space here for their tombs and the bigger the better. There was great prestige in being buried here.'

'Bit of a waste of time if you were dead. Not much chance to savour the moment,' he quips.

183

'True. Anyway, here are the sacred remains of Ramon Llull.'

A brief smile crosses my son's lips. 'And where's the proof?'

'As you're the one doing a special project on Llull for your final exams, you tell me.'

He leans forward to examine the Gothic alabaster tomb. 'According to popular myth, when Ramon Llull was eighty-two, he returned to North Africa where he'd previously gone to convert Muslims to Christianity, but this time he didn't go down quite so well as the locals stoned him. The story goes that Genoese merchants brought him back to Palma where he died and that he was buried here. The other theory is that he was killed by the Muslims and never made it back at all.'

'If that were true, what happened to his body?'

He shrugs. 'Some claim that he died on the voyage and was buried at sea. Who knows, or cares for that matter? It was seven hundred years ago, for heaven's sake.'

'Llull was a bit of a controversial figure, wasn't he?'

Ollie strolls over and studies a large contemporary piece of artwork behind the altar. 'Depends on what you call controversial. Apparently he had a religious epiphany, leaving his family and job as a tutor for King Jaume II, to become a virtual hermit. I doubt that made him too popular. Before then he was a complete hell-raiser and was probably a lot more fun.'

We walk back through the cloisters and out into the fresh air.

'So why have you chosen to study Ramon Llull?' I ask.

He laughs. 'Choice doesn't come into it at school. I'd have opted for Rafa Nadal and the tennis cult if I'd been allowed.'

'I guess you can't win them all.'

As I'm studying my map, Ollie nudges me. 'There's the woman who was praying in the front row of the church.'

I look up and see her heading towards us from the far end of the stone corridor. 'What about her?'

'She's wearing an identical dress to the one you used to wear in London. Remember? The grey one with black feathers sewn around the base.'

'How can she be? It was a sample dress. A one-off.'

'Thank heavens for small mercies,' he sniggers. 'There must have been more than one for sale, more's the pity. Mind you, she actually looks quite good in it.'

The woman approaches us and smiles. 'Isn't this a beautiful church?'

'It certainly is and with so much history.'

Ollie casts me a warning glance but it's too late. 'By the way, that dress looks wonderful on you.'

She beams. 'You like it? I'm so pleased. It was a gift from God at a time when I needed his help. That is all I can say.'

She gives a shy little smile and slips away through the exit.

'Why on earth did you comment on her dress? It could have been so embarrassing.'

'Well it wasn't, was it? And now I know why she was wearing my dress. I gave it to the local Red Cross. Catalina does a lot of work with the organisation and suggested I get rid of all my old suits from my London days. How cheering that my dress has found such a worthwhile owner.'

He saunters towards the huge wooden doors that lead to the street outside. 'You're not going to get all emotional, are you?'

I tap him on the head with the guide. 'I'm just happy that my dress has been so usefully recycled and it was obviously meant that we should see her today.'

'Was it?' He rolls his eyes and takes my arm. 'Don't go all cosmic on me!'

I laugh. There's nothing like a fiendishly waggish son to pull one up short. We head out into the spitting rain and find solace in Santa Eulàlia restaurant, just off the main *plaça* of the same name. Here we tuck into the plate of the day, *jamon Serrano*, fried eggs, sauté potatoes and salad – just the ticket on a wet day. After we have finished our coffees, owner, Jesus Maria Alonso, leads us downstairs to the cellars that have been lovingly refurbished and turned into an elegant, yet snug, dining room. The arches and walls have been formed from large honey-hued stones that have been beautifully restored.

'When we decided to develop this old cellar, we knocked through a wall and discovered these ancient stone structures – they must date back some three hundred years. They form part of the history of Santa Eulàlia church just across from us.'

I grin. 'What a find, though I hope you didn't unleash any medieval ghosts while you were about it.'

'Hopefully not, but as it was constructed back in the thirteenth century, it might well have a rich history with a few grim secrets.'

'Aren't there supposed to be old tunnels and catacombs under the church?' Ollie asks.

'So they say. This area of Palma is teeming with history.' He laughs. 'Mind you, we haven't found a tunnel yet.'

Stories of secret underground passageways in Mallorca are legion. It is believed that below Castell de Bellver, the unique circular castle that sits high on a hill outside Palma, there are deep tunnels running as far as the capital's Gothic cathedral of La Seu. There's also a legend about a witch named Joana who dwelt deep in a cave under the castle and fed poisonous figs to any unfortunate being who came her way. In other parts of the island there are believed to be labyrinths of military tunnels dating back to the Spanish Civil War, including those at the naval base in the port of Sóller. And of course in Moorish times, *qanats*, underground water channels, were created in hillsides for the use of local villages.

Ollie and I walk out into the cobbled street and are relieved to see a hesitant sun blinking behind an oyster-tinged cloud.

'Maybe we're in for a sunny afternoon,' I say cheerily.

Ollie shrugs. 'If we're going to see this exhibition, it doesn't really matter whether it's raining or not.'

Five minutes later we find ourselves standing outside the ancient arched doorway of the imposing Arxìu Municipal de Palma, the city's archives, and take the winding stone staircase up to the first floor. We are the sole visitors at this hour and are rather glad to have the run of the place.

'It's interesting that there's currently so much focus on writers of the past who visited Mallorca,' I say.

Ollie looks up from the catalogue that he's studying. 'Is there?'

'Well you may recall my mentioning that the Council of Mallorca and the Foundation of House Museums are launching literary walking routes island-wide under the acronym WOW. The official launch is coming up soon.'

'I remember.'

'There's also a reference book soon to be published by the university, all about English speaking authors who came here during the last few centuries.'

'Judging by this exhibition, a heck of a lot of them came here. It says in the catalogue that many international writers and artists started pitching up here from the turn of the last century.'

I nod. 'It helped that Palma's Gran Hotel opened around the same time, so there was somewhere quite elegant for visitors to stay. The early tourists, if you can call them that, were visiting Mallorca in the spirit of the Grand Tour. It must have seemed a very exotic and quaint destination in those days.'

'And fairly primitive in terms of visitor luxuries,' he opines.

'Very true. If you read *With a Camera in Majorca* by Margaret Este, written in 1906, or even *Jogging Round Majorca* by Gordon West, penned in the twenties, amenities were basic. Still, it was the charm of the island and its people that drew visitors here.'

'And of course it was cheap,' he says wryly.

I look at an old edition of *The White Goddess* by Robert Graves, erstwhile famed resident of Deia village. 'Yes, for impoverished artists and writers, it must have seemed like paradise. Think of the peace and beauty.'

He points to a book in a glass cabinet. 'These books and exhibits are about a man named Alan Hillgarth.'

Before World War Two, Captain Alan Hillgarth was British Consul in Mallorca, wrote adventure novels for fun and was a member of the British intelligence services. He was a close associate of Winston Churchill and, during the war, when posted to Madrid, was behind a secret mission called Operation Mincemeat, when faked documents were produced to fool the Germans.

'And what about local and Spanish authors on the island?'

'Ah, they are prolific. You must have heard of Blai Bonet, Miquel Bauçà, Bartomeu Pòrcel, Josep Pla and Miquel Riera?'

'Nope.'

'Well, get reading. I love *L'Illa de la Calma* by Santiago Rusiñol, a wonderful take on Mallorca.'

'We read that at school years ago,' he yawns.

'Of course the literary tradition is still alive and well here. *Nit de la Poesia*, the annual international poetry night, takes place at the Teatro Principal in Palma and the Santillana Foundation organises a huge literary conference at Formentor every year.'

'All the same, books aren't so popular now. Few of my friends buy books.'

'I find that rather depressing. Hopefully you'll all come to your senses one day and discover the pleasure of reading. You used to be an avid reader before becoming addicted to that wretched mobile phone.'

He gives a snort of derision. 'If you're lucky we might revert to oil lamps and horse and carts, too. Times have changed. Besides, we can download books in seconds via our iPhones. Actually, I'm reading an Andrea Camilleri novel at the moment, so don't put your head in a gas oven just yet.'

'Glad to hear it.'

We stare into another long cabinet that contains old copies of books by literary greats such as Evelyn Waugh, W.B. Yeats, Kingsley Amis and D.H. Lawrence, all of whom visited the island at one time or another. Although the exhibition only features writers from 1900 to 1965, I think of their predecessors, such as Archduke Ludwig Salvator of Austria, who lavished his time on Mallorca. The Archduke wrote *Die Balearen* in 1869, an authoritative five-volume guide to the fauna, flora and customs of the Balearic Islands and its original edition is housed in the Fundación Bartolomé March in Palma.

'I'm a big fan of all these writers,' I say, 'and of course others who visited the island. In fact, I know some interesting quirky facts about Lawrence...'

Ollie grimaces. 'OK, that's enough information for today, *gracias*. And if you mention Dorothea Bate and that wretched Myotragus mouse-goat again, I might just self combust.'

'Funny you should say that. Of course she wrote all about...'

He shakes his head and pulls a face. 'I'm off to look at the other cabinets. When you've taken your medicine, come and join me.'

I am standing by the pond, in deep conversation with Johnny, when my mobile phone gives a series of sharp squawks. It's an anxious-sounding Ed on the line.

'I've thrown in the towel, Scatters.'

It seems to be more appropriate than ever these days.

I gasp. 'What? But I thought things were improving at the school?'

He gives a long sigh. 'I'm afraid things went from bad to worse. I had a nightmare trying to fix a faulty speaker in the drama studio and then lost my way getting to one of the school's science labs and was very late.'

'Is the campus that large?'

'At least two acres, Scatters. Anyway, I had a slight panic attack when I eventually got there and had to have a cup of tea and some medication. My boss apparently told the head of human resources that I was a disaster.'

'Oh dear.'

'And then everything seemed to snowball. My boss told me that his department was no place for boffins. I've been so stressed that I decided that it was best I leave.'

I'm at a loss for words. 'But what about your mortgage?'

'We can manage for now and I've applied for some temporary work until I find something else…' He stops short. 'What's that weird noise I can hear?'

'My frogs singing.'

'Why don't you just move into a zoo while you're about it?' His voice rises in alarm. 'Don't tell me that they're all in your office along with that wretched hen?'

'Don't be absurd. Of course not. I'm talking to you by the pond.'

'Thank heavens for that.'

'What kind of job are you going to be looking for?' I ask.

'I'm not fussed, to be honest. Some place that can use my computer skills and isn't too stressful an environment.'

'And where MEK will be happy.'

'MEK is indeed a priority.'

'Maybe a sanatorium?' I suggest.

'Very funny.'

'How's Rela taking it?'

'Badly. She wants me to stop feeling sorry for myself and look for a job.'

I give a sniff. 'Wise woman. Send me your CV or anything else you'd like me to look over.'

He takes a sharp breath. 'With your gimlet eyes, that's asking for trouble, isn't it?'

I laugh. 'It most certainly is! I'm very exacting, as you know.'

'By the way, when are you and Jane setting off on your mad trek on the Spanish mainland?'

'You mean, El Camino de Santiago, St James's Way? Next month. It's come round so soon!'

'You're both insane. Two weeks of non-stop walking in the hills sounds hellish to me.'

'Nonsense, it'll prove wonderfully bracing and think how good it will be for our figures.'

'Rather you than me,' he says a touch sulkily. 'I'm panicked that while you're away I might have some trauma and neither you nor Jane, my two oldest uni friends, will be around to console me.'

'What about us? If we suffer some mishap, we'll be all on our own in the middle of nowhere.'

He gives a loud sniff. 'Well, on your own head be it. What does Alan think?'

'He's delighted to have two weeks of peace, quite frankly.'

When he's off the line, I sit on the edge of the pond and give a tut. 'Poor old Ed.'

There's a cackle. 'If you ask me, your old mate needs a kick up the derrière. Stress? Tell me about it. That heron was back again this morning, flying low over the pond. Nearly took my scalp off. For us amphibians, stress is a matter of life and death.'

'I know, but Ed is very sensitive and intellectual. I think that's the problem.'

'Gimme a break! Get him out gardening. He needs a pitchfork and a shovel in his hands and he'll be right as rain.'

'That's funny,' I say.

A voice interrupts me. 'What's funny?' It's Ollie.

There's a loud plop.

'I was just talking to Johnny. He's... well he was here.'

'Sure thing, mother,' he replies indulgently. 'Now you'd better get down to the *abajo*. The old Scotsman's having a fit about Carlos I setting up home there.'

I find my husband standing in his *abajo* with hands on hips, glaring across at Carlos I, who is sitting on a pile of straw in the far corner, next to a bowl of corn and water. I give the Scotsman a cheerful smile.

'Aha, I meant to mention that I set up Carlos I in here temporarily last night. His leg is so stiff that he's finding it hard to get into the hen house at night.'

'But he can't stay here. I've already got all Pep's *patxaran* bottles and paraphernalia clogging up the place and I don't want straw and corn everywhere.'

'Have a heart. If you were arthritic, how would you like having to climb up a ladder to get to your perch every night?'

'Luckily I don't need a perch in a hen house yet. As for Carlos I, he is not going to set up home here, thank you very much.'

'Well you'll have to find him a new lodging.'

'How about in a hot oven?'

I give a warning growl.

'OK, what about the old, wooden dog house that we found in the orchard when we bought the house? It needs repairing and painting but it might do.'

'Excellent! If you could fix that up, I'm sure he'd probably love it.'

'You expect me to do it now? Do you realise how busy I am? I've got so much pruning and grass cutting to do. It's growing like mad and I've got to get another bonfire going later.'

I shrug my shoulders. 'Up to you, but if you want Carlos I out of here, that's the only likely solution.'

'OK, you win,' he mutters. 'I'll fix the wretched dog house. Never a moment of peace in this house!'

With some satisfaction I leave him to his wizard-like mumblings and head off to the car. I've an important appointment to make.

Low cloud hangs over the fierce blue sea as Toful Colom and I clamber along the jagged rocks at the far end of the port. We have been granted permission to enter the naval base to see his two giant sculptures situated there. At one time this base would have been brimming with life and completely out of bounds to visitors. Even today, a uniformed officer stands guard at the towering gates, only naval personnel are admitted and any other visitors only under special circumstances. The remains of an old lighthouse can be found among steep rocks at the far end of the base as well as a handsome white building with red roof, now converted into a holiday residence for officers and their families.

In fact, the entire zone at the end of the port was once given over to military activities and served as the second naval base for the nationalist navy under Franco during the Spanish Civil War and World War Two. Topographically, the port of Sóller was deemed a perfect location for the base and so building began in the thirties. Established in 1937, its main purpose was to safeguard submarines and ships, allow for re-fuelling and to accommodate Italian seaplanes. Vast tunnels were created underground as a highly secure zone for torpedoes, although much mystery surrounded the exact use of these exceptionally guarded cavernous stores, and still does today. Toful and I examine the huge chain cross and abstract sculpture of a man with fishing rod that he created as a tribute to local fishermen. I take a photo of him standing by its side.

'It's such a landmark from the sea,' I say. 'You must be so proud to have it here.'

He shrugs and offers a modest smile. 'I'm happy that they've both found a good home. Shall we go and have coffee in the main building?'

'Am I allowed in there?'

He laughs. 'It's just a holiday home now. If you like, we may be able to see one of the tunnels you're so intrigued about.'

We follow a rocky path to the crumbling remains of Faro Viejo, the old, grey, stone lighthouse, built in 1864 by Emili Pou. Toful tells me to take care and I soon understand why. A swell of angry grey water and hissing white foam rushes up from a crater directly from the sea below. It makes me feel a bit giddy and I step back and crouch by some rocks.

'The problem with this lighthouse was that it was built next to this blowhole,' Toful says. 'In a storm, seawater could shoot thirty metres up the crater and crash on top of the lighthouse. In fact, during one bad storm, it shook so badly that the keeper and his family had to leave immediately.'

'And when was the newer La Creu built?'

He looks up at the black and white modern lighthouse higher up the hill behind us.

'That one replaced Faro Viejo in 1945.'

'So were keepers still living in this precarious lighthouse until then?' I ask in astonishment.

'Good heavens, no! They'd moved into safer fishermen's dwellings by then. It was unmanned.'

I look across at Cap Gros lighthouse, which stands aloft cliffs at Sa Muleta on the other side of the bay.

'So was this lighthouse older than Cap Gros?'

Toful shakes his head. 'That one was built in 1859. Its signals were fuelled by olive-oil-burning lamps originally. Imagine!'

We head off towards the main building, shadowed by scrubland and pine trees high above on the cliffs. Although the sun glimmers over the sea, a wild wind blows.

'I suppose Cap Gros was a better place to be based if you were a keeper.'

He puffs out his lower lip. 'It wasn't so great. In severe winters, it took a keeper about two and a half hours to reach the port because the terrain was so hazardous, so life was fairly solitary and basic up there.'

In the comfortable dining area of the base, we are offered warming coffees. The walls are covered with old historic images of the port and naval base before its change of use.

'I heard that the port was teeming with marines, from the period of the Spanish Civil War until the early seventies, maybe as many as a thousand at one time.'

He blows on his steaming coffee. 'It was an important military base and one got used to seeing uniformed officers around. There would have been Italian soldiers based here during the late thirties as they supported the Nationalists and Franco.'

'Wasn't there a terrible submarine accident here in the port?'

Toful frowns. 'That was back in 1946. A submarine was in deep waters near Sa Calobra and collided with a destroyer by the name of *Lepanto*. The crew of the submarine couldn't be reached as it ended up in an underwater rift and all forty-three hands died.'

'I remember the old naval building on the promontory that carried the motto, "*Todo por la Patria*". That wasn't pulled down until the late nineties.'

'It was used for military training purposes for some time and then fell into disuse. Its demolition was symbolic.'

I nod. 'I get the impression that many locals associated it with Franco and the Spanish Civil War and were glad to see its demise.'

He smiles. 'And now that it's gone we have better views out to sea.' He drains his cup. 'Come on, let's continue our tour.'

Out in the sunshine, a naval officer offers us a quick perusal of one of the long tunnels that stretches beneath the buildings situated in the harbour zone of Santa Catalina. To my disappointment, all I see before me is a huge and dingy man-made cave of exposed rock with a towering roof. There is nothing in its large swell of a belly that might give rise to fanciful notions and conjecture.

'There's not much to it, is there?' I say, my voice echoing in the cool, dry, musty air.

'It doesn't have any real use now,' Toful counters. 'I'm not sure what will happen to them.'

'So where are the other tunnels?'

'Dotted around.'

My eyes light up. 'Can we see some others?'

He laughs. 'No, just this one, today.'

We arrive at the entrance to the base where a cordial officer thanks us for our visit and sees us politely off the premises. Although he beams cheerily, I notice that he loses no time in locking the tall iron gates firmly behind us.

It is a balmy evening and the air is wonderfully still. In the shady gardens of the historic literary museum of Mallorcan writer Llorenç Villalonga, the mayor of Binissalem is speaking enthusiastically about the Festes des Vermar, the annual festival of the grape. As the celebrated wine region of the island, Binissalem and its wine producers have much to crow about. Tonight is the official launch of the event and at either end of the stage are young local women in traditional dress. Even the musicians, clad in historic garb, are circling the huge swell of guests, with their drums and *xeremies*, bagpipes.

'All the suits are out tonight,' whispers Ollie.

'Indeed, there's quite a line up on stage. It's nice to see the bagpipers out in force. You know the first bagpipe music was brought over by Jaume I at the time of the Spanish Conquest.'

He nudges his father. 'She's off again. I think I might go in search of a glass of wine.'

The Scotsman grins. 'Good thinking. I'll join you.'

As applause breaks out, the cicadas seem to hiss in approval from the dark, long grasses and, it could be my imagination, but I'm sure that I can hear a cockerel crowing. The boys head back, clutching glasses and offer me José Ferrer red wine. Always a safe bet.

I turn to them. 'We should go and find Carme and Carlotta from the House Museum Foundation. They've organised the launch of the exhibition tonight by Joan Benàssar.'

'Where is it?' asks Ollie warily.

'Just inside here. This museum was once the home of Llorenç Villalonga. He was born in 1897 and died about thirty years ago.

He was a prominent novelist in the Catalan language. Come on, let's have a wander.'

We pick our way through the crowd of guests and I suddenly see Carme waving to me across the room. She is in the company of Carlotta and the artist himself.

'Please meet Joan. He's very much in demand tonight but he just wanted to say *hola*.'

A man with a warm smile and intense dark eyes steps forward and kisses me on both cheeks.

'I do hope you enjoy the exhibition,' he says.

'Well I'm a fan of your sculptures but I'm less familiar with your paintings so I'm looking forward to it.'

We all chat for a few minutes before he is carried away on a sea of admirers.

'What kind of sculptures has he done?' asks Ollie.

'You've probably seen them gracing five-star hotels and country estates without knowing it. His stone figures, often of women, are very distinctive with fluid forms and pronounced features. They're very beautiful.'

Carlotta taps my arm and introduces me to Antoni Planas, whose foreword I've just read in the exhibition's catalogue. He explains to me that he, too, is a journalist but now works at the Institute of Balearic Studies. Both of us discuss the vagaries of the Spanish and English language and how important both have become in the world today. Of all the guests milling around the house, I deduce that, as a close friend and collaborator of the artist, he must be one of the most informed about his work.

In the refurbished cellar, once the preserve of huge wooden wine barrels, we find Joan Benàssar's series of colourful and dramatic works with bold literary slogans – some controversial, others contemplative. Despite the title of the exhibition – *Bellesa, Violència i Dolor*, Beauty, Violence and Pain, the prints have a distinctly Mediterranean and lyrical feel to them with their bright colours, themed images and slogans in the Catalan language.

'It's a bit of a cheerless title for an exhibition,' intones the Scotsman with a sigh. 'I might need another drink soon.'

I laugh. 'I think it's all about the marrying of art and literature, following Benàssar's participation in one of the annual literary festivals at Formentor. I think it's an inspirational exhibition.'

'Don't go all pretentious on us,' mumbles Ollie. He wanders off to examine the works and sometime later ambles back.

'For once I have to agree with you. I really like the naïve style of art and a lot of the literary quotes,' he says.

'I can't understand them all,' replies the Scotsman. 'Can you translate for me?'

He gives his father a withering look. 'No can do, old thing. You should be practising. Only way to learn Spanish, so you always told me.'

'Ha! That's got you,' I laugh.

Grumbling, the Scotsman gets out his mini Spanish dictionary and dons his reading glasses. 'You're both bullies, the pair of you.'

An hour later, once we've fully toured the exhibition space and listened to more speeches, we roam around the spacious property, exploring the various glass cabinets filled with historical artefacts and first editions of Llorenç Villalonga works. As we head down the rich mahogany staircase to the wide and elegant *entrada*, I notice the Scotsman whispering conspiratorially with Ollie. They both smile and nod.

'What's up?' I ask suspiciously.

The Scotsman grins. 'We know you like to lap up local culture but what about sliding off for a spot of dinner? It could be our last little celebration before you head off into the hills on your hiking adventure with Jane.'

Enthusiastically I follow them towards the front door. 'I thought you'd never ask.'

Thirteen

DOWNHILL ALL THE WAY

El Camino de Santiago – St James's Way

Sunday

A grey, marbled sky stretches out high above us and a spit of rain stings my cheek. Jane stops to adjust her small, black rucksack and flicks a quick look at our map, which she hangs in a plastic holder around her neck like a somewhat unwieldy necklace. It's 8:30 in the morning, we're feeling gung-ho and the air is crisp. It's our first day hoofing it along the famed Camino de Santiago, St James's Way, on the Spanish mainland, and having touched down in Leon for our first night's rest, we got up early, ready to begin our Thelma-and-Louise-style Spanish adventure.

They say all roads lead to Rome, but when it comes to Santiago, there are certainly more routes than you can shake a stick at – 12 as it happens – although the vast majority of the 200,000 international pilgrims choose to walk the traditional Camino Francés, which kicks off in the French Pyrenees at St-Jean-Pied-de-Port and ends 790 km – or 490 miles – later in northern Spain, in the blessed city that bears the saint's name, James in English, Jaime in Spanish or Iago in Gallegan. As we don't have the luxury of time on our hands, we have opted to spend two weeks on this famed road, aiming to cover more than 300 km in the northwest of the country, from Leon to Santiago, at a steady 20 to 30 km each day.

Of course people choose to walk the Way for all manner of reasons. Some seek spiritual clarity in their lives, others desire a few weeks or months of contemplative time away from the bustle of everyday life, while others just want to enjoy a jolly jaunt in the magnificent Spanish countryside. St James's Way began life with a lucky hermit who, in the ninth century, was apparently guided by an eerie light to the burial site of St James, the apostle. Admittedly, the good saint hadn't fared too well in life. After an unsuccessful time attempting to evangelise Spain, he was recalled to Jerusalem whereupon he was martyred on the orders of King Herod and his decapitated body left unburied. Eventually a group of Christians managed to smuggle the corpse onto a boat where it floated under the guidance of an angel across the sea, up the River Ulla, and finally to Galicia where it rested in Compostum, which in time became known as Compostela.

The popularity of The French Way – the route which Jane and I have decided to follow – began life in *Calixtine Codex*, a tome by the French priest Aymeric Picaud, which listed the main pilgrim routes to the cathedral of Santiago de Compostela where the remains of St James were supposedly laid to rest. In the good old days, medieval pilgrims would set off in a simple tunic and cloak, with a gourd full of water attached to their waists and a scallop shell dangling from a scrip, or deerskin bag. Even to this day the scallop shell serves as a powerful metaphor, its grooves meeting at a single point, which represents the eventual convening of all pilgrims at the tomb of St James in Santiago.

As Jane and I stand uncertainly on the pavement outside the imposing thirteenth-century Gothic cathedral in Leon, we notice an assured-looking older woman bearing a hefty rucksack. A large scallop shell swings from her waist and, without a map in sight, she heads off breezily along the street.

'I think we should follow her,' I lazily suggest.

'But we should be able to see brass scallop-shell signs embedded in the pavement. Where have they all gone?' Jane asks in some frustration.

'Lord knows,' I say. 'Maybe the town planners ran out of shells. Let's just shadow Miss Confident.'

'I think she's carrying all her belongings, unlike us. All the same, I'm glad we're using the bag carrying service. My rucksack feels heavy enough.'

'Mine too.'

We wander along, admiring the historic buildings and suddenly lose sight of our female guide.

'Oh bother,' I tut.

Jane sees a yellow arrow painted on the ground. 'This must be a sign. Come on.'

Distracted by our glorious surroundings and festive preparations in the town for an imminent marathon, we end up at a rather perfunctory roundabout where a local policeman attempts politely to guide us back on course.

'Hurry,' he urges. 'The marathon will be underway soon.'

Somewhat wistfully my eyes rove the bright blue-and-white police tape cordoning off one of the roundabout's arterial roads along which runners will presumably soon pound.

Jane shoots me a wry grin. 'Thinking of gate-crashing the event?'

'Tempting, but a long and leisurely hike with you sounds more appealing,' I reply.

Soon, we find ourselves in a tranquil square where a road sweeper in a luminous jacket cleans between cars in lacklustre fashion.

I engage him in conversation and, reeling from his detailed and rather bizarre instructions, lead Jane along a broad road in what I hope is the direction for the landmark San Marcos building.

'He seemed a trifle odd, so heaven knows if this is right,' I say.

'Perhaps we'll never leave Leon. Think of the humiliation,' she groans.

And yet, 15 minutes later, we stumble upon a brass scallop-shell sign and are soon crossing the medieval bridge that runs over the regal River Bernesga and are on our way. Despite the gloomy skies, I am feeling chipper and full of energy. There is something wonderfully liberating and exhilarating about striding forth into the unknown, encountering new cities and wild terrain on foot with just a rucksack on one's back. It is so long since I've had the luxury of space and time just to drink in heavenly new landscapes, reflect and walk and talk with a good old chum. The thought of having two whole weeks for our grand adventure makes my stomach flutter with excitement like a restless bird.

By now the rain is falling steadily and in the early morning haze we see before us several pilgrims, their lumpy rucksacks hidden under voluminous green plastic shrouds, giving them the appearance of lumbering turtles. On the outskirts of the city, we are amused to see a series of what look like Hobbit homes buried in undulating small hills, their roofs covered in soft grass. They are in fact disused wine and victual stores, but we prefer to think of them as miniature homes. As we plod on, my right walking boot becomes uncomfortable around the ankle and Jane's is nipping on the left side. Soon we are flanked by the Cantabrian Mountains and rolling out in front of us are the verdant Leonese moors.

'We've only got to complete twenty-one kilometres to Villadangos,' I say. 'A doddle.'

'Yes, we'll be there early and can have a good soak. Let's stop for a coffee in an hour or so.'

We plough on, congratulating ourselves on our level of fitness until our limbs begin to ache and our boots gnaw at our toes. Some miles later, we happen across Diane, a sprightly and graceful 78 year old from Alaska who, having lost both her husband and 50-year-old son to illness, decided to walk the Camino in their memory.

'Well girls,' she drawls with a smile, 'I've walked all the way from Pamplona, so if I can do it, you can. You'll feel it tonight as it's your first day but it'll get easier.'

Some 22 kilometres later we arrive in Villadangos, a one-horse town, where even the horse appears to have bolted. Sitting on the edge of a motorway intersection amid dreary pastureland and warehouses, the town seems to have been abandoned by most of its citizens. Scores of houses are boarded up, shops and restaurants gather dust and anyone with a pulse seems to have gravitated to our modest hotel where the simple yet cosy restaurant unsurprisingly does a brisk trade. At eight euros for a fantastic three-course meal with bottle of red wine and bread thrown in for good measure, it's tempting to ditch the rucksacks and stay here for two weeks, despite the insalubrious surroundings. And it's here, at Hotel Avenida, where my pilgrim passport obsession begins. In order to receive the official Compostela certificate in Santiago at the end of our trip, Jane and I need to get our little pilgrim passports stamped every day in hotels and cafés en route. All the same, what I consider to be an exciting challenge, Jane views as a bit of a drag.

'Our second stamp!' I cry delightedly as we head out of the restaurant in the falling rain. I peer at the inky, black shell-shaped mark in delight.

Jane rolls her eyes. 'You're not going to do somersaults every time we get a stamp, are you?'

'Of course,' I retort. 'Something's got to distract me from the pain and rain.'

After our delicious and substantial dinner, we dart into the hotel accommodation block, bathe our aching limbs and fall into a peaceful and deep slumber.

Monday

It's been a couple of hours since we willingly waved adios to deserted Villadangos and have picked up a new American friend on the road. Sassy Dawn runs a dog-walking business in New York and has chosen to go the whole distance on her own. In some admiration we listen to her anecdotes about crazy fellow hikers and some of the more challenging hostels she has slept in en route from Pamplona. Unlike the intrepid New Yorker, Jane and I have opted for simple hotels and private hostels on the road, where we are guaranteed our own bathroom and don't have to share dormitories with heavy snorers, sleep walkers and potential lunatics. She's carrying an enormous rucksack with just about everything but the kitchen sink and is full of the joys of the journey. The sky has brightened as we follow the clearly marked blue pilgrim signs with yellow arrows along the road and cross the famed Roman bridge, with its 19 arches over the river Órbigo.

'You know this was declared a national monument in 1939?' I say.

'Why?' asks Jane.

'Apparently it's known as the Puente del Paso Honroso, in memory of a medieval knight who set up a major jousting event here in the fifteenth century. It was all in honour of his lady love.'

Dawn laughs. 'Romantic knights are thin on the ground these days. How about we look for a café in the town instead?'

After a warming coffee and sugary *churro* doughnut, one of the delicious indulgences in this part of Spain, we head on towards the ruddy plains of Villares de Órbigo, where the rain-soaked soil proves a challenge for our hiking boots. My left ankle is still feeling bruised from where the boot is rubbing, but so far no blisters. In spite of the slight discomfort I continue to feel full of energy and good humour, reminding myself, not for the first time, how lucky I am to be able to share an indulgent and carefree time in the lush Spanish countryside with my old pal. Ahead of us on the muddy track we are reunited with Alaskan Diane, who uses hiking poles in each hand to stab at the thick mud beneath her feet. Laboriously she ploughs on with a sublime smile and merry demeanour, seemingly much cheered to encounter the three of us on the path. It seems that she rose early to give herself a head start. While Dawn and she become acquainted, I stop to take a few magical shots of the rugged and uncompromising landscape, images I will no doubt treasure on my return to so-called civilisation. As the track steepens, Diane waves us ahead.

'Go for it, girls!' she yells. 'Remember the hare and the tortoise? I'll catch you all up in my own good time.'

In a seemingly barren strip of terrain we suddenly alight upon Susie, a statuesque Briton, living in the wilds with her partner David. She has set up a stall of complimentary juices, cakes and fruit for the benefit of pilgrims that stands alone in the sea of rich vermillion soil like an oasis in a desert. Surrounding us are small wooded areas of pine trees and, in the far distance, the mountains of Asturias.

'But why are you doing all this for complete strangers?' I ask her in some incredulity.

She shrugs. 'It's nice to support you all in your quest. David and I like to give back.'

As we tuck into fresh figs and peaches, Dawn, Jane and I are somewhat nonplussed. It's a chilly autumnal day and we're wondering where Susie and her partner actually live. She wafts a hand vaguely towards what looks like a draughty old stable. 'We sleep here and we've got a stove to cook on, too.'

We peer into a small, tented area where a fire burns. There's no water nearby so they apparently carry supplies some distance to their encampment every day. I don't find the idea remotely appealing, especially with the prospect of inclement weather.

'Won't it be freezing in the winter?' Jane shivers, as if echoing my thoughts.

'Probably, but we'll cope. Life's an adventure, isn't it?'

I watch her washing plates in cool, mud-tinged water, ready to sleep under the stars, and accept somewhat guiltily that my idea of adventure on this trip will come with successfully finding a warm bed and hot meal for the night, preferably accompanied by a warming tipple.

Astorga, our next port of call, was once a staging post over the centuries for Roman legionaries and pilgrims and boasts a vast cathedral that was begun in the fifteenth century and some impressive Roman remains. Dawn has left us to travel on to the next town, but happily we cross paths again with Alaskan Diane who is staying in a local hotel. As we head into the porticoed main *plaça*, Jane and I pass the bijoux Chapel of St Vera, built in 1816, and a lifelike statue of a pilgrim holding his hat against the wind. Ominously, this proves to be a popular pose for statues in this part of the world. In a local grocery shop I opt to buy a walking stick, a snip at just seven euros, having been warned that we are soon to encounter some stiff climbs and descents. Jane already has a rather smart metal hiking pole, although bizarrely it's already given her a blister on her hand. Our eyes feast on a counter of home-made chocolates and *holarones*, small sponge cakes, the local Astorga delicacy, and soon we are stuffing the sweet provisions into our rucksacks.

'So much for losing weight,' puffs Jane. 'Even if we have just walked another thirty kilometres today.'

'We'll be lean and healthy-looking in two weeks' time,' I rejoice cheerily.

She offers me a bleak stare. 'That all depends on how many *churros* we get through at breakfast and Pilgrim menus by night.'

As we search for our hotel, we stop to admire the white granite Bishop's Palace, created by Catalan architect, Antoni Gaudí, that rises like a giant ghostly spectre over the city wall.

'It looks quite unreal,' muses Jane.

'Rather like a Disney castle, isn't it?'

She gives a yawn. 'Impressive though. So where's this hotel you booked?'

Jane and I agreed that we would share the booking of accommodation, reserving rooms in advance. Rather unnervingly I'm responsible for the first week, so if any of the lodgings are well below par, the buck will stop firmly at my door. We consult our map and soon find ourselves outside a rather grown-up hotel.

'What do you think? Not a bad deal for the price, eh?'

She grins. 'You're just trying to show me up. I'm not sure the ones I booked will be able to compete with this.'

At the desk, the receptionist shakes her head. 'I hope you won't mind but we had a double booking so we've had to upgrade you to a suite.'

We can hardly contain our joy. A few moments later we stand in the airy deluxe bedroom, casting our eyes about us.

'Where's the hairdryer?'

'Hairdryer? You can't be serious! We're on a walking holiday in the wilds.'

She narrows her eyes. 'I want a hairdryer.'

'OK, ask the desk staff.'

'What is it in Spanish?'

'Yo quiero un secador de pelo, por favor.'

She stares at me is some horror. 'You expect me to remember that?'

'Well it would be a good idea to learn a few basic words while we're on the trip.'

She puffs out her cheeks, and stretches her stiff legs on the bed. 'I'll have a go. Why not teach me a useful phrase every few days.'

'Oh come on! One a day, at least,' I protest.

'Trust me, I have zero language skills. When you hear my pronunciation, you'll be begging me to stop. One new word every two days.'

I laugh. 'That's a deal.'

'OK, let's start tomorrow.' She smiles across at me. 'So, fancy ringing down for that hairdryer for me now?'

Tuesday

'*Iz possible tenner un sickador*? Is it possible to have a hairdryer? *Una café con letcher, por favor*. A coffee with milk please,' Jane eyes me hopefully.

'No. Start again.'

She sighs. 'This language-learning is exhausting. How about I want a cup of hot water?'

'Why would you want to know that?' I ask.

'It's for my cleansing Chinese medicine tea. I should be taking it every morning.'

'OK. *Una taza de agua caliente, por favor…* The z is pronounced as *th…*'

'*Un tatha aga catala…*'

'WHAT?!' Judas rings. It's the Scotsman.

'What ho! Where are you?'

I look around us in the crisp morning air. 'We left Astorga a while ago and are en route to Rabanal. It's only about twenty kilometres altogether. Earlier we popped into an idyllic little village in the middle of nowhere called Castrillo de los Polvazares, where we scoffed some wonderful coffees and home-made cake at a small hotel called Cuca La Vaina…'

'This trip sounds like one long eating marathon with a few sightseeing trips in-between. What's that strange groaning sound I can hear?'

'That's Jane practising her Spanish. She's coming on leaps and bounds.'

'Just to report that Carlos I is on the mend and he's moved back into the hen house with Cordelia, thank heavens. And before I forget, Tomeu Deya has invited us up to the Can Det mill in Biniaraix to see the new season's olive oil being produced.'

'That we must see. And how's Johnny and the frogs?'

'Sorry to report that they've just left for their hols. Won't be back till the spring now.'

I'm momentarily disappointed to think that I will need to wait some months to hear my beloved *chanteurs* again, but the wait will make their return all the more magical.

'So tell me about the landscape,' he asks.

'It's breathtakingly beautiful. We're walking through a lot of forests of holm oaks and pines now and we're starting to climb some fairly steep hills. It's getting cooler, too, but no rain.'

'How are the boots holding out?'

'A bit of rubbing but nothing too bad. Always got my trainers if all else fails.'

After the Scotsman rings off, Jane and I march on. There isn't a soul about and all we can hear is the chirping of the birds and the leaves shimmering in the breeze. Rather goonishly I seem to have a permanent smile slapped on my face, such is the sheer pleasure of our fragrant and harmonious surroundings. After another hour along the route, we allow ourselves a brief pit stop at a tiny café in the woods, where the welcoming owner plies us with freshly baked *churros* and hot coffee. Better still, he rubber-stamps our pilgrim passports.

'Ten stamps already,' I trill, flapping the little book in the air to dry the ink.

Jane shakes her head pityingly. 'I'm glad it makes you happy. Now back to my Spanish lesson. Where were we? *Iz possible un tatha aga...*'

Wednesday

Having just left La Posada de Gaspar, a cosy and traditional stone-built guesthouse in the picturesque village of Rabanal, we take a steep path in the direction of our next overnight stop, Molinaseca. We have enjoyed being in the ancient Leonese historical region known as Maragateria, with its hearty gastronomy and original stone architecture and cobbled streets and paths. The sky is inky as we set off in the icy morning air, a strong and blustery gale whistling in our ears, and follow a small huddle of fellow pilgrims along the upward slope. Barely 5 kilometres along the stony track we meet up with Dawn and together arrive in Foncebadón, a barren zone where we stop at a height of 1,500 metres to inspect La Cruz de Ferro, a small iron cross raised high on a wooden pole of uncertain epoch. It sits on a sizeable hillock of cairns that have been placed there by pilgrims over the centuries. The air is freezing as we clamber over the rocks to the top, muffled up in fleeces, jackets, woolly hats and scarves. Later, we examine the many keepsakes and small mementos left by passing pilgrims at its base, speculating on their personal stories and what motivated them to make the trip.

'Legend has it that a hermit called Gaucelmo founded an inn around here in the eleventh century,' says Jane, looking up from her favourite guidebook by Spanish author Sergi Ramis.

'But why would a hermit want to do that?' I ask.

'I've no idea,' shrugs Jane. 'Sergi doesn't say.'

'I think most people would want a drink by the time they got up here,' counters Dawn. 'The hermit certainly got it right.'

Onwards we go, stopping for a welcome coffee at a tiny mountain café a few hours later. Here, surrounded by unforgiving and austere terrain, we are delighted to meet up once again with hardy Australian Tony, whom we met in Rabanal, and cheery Canadians Lael and Richard, with whom we hooked up back in Astorga. There is a feeling of immediate kinship with many of the pilgrims we meet en route and an easy camaraderie born of sharing an inspirational joint goal in unfamiliar terrain. If there's one thing I've learnt so far on this trip, it is that the 'whys' and 'wherefores' are immaterial. Those walking the Camino seem to accept that their fellow pilgrims are making the journey for a variety of reasons and are therefore content just to extend uncomplicated friendship and bonhomie along the way. We've yet to meet another Briton but learn from our American chums that the Hollywood film, *The Way*, is partly responsible for the vast number of Americans participating on the route.

'The film is about a father who carries his son's ashes along the Way,' says Dawn. 'So it's become a pilgrimage for some who've lost loved ones.'

'That's rather sad,' I mumble. 'And then you get people like us, going for peace, enlightenment and a chance to get fit.'

'Fit?' laughs Jane. 'Wait till we get on the scales back home before you say that.'

Thursday

Jane is standing at the reception desk of The Way Hotel in Molinaseca that looks out over the pretty River Meruelo. We are in the El Bierzo region of Castile and León, shortly to progress into Galicia.

'*Un secador*? You want a hairdryer?' says owner, Matti Elizalde, in perfect English. 'I have at least four models. Take your pick.'

Jane is a picture of happiness. 'Why is it so difficult to find these in hotel bedrooms?'

He shrugs. 'Many pilgrims use them to dry clothes and that doesn't go down well with hoteliers. The less spiritual ones take them away in their luggage. That's why they are not offered or are kept at reception.'

'How terrible to steal them,' I say.

'That's human nature for you,' he smiles. 'But you know, I like pilgrims. I am from the Basque area and have done the St James's

Way many times, but when I had a bad accident, I couldn't walk such distances any more. I was very downbeat but a good doctor told me to open a pilgrim hotel instead. So I did and I've never been happier.'

'It's such a beautiful town, too,' Jane enthuses, waving her guidebook in front of us. 'Sergi Ramis has only good things to say about it.'

'Oh well, if Sergi likes it, then it surely must be a wonder,' I wink.

'I hope you lovely ladies will be careful on the journey. Don't talk to any strange men and be vigilant even though it is a very safe route.'

'I've got a good stick to ward off trouble,' I laugh, shaking my faithful curved crook in the air.

'And what about you?' he asks Jane in some concern. 'Aside from hairdryers I do a good line in walking sticks.'

He opens a cupboard and a whole load tumble out. They are of different heights and hues. He gives a wry chuckle. 'Although most pilgrims remember to take hairdryers with them, you'd be surprised how many leave their sticks behind!'

Friday

A white mist blinds the higher peaks from view as Jane and I soldier on in the bitter, early-morning cold. The previous day we walked another 31 kilometres and have 30 to complete today. We have left the charming town of Villafranca del Bierzo far behind us and now strike on to O'Cebreiro, a small hamlet nestling in the Galician hills. This is likely to be our toughest day of walking as there are steep inclines and sharp descents, but this fails to dull my ardour. The simple routine that Jane and I have developed each day, often involving challenging hikes, has become so pleasurable and satisfying that we wear our aches and pains like badges of honour. In a tiny village en route we break our journey to enjoy a cup of hot coffee and are pleased to see Australian Tony sitting inside. He gives us a friendly nod.

'You two are on a roll,' he smiles. 'I bet you'll take the next tough stretch in your stride.' Somewhat reassured, we give him the thumbs up as he zips up his weatherproof jacket and heads out into the chilly air. Some time later, as we plough up the curling track near several farm buildings, a snow-white, wild hen with a lush plumage of feathers and fluffy, hairy feet runs out in front of us.

'Isn't he gorgeous!' I exclaim.

Jane is still muttering her mantra of '*una taza de agua caliente por favor*' while studiously studying the editorial pearls of Sergi Ramis, so shows little excitement. However, an elderly woman dressed in black woollens comes over to greet us and tells me that the chicken is a rare exotic breed, a gift from a friend. All the same, it is apparently useless as a layer. She offers to let me take it but perhaps heeding the motto 'two's company, three's a crowd', Jane balks at the idea and informs me that it's out of the question.

'Spoilsport,' I moan as we stop to catch our breath. I point to one of the many stone and wooden *hórreos*, ancient thatched granary stores, that are now a common motif of many of the rural villages we pass through.

'The round basketwork ones are called *cabaceiras*,' I say.

'Ah, yes, I think Sergi comments on that somewhere...'

'He would! But does your beloved Sergi mention anything about those little Hobbit homes that we keep passing with thatched roofs and round stone bases?'

She flicks through the pages of her book in some angst until triumphantly pointing at a page. 'There! Sergi gives them a mention here. Apparently they are known as *pallozas* and are characteristic of pre-Roman culture, possibly Celtic. He says here that they were used as dwellings until the twentieth century, after which time they were transformed into storehouses. What would we do without him?'

'Heaven knows,' I say under my breath as I fantasise about hurling the book down the nearest ravine.

As we head up into the hills, we espy a frail-looking elderly matron in black garb collecting chestnuts in a huge wicker basket that she effortlessly lifts onto one shoulder. It is filled to the brim and, without a groan, she sets off at a fast pace along the track. Some hours later we reach Las Herrerias, where a sign offers pilgrims the chance to ride a horse up the final helter-skelter pathway into the mountains to O'Cebreiro. Jane looks longingly at the horses and takes a glug from the water bottle in her rucksack. 'What do you say, Ans?' She always sweetly uses her old nickname for me when she wants to get her way.

I stand firm. 'Nope. We've got to walk it. We're pilgrims, aren't we?'

'Who's going to know if we take the easy option?' she giggles.

'It's the principle that counts,' I reply staunchly, grabbing her arm and leading her away from temptation.

Two hours later, when I suddenly discover that I foolishly left my beloved walking stick against a fence way back on the track, I begin to regret the decision. With wobbly knees, aching backs and numb legs we slog on over the hills and through miniscule, mostly abandoned hamlets and villages where stray dogs and cats amble over to greet us. I feel sadness that due to the country's economic constraints so many rural folk, particularly young people, have felt compelled to seek work in cities or even overseas, with the result that some villages resemble ghost towns. To our delight, we soon reach a sign officially informing us that we have now entered the region of Galicia. So far we have travelled about 125 kilometres and, despite enjoying our early-morning starts and all-day hikes, find this latest stage somewhat testing. Finally, in spitting rain and with fretful dark skies above us, we hobble into O'Cebreiro, the tiny outpost high on a hill that offers just a small hotel, gift shop and a few hostels to weary pilgrims. In the wild gale we throw open the front door of the dwelling where I've booked a room for the night and find three amply built local women scrubbing and peeling potatoes and apples together, rather like characters out of a bucolic work by Jean-François Millet. They barely look up when I offer a greeting as they sit huddled over their buckets, their fingers red and chapped with the cold.

'You're late,' huffs one. 'We nearly gave your room away. You should have called earlier today to reconfirm.'

'That would have been a trifle difficult without phone connection,' I say in some consternation.

Another wipes her hands and takes a key from a shelf and leads us out of the warm reception into the freezing wind. We are to be housed in what appears to be an annex in a graveyard, but fortunately it turns out to be a strip of land housing the Royal St Mary's Church. The room is basic and freezing cold.

'This has to be one of your worst choices,' says Jane sadly. 'No heating and…' She returns from the miniscule shower room. 'No hairdryer.'

Shivering, we close the open window and watch as the hamlet is soon veiled in unremitting darkness. In need of a walking stick, I venture out to the shop, promising to enquire about hairdryers on the way. A pleasant man finds me a sturdy stick and I buy a T-shirt for Ollie. At the reception desk of our hostel, my request is met with merriment.

'A hairdryer? You think we have hairdryers here?'

At least I've livened these women up. 'It's for my friend…' I bleat, watching them convulse with giggles.

Back in the bedroom where Jane is submerged beneath cold sheets, I suggest that we comfort ourselves with a hot dinner and a bottle of robust country red wine – even if the red wine around here is always served cold.

She nods. 'Wine is definitely needed. I can forgive the lack of a warm welcome but the absence of a hairdryer really takes the biscuit!'

215

Monday

Rain is pouring from the heavens and Jane and I, like many of our fellow pilgrims plodding along through the dark forests on the outskirts of Sarria, have donned plastic, bat-like rain capes. Our last two nights were spent in tranquil Triacastela and rainy Sarria, where we were fortunate enough to witness a wonderful local wedding. There was something quite surreal yet magical about standing voyeuristically by the church steps celebrating the nuptials of a couple of happy strangers. I found it touching that one of the local guests stopped to chat with me in Spanish, explaining proudly that the beaming pair were both close friends. En route, we met Simon and Jenny, a young Australian couple living in a tiny hamlet in the hills, who open their doors to pilgrims and while away their time making elderflower wine and quince jelly. As we strolled by the entrance to their dilapidated old stone house, they warmly welcomed us into the courtyard and plied us with damsons in syrup and sought my advice about the consistency of their home-made quince jelly bubbling on a makeshift stove. Much as I marvelled at how rudimentary and cold the dwelling was, I was relieved to see that in the kitchen area they had several crates of home-made hooch to keep their toes warm on a cold night.

We march on in the chill, hoping that the sullen sky will transform into a carpet of blue silk, but the bad weather seems set for the day. To our relief, in a small café in the woods, we come across Dawn, Tony and our Canadian buddies, all shivering in the chill, and vow to meet up at Santiago Cathedral for the famed Friday pilgrim mass. Laughingly, we share anecdotes and compare minor injuries over warming coffees and home-made cake, assuring one another that the rain will soon pass. I find myself genuinely looking forward to catching up with our new buddies along the journey and marvel at how quickly new friendships can be forged when a singular quest is shared. In Sarria, we got talking to a

Californian couple named Ronnie and Martin and are pleased to see them waving cheerily at us from the track. As a vegetarian, Ronnie had entertained us with tales of the meagre fare dished up to her so far en route. When she sees us, she rolls her eyes.

'Hey! Guess what they served me last night – that's right, another omelette! I tell you guys, if I see another egg or tuna salad, I might just go mad.'

Her husband, Martin, chortles happily. 'You're way past that post!'

Some time later, as we battle against the wind and lashing rain, I feel a strange sensation in my hiking boot and discover that water is seeping inside. Worse still is that the entire rubber sole is peeling off. It is the very same problem that occurred on my infamous walk to Lluc Monastery with my friends Ignacio and Cristina. On that occasion, it transpired that my walking boots had been affected by a small bug that eats into rubber in humid conditions. It was evidently happening again. This is the first time on the trip that I feel somewhat disheartened. My main concern is that if my boot gives way entirely, I might be forced to take public transport to our next port of call. Not wanting to worry Jane with my woes, I soldier on in the icy water, miserably listening to the squelch of my boot as it thirstily gulps in water at every puddle it greets. The rain continues to fall in sheets, and yet we stumble on, unable to converse and blinded by the onslaught of water. Shaking with cold, I try not to focus on the elements and my numb foot and instead visualise a warm and toasty fire in a grate and a welcome glass of *vino tinto* at the side of a warm and comfortable bed. I say a little prayer that my sole will hold out until our next night-time stopover.

Some hours later, as Portmarin comes into view over the river Miño, I admit to Jane that my boot is just about to separate from its sole and that my foot has been resting in a pool of icy rainwater for some distance. Somewhat horrified but amazed that it's survived this far, she guides me to our warm and friendly hotel – a good choice on Jane's part – before it completely comes apart. I say a silent prayer and cheer up when I see in the lobby that our luggage has arrived before us. It won't be long before I'll be able to unearth my trusty trainers from my rucksack to keep me on my toes. In a lively restaurant some hours later we relax over red wine and warm food, toasting our toes by the fire, and suddenly life has never seemed quite so good.

Wednesday

The sun is shining as Jane and I arrive in Ribadiso, a peaceful hamlet with a basic, though clean, hostel and a cheery café. We have walked 25 kilometres from Palas de Rei, where we had an overnight stay and where we were given a warm welcome at snug Hotel Benilde by desk staff Pilar and Alessandro. So accommodating were they that they even carried our luggage upstairs and left a hairdryer in the bathroom for Jane.

Many pilgrims stay overnight in Ribadiso as the holy grail of Santiago looms ever nearer. In the local bar we meet up with our various chums and a German named Henning and his grey hunting dog Alf, who carries a pouch of dog food on either side of his back. The two have walked for many miles and look none the worse for wear. Like me, Henning takes great delight in studying all the stamps in his pilgrim passport and we sit comparing them as Jane tuts and tells Dawn that I am just a child at heart. Together we all sit in the glorious sunshine, sharing happy memories and funny anecdotes about our trip thus far. Jane has nipped inside the bar and soon returns with a tray of beers.

'Do they speak English?' I ask suspiciously.

With a superior smile, she shakes her head. 'Actually, I'll have you know, I asked in Spanish.'

'Amazing!' I exclaim.

'I may not be able to ask for a cup of hot water, but when it comes to alcohol, there's no stopping me,' she beams.

Friday

After a night spent in Pedrouzo, a perfunctory little town where we found cheap and cheerful lodgings, we set off under sombre skies just after 7:30, eager to reach our much-heralded final destination. We have barely 20 kilometres left to complete on foot and we enjoy the tranquil stretch, passing tiny hamlets and villages en route as we near our goal. After 7 kilometres, we reach the modest airport of Lavacolla on the outskirts of Santiago and, an hour later, Monte de Gozo, meaning Hill of Joy. Here, a giant, modern religious creation by sculptor Jose Maria Acuña, graces the summit of a grassy hill. Pilgrims swarm its base, taking selfies and allowing themselves a few minutes respite before continuing their journey. Surrounded by bushy eucalyptus trees, the once much-anticipated distant view of the three spires of Santiago Cathedral is now obscured. There is a whiff of modernity and commercialisation about the place, which I find unsettling, and so we take refuge at the bijoux and peaceful chapel of San Marcos, which still retains historic authenticity. We are now just 3 kilometres from the city.

As hundreds of pilgrims converge on Santiago de Compostela, the excitement is palpable. It is a breezy sunny afternoon and so warm that our fleeces are consigned to our rucksacks. Following the faithful blue signs with yellow fletches, we finally see the giant gate leading into Obradoiro Square. A lone piper serenades us as, with joy, we acknowledge the end of our thirteen-day walk that has taken us 311 kilometres across the north-west of Spain and through some of the most beautiful countryside that I can remember. After leaving our rucksacks and belongings in a local hotel, we set off to the official cathedral office to receive our

Compostela certificates. To my relief, we are allowed to keep our little pilgrim passports that have faithfully recorded every stop taken on our long and memorable journey. In the magnificent baroque cathedral, as tradition dictates, we queue with other pilgrims to embrace the statue of St James, the apostle, and soon the service begins. The pews are tightly packed with pilgrims of every nationality and, as our eyes search the throng, we see many a smiling face. There's Tony from Australia, Lael and Richard, Dawn and Ronnie and Martin, and other pilgrims we've enjoyed chatting with along the Way. At the close of the service, the magnificent *botafumeiro*, an antique thurible weighing 80 kilos, is swung by a group of six priests and sweet incense suddenly fills the aisles. As the organ plays, we file out of the stone arched portals into the night air, ready to share hugs, drinks and laughter with our walking companions who will soon be setting off to their respective homes all over the globe. Jane and I share a hug and congratulate ourselves on our feat.

'Well, it's been a blast!' I say. 'Even if I have had to cope with your appalling Spanish and obsession with hairdryers. Oh and let's not even mention old Sergi Ramis.'

She laughs. 'And what about you with those wretched stamps?! And your, er, choice of hiking boots.'

'Oh come on! How was I to know that a fiendish rubber bug was secretly chomping away at my soles?'

We giggle.

'To be honest, I never would have believed that walking could be such fun.' I give a sigh. 'I'm really sad it's all over.'

'But is it?' she says with a gleam in her eye. 'I mean we still have four hundred and seventy-nine kilometres left to complete the entire length of St James's Way.'

I turn to her. 'You mean we could walk from St-Jean-Pied-de-Port in the French Pyrenees all the way to Leon?'

'Why not? Then we could take the train to Santiago, having already walked that stretch.'

'But it would be tougher than this trip and longer. In fact, another hundred and sixty-eight kilometres more.'

'A breeze,' she insists. 'And you know the best thing about it?'

'What?' I say, full of anticipation.

'My old friend Sergi Ramis can join us again as he extensively covers the whole journey in his guide book and...'

I give a groan.

She holds up her hand, laughing. 'But most important of all, I'm going to invest in a travel hairdryer and a Spanish dictionary. What can possibly go wrong?'

Fourteen

OILING THE WHEELS

A steady downpour of gentle rain caresses the orange and lemon trees and drenches the orchard's carpet of soft, pale grass. Sitting in a wicker shopping basket on the windowsill of Alan's *abajo,* Inko looks out across the valley and gives a hearty yawn. From her eyrie, she can keep a beady eye on our industrious and chatty hens that are digging the soil beneath a clump of algarroba trees. A stream of tiny charcoal-hued chicks peep out from beneath the wings of a fat black hen, and, sensing rain, disappear into the warm and downy depths once more. Our two new snowy Silkies, purchased from Nacho Pons a few months earlier, are clucking loudly, their fluffy plumage somewhat flattened by the incessant rain. In a short space of time, they have blended in with the rest of the flock and are wonderfully tame. The only problem has been in remembering their Buddhist names, so Aye Thin Zar has simply become AZ, and Cudabhiksuni, Sunny.

Marching about the vegetable patch in green wellies and a cagoule is the Scotsman. He is wearing an old tweed cap and puffing on a *puro* with seemingly no care about the inclement weather. Pressing his mobile phone to one ear, he offers a series of enthusiastic *si-si-si's* to the caller on the other end of the line. I stride along the gravel path in my running gear and tip some cooked spaghetti into the hens' feeding bowl and watch as they scurry towards me, clucking excitedly. If there's one thing our hens love, it is spaghetti, which presumably they mistake for long and lifeless worms.

The Scotsman beckons me over and beams happily. 'Good run?'

'Wonderfully wet and invigorating.'

'You'll never guess who that was on the blower. It was a chap from Focus Films inviting me to audition for a holiday brochure. It's a very well-known company.'

'What do you have to do?'

He hesitates and then gives a nonchalant shrug. 'Dance.'

'You're kidding?'

'Not at all. Apparently I have to dance around in summer clothes as if I'm on holiday and having a raucous time. I'm off for the audition tomorrow.'

I can't hide my mirth. 'Will I be able to download a video afterwards?'

'In your dreams,' he growls.

'What kind of dancing is required?'

'Who knows, but I'm sure I can *writhe* to the occasion,' he sniggers.

'Boom boom!' I reply.

He waves his *puro* about in the air. 'Can you see all the rows of broad beans I've just planted? And I've dug up all the weeds, too. It's back-breaking work.'

'Well done. You're also getting wet. Would you like a coffee and muffin break?'

He nods. 'Good idea. We've got to visit Tomeu Deya in an hour and you need to get out of those wet running clothes first or you'll catch your death.'

We walk up the stone steps to the back terrace where greeny-brown water sits in the base of the forlorn swimming pool. Crisp autumnal leaves float on its surface, twirling round and round with the force of the rain. Catalina's brother, Stefan, our builder, thinks that we have a small leak so we need to keep the pool partially filled to check its level before repairs can be made.

In the snug kitchen, Minky, Doughnut and Orlando sit curled up on cushioned chairs, slumbering deeply, not even stirring when I make coffee and set out a plate of pecan and apple muffins on the table. I throw off my trainers and peel the soaking socks from my feet and rest them on the tiles. A hot and invigorating shower is my next port of call. I turn to the Scotsman.

'You know, while running I bumped into Tomeu, an old friend of Neus', and he told me that at one time Sóller valley had twenty-two practising priests.'

He frowns. 'What an odd thing to mention in passing on a rainy day.'

'Ah, but I met him outside the local church and commented on the fact that it was mostly closed, similarly to many of the churches Jane and I passed on the Camino de Santiago last month.'

'So how many priests are there now?'

'Only two in the valley apparently, meaning that most of our local churches are unattended and therefore kept closed. That also explains why on a Sunday the main church in Sóller is always packed.'

'It's a bit like trying to find a garage open on a Sunday,' he muses before popping a morsel of muffin into his mouth.

'Any news of Juana and Pep? Aren't they coming round for supper at the weekend?' I say.

'Funny you should mention them. I caught Juana buying Venezuelan oranges in Carrefour the other day. There I was browsing the wine section when she rolled by with her trolley full of foreign fruit.'

'What do you mean, foreign?' I ask.

'I mean non-indigenous. Here we are on an island that produces the very best oranges, lemons, olives, almonds, figs and other fruit and there she was buying imported stuff. Madness!'

'Did you tell her off?' I laugh.

'Indeed. I lectured her for about five minutes on the value of buying local products and told her that it was about time she joined our Sóller Alma Eco group. She argued that the imported oranges were bigger and juicier.'

'And no doubt cheaper.'

'Not always,' he replies thoughtfully. 'Pep says she's got a bee in her bonnet about buying imported goods. He says it's the novelty factor.'

'In that case let's take her to task at supper.'

'As long as you're not too evangelical about it,' he smirks. 'Going off at a tangent, it's only a month until Christmas and we still haven't finished painting Ollie's room. I think we need to get cracking.'

Our ambitious plan to transform Ollie's bedroom into a temple of cool has proven more labour-intensive than either of us had envisaged. Having managed to haul the spare double bed up from the Scotsman's *abajo*, we set to work on repainting the walls and all the furniture, after sanding down the various cupboards and the chest of drawers and changing their handles. Next came the light fittings and the purchasing of a pewter-hued sisal rug to adorn the old pinewood floor.

'Let's hope he likes charcoal and grey,' the Scotsman remarks.

'Trust me he'll love it and if he doesn't, he can swap digs with Carlos I.'

Once showered and changed, I check my e-mails and make a few phone calls before setting off with the Scotsman to visit Tomeu Deya in the village of Biniaraix. Can Det, which has been in the hands of the Deya family since 1561, is now the oldest working commercial olive mill in Mallorca. To this day, from November through to January, local families of the Sóller valley bring their olive harvests to brothers Guillermo and Tomeu Deya and their team of five workers to transform it into liquid gold. There are commercial clients, too, who bring larger quantities of olives for milling. As we walk into the airy and darkened *entrada* of Can Det, with its huge slate-coloured flagstones, Tomeu steps forward to greet us at the sound of the shrill doorbell. Having been assigned the task of coordinating the promotion of the Tramuntanas UNESCO Heritage status for the last few years, he is now handing over the baton to another specialist within the regional government. This means that he can devote more time to the family olive mill and his other commercial ventures. Before ushering us through into the factory, he points to an engraving on one of the heavy wooden front doors.

'You see this? The year 1791 is engraved here, the date when these doors were constructed, and the cobbled stones on the floor of the *entrada* were once used by animals and horses. In former times, horses or donkeys would have been led through here to the rear patio.'

We follow him through a low door to the factory where the sound of frantic machinery suddenly fills our ears. This is the throbbing heart of the oil production, where workers in blue overalls wash and prepare the olives for milling. Tomeu's older brother Guillermo joins us and points out the different processes of the mill. First he shows us the massive baskets of olives that have arrived straight from local orchards. The fruit is of many hues – bright green, black, brown, red and beige, and twigs and leaves are thrown into the mix, too.

'The more mature olives here are better for oil,' asserts Tomeu. 'All of them need to be thoroughly washed first.'

Guillermo taps one of the machines where three conical stone blocks move round on top of a circular base. 'Here the olives are crushed. The *truis* are made of stone because if they were made of metal, the taste of the oil could be tainted.'

'Next,' says Tomeu, 'the olive mush or pâté is squeezed through these coco fibre mats, known as *esportins*. The mats are stacked up and pressed hard.'

Guillermo shows us browny water and oil that run along steel channels in another part of the room. 'The oil and olive juices, mostly water, need to be separated, which we do by centrifugal force in this machine.'

We peer into the large metal cylinder.

'You'll see that the oil rises to the top,' he continues. 'When the oil runs golden, we know that it is ready.'

'What is the minimum number of olives that someone can bring you?' I ask.

Tomeu shrugs. 'Well, we're not going to count every one. What we call a *truada*, two hundred and seventy kilos, which produce a hundred and seventy litres of oil, is a good amount. Even if someone doesn't produce enough olives on their own land, they can share a load with another family member or neighbour. It's not a huge amount.'

The Scotsman is fascinated by a pile of rough, dried debris left by the olive husks. It reminds me of elephant dung but I decide not to make the comparison.

'What happens to these?' he enquires.

Tomeu gives him a piece. 'This is used as carbon for fires. It's totally natural so it burns well. Nothing goes to waste, which is the important thing.'

'You have to remember,' chips in Guillermo, 'that we do this for love. We are artisanal olive oil producers and cannot compete with modern mechanised processes that require just one person to operate the machines.'

'Our oil has a different taste,' smiles Tomeu.

'Because it's made with love?' I hazard.

They laugh. 'You could say that. We're proud that this mill has been in our family for so many years and we'd like the tradition to continue. We run other businesses, but this is our passion.'

Tomeu takes us into a small cellar where there are bottles lining every wall. 'This is where the olive oil rests. Like a good wine, it's good to let it settle. We usually recommend leaving the bottles a month or two in order to let the cloudy appearance of the oil disappear.'

I'm envious of local friends who have a sufficient number of olive trees on their land to produce their own oil. Our own trees are too sparse to produce enough fruit for a batch, so for now we buy Can Det's own harvested olive oil. Tomeu passes the Scotsman a 5-litre plastic bottle of oil and gratefully takes the notes he offers in return.

'That should keep you going for a while,' he says.

'I should think so,' replies the Scotsman, adding wryly, 'Mind you, my wife goes through it like a dose of salts.'

Before we leave, I ask Tomeu about the UNESCO award. 'I know that you're stepping down from the project now that the main strategy is in place, but how will the heritage status affect our valley?'

He shrugs. 'It's complicated. Hopefully receiving this accolade from UNESCO will mean that visitors to the island will respect the Tramuntanas and their heritage and want to explore them, too. The award celebrates human activity in the mountains – the ice houses, charcoal-burners legacy, agriculture – such as olive oil, citrus fruit and almond production. It's really about how man has interacted with nature over the centuries here in Mallorca. Quite some feat.'

'And it's still going on today,' I reply.

'Of course, but not quite to the extent it once has. It's important to cherish the Tramuntanas and to protect them while seeing them as a living thing that people can enjoy.'

'Hence the expression "the hills are alive",' adds the Scotsman somewhat inanely.

'I suppose so,' laughs Tomeu.

At the enormous front doors made from cherry wood, the very ones that date back more than 200 years, Guillermo appears with a bottle of golden olive oil. It isn't labelled and is all the more special for that.

'Enjoy it,' he says as we head off into the street with our two precious bottles of oil. 'And remember that it was made with passion and love.'

Despite Pollença being but an hour's drive through the Tramuntanas from my home in Sóller, it always somehow feels as though I'm setting off on a grand adventure when popping over to the historic town in the north of the island. It is a luxurious and visual feast of a journey by car, coursing up the winding and leafy American Road and enjoying magnificent mountain vistas along the way. As it is Sunday, the car park of the Mirador de ses Barques, a popular staging post for weekend hikes, is already groaning with cars and bikes. Dog walkers and families buzz about the place and a couple of horse riders stop by the road, seemingly sharing a joke with one of our local, blue-uniformed police officers. A warm sun glimmers on the horizon and a flock of starlings flit across the azure sky. It's hard to believe that we are in the grip of autumn when normally rain is the hallmark of the season.

Today, the Scotsman and I have been invited to attend the official launch of Walking on Words, which is being held at the iconic Illa d'Or Hotel in Pollença port. This elegant and historic white edifice that reaches out to the sea at the tranquil far end of the port was at one time visited by the likes of Winston Churchill and Agatha Christie. Indeed, it is the very connection with the writer that has proven the reason for the Council of Mallorca's choice of venue.

Leaving the Mirador de ses Barques behind, we follow the contours of the road and are soon at the placid Cuber Reservoir, its dark water tinged with sunlight and shadow from the rocky corona of mountains that embrace it. Just a few kilometres further is the spectacular Gorg Blau lake, overlooked by Puig Major, the highest peak in the Tramuntanas.

I turn to the Scotsman. 'I read a fascinating article in the *Diario de Mallorca* last week about an ancient Islamic settlement recently discovered beneath the waters of Gorg Blau. Amazingly, it harks back to the thirteenth century.'

He steals a glance at me from the driver's seat. 'I hadn't realised that the Moors set up home this far into the Tramuntanas.'

'According to the article, it wasn't exactly voluntary. When Jaume I landed in Mallorca in 1229, there was a huge battle in Palma at which the Moors were defeated. Apparently an estimated forty thousand people escaped to the hills and held out for as long as they could. As it happened, barely a few years.'

'What happened to those who weren't killed or didn't manage to run away?'

'The newspaper piece surmised that they were mostly enslaved. Some left the island by boat and sailed for Africa. It seems that the settlement under Gorg Blau lake has been named the Vall de Almallutx and is now the most significant Moorish city discovered in the Baleares, perhaps the whole of Spain.'

'Did the article say when the site was discovered?'

'Well it seems to have been known about before, but in 2011 local archaeologist Jaume Deyà did an extensive search of the zone and found a remarkable number of Islamic burial sites, sanctuaries, buildings and ceramics. They must have had to involve divers. What is interesting is that Deyà noticed that many of the items found had been badly charred, which has led them to believe that the city was attacked and burnt down in 1232, when the fleeing Moorish rebels were finally crushed.'

'A rather sad end to what was probably a beautiful city. I wonder how the archaeological dig is being financed.'

I look over the shimmering lake. 'Since the economic crisis in Spain, there hasn't been much money swilling around for such research but the article mentioned that La Caixa Bank and private local companies in the area have chipped in.'

'Thank heavens. Otherwise such a jewel might never have been brought to light.'

'The good news is that many of the artefacts are apparently being housed safely in local museums.'

Further on, we pass the elegant grounds of Lluc Monastery on our left and are soon heading towards Pollença town and its sunny port.

Luckily we find a parking space tucked away in a quiet cul-de-sac close to the hotel and pass through the airy lobby to the sunny rear terrace, marvelling at the mesmerising seascape beyond.

Already guests are excitedly buzzing about the seats in front of the stage and a musical quartet is poised for action. Curious holidaymakers and dog walkers breeze along the promenade, wondering what spectacle is about to take place, while two young actors read through their scripts. Carme and Carlotta from the foundation of house museums welcome us with hugs at the registration desk and soon we are seated. It's not long before our Pollença-based chums, Donald and Claire Trelford and Andrew Ede, arrive. As it happens, both men are also columnists for the local expat newspaper, *Majorca Daily Bulletin*, and have come to support the event. Alan leans over to me.

'When do we get a drink? I'm parched.'

I give him a nudge. 'All good things come to those who wait.'

The band strikes up and soon the performance begins. I settle in my seat in the sunshine, enjoying the combination of glorious weather, literature and music.

At the end of the performance, canapés and drinks are offered and I catch up with guests while the Scotsman furtively disappears behind a bush to take a call. He returns with a smile on his face.

'You'll never guess! I've won the audition for the holiday brochure advert. Those natty moves I did to Mick Jagger's "Dancing in the Street" evidently went down a storm at Focus Films.'

I give a sigh. 'Are you sure it's not going to be one of those embarrassing dancing-pensioner-type adverts?'

He seems affronted. 'Of course not! Don't forget that at the audition I was dancing with a nubile twenty-year-old Latino.'

'If you say so.'

He shoots me a wary look. 'I'm not sure why you're so concerned. I mean the wurst sausage advert was a resounding success, wasn't it?'

'Indeed, but there's something about this one that doesn't sound quite so straightforward.'

Carme and Carlotta come over to join us and proffer glasses of red wine. 'Did you understand everything?'

The Scotsman throws his hands out expansively. 'Well the Mallorquin was OK, but I had a few problems with the English.'

They laugh and thrust a catalogue in our hands. 'This shows you all the WOW literary routes around the island. We're counting on you to set a good example by trying them out.'

'*No problema*,' replies the Scotsman, jauntily giving me a nudge. 'I'll try to fit them in between acting commitments.'

They stare at him. 'Gosh, you act?'

His mobile phone rings. It's Ollie on the line, calling from his school. In some confusion he apologises and strides off to the promenade to speak to his beloved son. Saved by the bell. He returns in high spirits.

'Now where's he going?' he asks. 'Should we wait?'

'I think so.'

A moment later he reappears, this time with a jar of honey and a round parcel. 'It's my home-made sheep cheese and flower honey. I keep my own bees.'

'Are you sure?' I ask.

'Please take them, it's the least I can do. I have something else you might like.'

He dips into a cloth satchel around his neck. 'Do you like *bolets*, the wild mushrooms?'

I nod.

'These are fresh from the mountains today. It's not been a good season with so little rain but I get up early and beat the sheep to the best crops.'

As we wave goodbye, I see him scoop up a tiny black lamb with a wiggly tail and place it over his shoulders. And, without looking back, he strides up the hill, singing as he goes.

I'm sitting with my friend Isabel Moreno in the stylish café of the Fundacio La Caixa, housed in one of Palma's most distinctive edifices of the modernist period. Designed by Catalan architect Lluís Domènech i Montaner in 1903, this was Palma's first luxury hotel and proved a huge draw for celebrated international writers and visitors at the time. In 1993, the old building was restored and transformed into a vibrant art space running across several floors. Today, aside from the permanent and new exhibitions, its magnificent wrought-iron work, sculptures, grand balconies and intricately designed tiles attract thousands of visitors each year. Isabel and I look out at the falling rain.

'What a day!' I exclaim.

'Ah, but we need rain. The *bolets* and *setas* have been poor this autumn, and the reservoirs have to be kept filled.'

I take a sip of my hot coffee. 'True enough. I'm a fan of the wild mushrooms, but even in Sóller the *setas* have been few and far between.'

She nods. 'I love the sun but our fauna and flora need rain, something visitors on holiday here don't always seem to understand. Now, before I forget, here is the copy of my new book. It gives a taste of all my international adventures as a biologist.'

I examine the substantial white tome. Isabel was for many years the revered director of marine biology at the University of the Baleares before retiring in 2009. All the same, she had no intention of hanging up her white lab coat quite so soon. To this day she conducts biology lectures and is a valued member of various oceanographic committees whose aim is to protect marine life around the Baleares. The Scotsman and I were lucky enough to have met Isabel when, together with some friends, she took us on a tour of Cabrera Island, explaining the fauna and flora and underlining how critical it was to preserve the biodiversity of Mallorca's most cherished national park. By chance we discovered that a mutual contact, Dr Salud Deudero, studied under Isabel at the local university. She is now one of the leading lights of the Spanish Institute of Oceanography in the Baleares.

'Have you seen Salud and her husband Mimo recently?' she asks.

'We had supper with them over at the home of our friends, Ignacio and Cristina, not too long ago. They were teaching me how to make animal noises in Spanish.'

She laughs. 'Salud was one of my most gifted students and now she is conducting brilliant research in the field.'

I tut. 'Why is it that I know so many brilliant biologists and was a complete dud at science at school?'

'You probably weren't inspired by your teachers. But think of the scientific expeditions you've been on with that British explorer friend of yours, Colonel John Blashford-Snell?'

'Yes, but that's live science in the field, which is so much more fun.'

'That's the point. Science should be fun! You know, I have been all over the world for my work – I visited Antarctica three times, staying for two months each time, and South East Asia, the Galapagos, the Middle East, South America and the Seychelles. Science opens doors to wonderful cultures and experiences.'

'Were you not born in London?'

She nods. 'I suppose I've always been a traveller. My father was offered a professorship at Cambridge University, so I spent my youth in the UK before studying in Madrid, Santiago, Oviedo and the Canary Islands. Eventually I married and ended up here in Mallorca.'

'There are worse places to end up,' I smile.

'It is a paradise for biologists, despite heavy tourism. In between learning to play the piano these days and spending time with my grandchildren, I like to be involved in marine-life preservation. It's so important for the future of the Balearic Islands that we educate residents and visitors about the importance of maintaining the natural harmony of the islands for future generations.'

She stands up and stretches. 'And now the rain has ceased, I must get home to see my grandchildren. Where are you going now?'

'To the launch of a new book entitled, *Entre la Calma y la Inspiracion*. You'd be interested because it's the brainchild of two lecturers, Dr Juana Maria Segui Aznar and Dr Patricia Rodriguez of the University's philology department.'

'Between the Calm and the Inspiration – that's a good title. So what's the subject matter?'

'It's a dictionary of notable English-speaking writers who visited the Baleares from the nineteenth century to the present day.'

'It's extraordinary how much of a literary tradition there is here on Mallorca.'

'Actually, it's becoming quite a hobby of late finding out about the many historic writers who visited the island, let alone discovering Mallorca's own celebrated authors and poets. I used to seek advice on such matters from Margalida who ran Calabruix, our local bookshop, but sadly she died last year. Now I've got to fend for myself.'

She gives a wry smile. 'I'm sure as a journalist you're used to carrying out your own research, just like us scientists.'

We head out into Plaça Weyler and peer up at the slate-grey sky.

'More rain on the way,' she remarks cheerfully and then, seeing her bus slowly progressing along the street, offers me a hug and scurries across the street. I am relieved to see her reach the bus door before it pulls away from the stop. As I head off in the direction of the Misericordia monastery building, where the book launch is to be held, Judas trills.

The Scotsman sounds somewhat coy.

'I've just finished the filming for the holiday brochure advert.'

'Wonderful. How did it go?'

'Fine,' he says a little flatly.

'Anything wrong?'

'No, but I didn't get to dance with the twenty-year-old woman again.'

'Oh?'

'Instead I was paired with a very nice lady more my own age. In truth, she's probably a fair bit younger, and we had to pretend to dance and laugh.'

I giggle. 'So you *are* going to be in the oldie section of the brochure!'

He sounds indignant. 'I'll have you know that it will be the senior-citizen section. And as the casting director said, these days, older people are so young for their ages.'

'Diplomatic of him,' I retort. 'So this time you were doing the foxtrot rather than jiggling around to "Dancing in the Street"?'

He gives a sniff. 'Not at all!'

'So when will we get to see this brochure?'

There's a pause. 'Not for some time,' he replies robustly. 'In fact, I'm rather hopeful it may never see the light of day. I'll never live it down with Pep.'

'But think of the money.'

He brightens. 'Indeed. After our wonderful visit to Can Det, I was thinking of treating us to a few new olive trees.'

'So that we can eventually make our own olive oil?'

'Why not? Pep and I have made our *patxaran* in time for Christmas, so what's to stop us making our own oil? We could pool resources.'

I give a groan. If I thought the joint follies and dubious enterprises of these two overgrown schoolboys were at an end, I was evidently sorely mistaken.

Fifteen

CRUNCH TIME

It's a crisp, wintry day and yet a lemon sun smiles down on the orchard, casting hazy light on the vast dewy cobwebs that cling to the branches of orange and lemon trees. The sky is a pale blue strewn with clouds that form a soft white corona around the highest peaks of the Tramuntanas. From my office window I watch the antics of our resident robin as it pecks in the stubborn and cold soil for grubs while keeping a stealthy eye on the movements of Inko, who is nonchalantly prowling along the wall above the pond, her gimlet eyes fixed on the frisky little red-breasted bird in the garden below. As the robin hops onto the gravel path, Inko suddenly descends at break-neck speed and leaps forward, missing her prize by a fraction. With evident satisfaction, the robin flits into our silvery olive tree in the centre of the lawn and utters what sounds like a titter. Inko stalks off, a sulky expression on her face. I look towards the still pond. Dark green lily pads float serenely on the surface while the wispy reeds have grown so tall that they touch the mouth of the rocky ledge high above from where fresh water cascades down the wall into the pond below. I miss our singing frogs and my conversations with

Johnny and so, instead, content myself with the daily visitations beneath my window of Franco, Cordelia, and Carlos I and his paramour Negrita. They cluck and cry with gusto, usually just as I'm attempting to write a particularly tricky newspaper article that requires deep concentration.

I turn to the pile of papers on my desk. Greedy George is delighted with the pre-press coverage I have drummed up for Havana Leather's chicken cape-ons and Hennie Driscoll's Chick-Knitathon is gaining many column inches as scores of volunteers step forward to offer their services, knitting jumpers for her scrawny wards. George, Hennie and I have agreed on a joint press launch for the Chick-Knitathon that will be held at Havana's flagship London store in February. The Chick-Knit itself will be held the next day at a pub in Chelsea, called the The Cock and Bull. Meanwhile, the opening of Manuel Ramirez's new hotel in Moscow, Le Coq d'Or has been scheduled for early March.

The Christmas season is nearly upon us and many local events are happening across the valley. Tonight we will be popping by La Residencia Hotel in Deia village to view a new exhibition by Colin Hunt, a local British artist and sculptor, and then there's our friend Paul Archer's annual Christmas Carol Concert at which favourite international carols are sung. Ollie is arriving in a few days' time for his school holidays and my sister, Cecilia, and nephew, Alexander, will be arriving soon after. In fact, there's so much going on that it's easy to be distracted from productive work.

An hour or so later, as I put my newspaper column for the *Majorca Daily Bulletin* to bed, the telephone rings and in some good cheer I expect to hear Ed's voice on the line. He sounds panicky.

'I have some terrible news!' he wails. 'I've lost my wedding ring and Rela's furious!'

'How on earth have you done that?' I say.

'I must have taken it off before I went to bed but this morning it was nowhere to be seen. I've looked everywhere.'

'I never take mine off,' I reply. 'You should just leave it on.'

'But what if it grows into my finger and one day has to be gouged out by a doctor or, worse, it causes gangrene and I end up losing a finger? It would end my piano playing.'

I give a sigh. 'You really have worrying mental-thought processes, Ed.'

'So what shall I do?'

I pace about the room. 'The best thing is to sit down with a cup of tea and retrace your movements over the last evening. Are you sure you left it by your bed?'

He exhales deeply. 'Where else would I have left it?'

'I've no idea. Have a mull and re-search the entire house.'

'It's bad enough no longer having a job without this latest disaster.'

'What are you doing about that?'

He sounds glum. 'I'm applying for loads of things but nothing's come of it so far.'

'Keep your chin up. It's nearly Christmas. Something will turn up soon, mark my words.'

I replace the receiver and potter downstairs to the kitchen. Pep and the Scotsman are sitting at the table, sifting through a wicker basket full of olives that they have picked from our own trees and those in Pep and Juana's *olivar*, their orchard near Fornalutx.

'Look what we've picked between us,' says Pep proudly. 'This represents four days back-breaking work.'

I raise an eyebrow. 'Quite frankly, I don't think you'll get more than about two bottles of olive oil out of that basket.'

'Nonsense!' he cries. 'We're going to Can Det with our booty and when we return you won't believe how many bottles we'll have. You and Juana will be in awe.'

The Scotsman nods. 'I think we could have enough for a good six months' supply here. To think that it'll be our first production of pure virgin oil.'

Pep gets up and switches on the coffee machine. 'I think a celebratory coffee is called for. Let us drink to olive oil from the house of Pep and Alan.'

He offers me an espresso and does a little dance around the kitchen. The Scotsman shakes his head and laughs. 'He gets worse with age.'

'Too true,' I say. 'So what's happening with the *patxaran*? Is it going to be ready for Christmas?'

'Of course!' bellows Pep. 'We shall be unveiling it at Christmas. It will be fantastic.'

'I'll be the judge of that,' I reply.

Pep makes two more coffees and passes one to the Scotsman before picking up a savoury biscuit from a plate on the table and slapping a piece of sheep's cheese onto it.

'This cheese of yours is nectar from the gods.'

I nod. 'It's from Llorenc Payeras in Lloseta. We order it through our local eco group.'

'I know. I have told Juana that we must join. I can't stop eating it.'

Half the new cheese appears to have vanished.

'Have you eaten all that?' I ask Pep.

'What kind of a hostess are you? You tempt me with heavenly cheese and savoury biscuits, then admonish me.'

I give a tut. 'Those Gori biscuits were new yesterday. Have you wolfed down the whole packet this morning?'

He gives me a wink. 'Alan helped me. Sifting through olives is hard work.'

I smooth out the packet. 'You know I've always wanted to visit the factory that makes these biscuits. It's in Muro.'

Pep nods. Gori de Muro is a well-established local brand. In the old days, this type of simple, savoury biscuit was cherished by seafarers as it lasted a long time and could be stored successfully on board. 'I like the biscuits by Quely, too.'

'Yes, but Gori is more artisanal. I get the impression that it's just a small business. And now they're doing rosemary and chilli varieties.'

Pep smears cheese on the remaining biscuit on his plate. 'Here, for you, *chérie*.'

'Too kind,' I reply. 'So why are these biscuits so popular in Mallorca? I mean you all eat them with *sobrasada* and cheese and they form part of the staple diet of most locals.'

He shrugs. 'They're such an important part of our culture and they also fill you up! The only ingredients are wheat flour, salt and olive oil so they are cheap and adaptable and don't spoil the taste of whatever you spread on them. I should think that, historically, they were made by hand and baked in the oven and preserved for a long time.'

I stand up. 'That's it. I'm going to visit Gori in Muro.'

'What for?' asks the Scotsman.

'To see how the biscuits are made of course and to meet Senyor Gori.'

Pep laughs. 'And what if there is no Senyor Gori?'

'Then I'll be disappointed but at least I'll know.'

'That's not a very lucid response,' he taunts.

'Too bad,' I reply briskly, slinging my rucksack over my shoulder. These days I find it a far more useful companion than a traditional handbag. For one thing, I can squeeze a sizable bag of hay into it.

'Where are you going?' asks Pep.

'Not that it's your concern, but I'm going to buy some hay from Sebastian at Hens.'

The Scotsman drains his cup. 'Pep and I are off to Can Det so I'll see you later. Don't forget that we're all dining at Sa Teulera tonight.'

Sa Teulera is our nearest restaurant and used to belong to one of the family members who originally occupied our *finca*. It was renowned for its meat grilled on a wood stove but when the owner sadly died, it fell into abeyance. Recently, Juan, the restaurant's new proprietor, has revived its spirits with a massive refurbishment and restored its erstwhile reputation.

I make my way to the front courtyard and jump into the car. For a few seconds I breathe in the soothing, dry and woody aroma of rosemary that wafts through the open windows. Our silvery green bushes form an aromatic border around the lawn and the pungent fragrance is ever present. As I bump along the track, waving at Rafael as I pass his *finca*, I suddenly hear a strangled squawk from the back seat. I brake and flick my gaze to the driver's mirror only to see a feathery face staring back at me. Cordelia is sitting on the back seat and clucking vociferously. I hesitate and consider turning back but change my mind. After all, if I'm off to Hens, it seems somewhat fitting that my faithful feathered companion be allowed to share the ride.

With only a mantle of grubby white sky for company, we potter along empty rural roads, flanked by verdant fields and lush orchards that are the hallmark of the Es Pla region. At intervals, ancient windmills pop up between soft, undulating, pine-clad hills, offering a nod to the island's rich agricultural past. The northern town of Inca is bustling with life and its famed Thursday market is in full swing as we drive through the busy centre in the direction of Muro. Christmas is but a week away and there is palpable excitement in the air. Once out of the town, our gaze falls on the rich arable pastures that line both sides of the road. In several of those sheep amble about the terrain, munching on patches of grass or standing in groups like aimless teenagers under the bushy olive trees.

The air is sweet and aromatic as we head up to Muro, a modest and sleepy little town perched perkily on a hill. The Scotsman effortlessly finds a parking place by Plaça Constitució, the main square, and together we consult our street map. Before us, the imposing Gothic sandstone church of San Joan Baptista seems overwhelming, flanked as it is by towering, mature palm trees and a seven-storey belfry. The church, like so many across the island, has attracted various additions over the centuries, from Gothic splendour to baroque and Renaissance flourishes. To its left, a small statue of a young boy catches my eye. He is holding a flute and has his legs crossed casually, his wide-brimmed hat thrown back on his head. He wears shorts and sandals and has a pouch slung over one shoulder. Most extraordinary is that he sports wings on his back.

I touch the greeny-grey cool metal. 'Isn't this sculpture imaginative? It's called Porqueret, which I suppose must mean swineherd in Mallorquin.'

The Scotsman steps closer. 'I see it's by Pere Pujol, the sculptor from Arta you once told me about.'

'Of course, that would explain its mythical quality. It must be a story from one of the *rondalles*.'

His eyes search the facades of the old stone houses that line several nearby streets. 'Now where is the Gori biscuit factory? I can't see any signs for it.'

An elderly man with a *ca rater*, the little beloved Mallorcan hunting dog, walks by and immediately offers directions. 'It's well known around here but there's not much to see. Why not visit our local museum instead, it's just over there.' He points vaguely into the middle distance and so, with a wave, we set off and soon see a sign for the Museu Ethnològic.

'Let's have a quick look here and then we'll hunt for Senyor Gori's emporium.'

The Scotsman sighs. 'Fine, but don't forget that we've got to pick up Ollie from his chum's house in Palma, and later Pep and Juana will be coming around for drinks and dinner at eight.'

'We've got bags of time,' I retort.

At the entrance to the old mansion, the custodian expresses surprise to see visitors and eagerly hands us a pamphlet of information. Few tourists venture to this part of the island, which is a shame as there are many jewels to be savoured. We spend 30 minutes examining the old artefacts – sets of traditional Mallorcan bagpipes known as *xeremias,* historic costumes and ancient agricultural items.

'I wonder when *xeremias* were first played here on the island,' ponders the Scotsman.

I consult the leaflet. 'Apparently King Jaume I introduced them to the island once he'd conquered the Moors. They used to be called *sac de gemecs*, meaning bag of groans. It says here that there's evidence that Islamists played bagpipes as early as the ninth century.'

'Bag of groans indeed!' he laughs. 'As a Scot I feel it my duty to defend them.'

My attention is caught by an old water wheel, a creation brought to the island by the Moors.

'That's a beauty,' remarks the Scotsman. 'Isn't it called a *noria* in Mallorcan?'

'Spot on,' I reply.

'The Moors were such agricultural experts,' opines the museum's custodian. 'Think of all the practices, such as terracing, that we've adopted here even to this day.'

As I begin cooing over a cluster of colourful and ancient *siurell* figurines in a glass case, the Scotsman pointedly reminds me that we should be on our way. After offering farewells to the museum's custodian, we follow his directions to the Gori factory and soon find ourselves in the tiny square of Sant Marti. A bar sprawls out onto the grey paving stones and for a moment I look around in bewilderment, wondering if we've come to the right place, but suddenly the Scotsman grabs my arm and leads me to a modest pair of glass doors flanked by green shutters. A sign in bold brown letters announces that this is Gori de Muro, established in 1890.

'How thrilling!' I chirrup and, pushing the doors open, I bound in. A bell tinkles and an affable-looking man wearing a light-blue polo and beige trousers offers a friendly welcome from a doorway at the rear of the room. He is balding and his eyes smile behind heavy-rimmed glasses, but it's evident that he is curious about our mission. No doubt he thinks we are tourists who have lost their way. I look around the narrow white-walled room lined with boxes of biscuits of every kind, thinking it resembles a storeroom, rather than a shop. In Spanish I explain that I'm a fan of Gori biscuits and have travelled from Sóller to see the factory and if possible to meet Senyor Gori himself. He seems bemused and somewhat abashed.

'I am Senyor Gori,' he tells me. 'Gregori Gori. My grandfather founded the company.'

I am overcome with delight. I somehow knew that there had to be a Senyor Gori, even better that his parents had wittily named him Gregori.

'Would you like to see the factory?' he asks.

I can hardly contain my excitement. The Scotsman shakes his head in amusement.

'You're easily pleased.'

Gregori Gori apologises that the factory is so quiet but his five co-workers have all gone home. All the same it is fascinating to see the giant ovens and area where the biscuits are made and packaged.

'Do you do everything here?'

'We certainly do. And we even arrange exports to other countries. We sell in many places and now I'm experimenting with new flavours such as chilli, which has gone down well.'

'Oh I love the rosemary ones, too,' I enthuse.

'I'm glad you like them,' he beams.

After our visit to the factory, we are led back out to the shop.

'Thank you so much for popping by,' he says. 'It's good to know that we have British fans on the island. Keep an eye out for our new varieties.'

The Scotsman laughs as we walk up the street. 'You know there are people who would give their right arm to meet a celebrated actor or musician but you'd be just as happy meeting the manufacturer of one of your favourite local products.'

'You're absolutely right.'

Just as we reach the car, my telephone rings. It's Ed.

'Scatters! Fantastic tidings. I've found my wedding ring and Rela is speaking to me again.'

'Thank heavens for that. Where was it?'

'Amazingly a man called from a small guesthouse in Sussex where we'd stayed a few weeks ago. One of his chambermaids found it by chance under the bed.'

'This time never take it off your finger.'

He gives a nervous cough. 'I suppose I have no choice. If I lost it again I think Rela might file for divorce!'

The Scotsman turns to me in the car. 'A happy ending, that's what I like to hear. Ed deserves it after the problems he's had with his job. Perhaps his luck is about to change.'

'You never know what drama will strike Ed next, but as they say, hope springs eternal.' I give him a wink. 'Finding a new job would be a good way to ring in the New Year.'

'Ho ho ho,' he counters.

We drive out of the little town. In my hands is a packet of flat white rosemary biscuits. A small memento of our visit to Muro and our encounter with the one and only Gregori Gori.

A fire crackles in the grate and the tiny white lights adorning the bushy fir tree twinkle like diamonds among the branches. Christmas is nearly upon us and already we are in celebratory mood, gearing up for the big event. The house feels festive and cosy and, after a comforting roast dinner and more than a few glasses of Rioja, I am well into the Christmas spirit. All four cats are curled up on chairs in the kitchen and the remnants of dinner have been cleared away. Ollie and Angel are happily watching a film together in Ollie's newly decorated bedroom upstairs. After his initial shock and delight at the room's massive leap from boy to man-den, he has enjoyed showcasing it to his local Spanish friends, spreading his computer and books over the double bed and luxuriating in having his own television and DVD player. Juana and I sit nursing untouched glasses of home-made *patxaran*, while exchanging Christmas recipes. The Scotsman and Pep look on with a hint of anxiety in their eyes.

'*Por favor*! When are you going to try it?' puffs Pep. 'We're not trying to poison you.'

I take a tentative sniff while Juana takes her first sip and swills the liquid around in her mouth.

'Well, do you like it?' asks the Scotsman.

She pulls a face. 'Terrible!'

I take a gulp. 'So sweet. It's intolerable.'

The two men stare at us in confusion until they realise that we are both teasing them.

'It's delicious,' I say.

'A perfect balance of flavours,' rejoins Juana.

Relief is etched on their faces as, suitably mollified, they relax into the cream cushions of the sofa and offer tentative smiles.

'Perhaps we can start making wine again given our success with *patxaran*,' says Pep hopefully.

'In your dreams,' replies Juana firmly.

'And forget limoncello, after the mess you made with lemons in my kitchen,' I chip in.

'The grapes were worse!' exclaims Juana.

I give a sigh. 'Don't remind me. I'm still finding red juice marks on the skirting boards.'

The Scotsman tuts. 'Such an exaggeration. Never did mockers waste more idle breath, Pep.'

'What does that mean?' he asks.

'Read Shakespeare's *A Midsummer Night's Dream* and you'll find out,' I quip.

'I stand at your literary shrine,' Pep retorts in an attempt at a refined British accent. 'We humble Mallorcans are so ill read.'

I give him a playful kick under the table. 'So what happened with the olive oil? I take it that, as I warned, you didn't have enough olives to make as much as a litre.'

Juana laughs. 'Maybe if you start growing more olive trees now, we might be able to cultivate our own oil in another decade.'

Pep gives an impish smile and disappears into the dark courtyard with Alan. I hear the door of Pep's van slamming. Moments later they return with two large brown boxes. To Juana and my amazement they place them in front of us.

'Take a look inside,' says Pep.

We each pull out a bottle of what appears to be golden olive oil. Labels have been affixed to the front of each one inscribed in ink with the words '*Aceite de la casa de* Alan y Pep'.

'You really did it?' says Juana in surprise. 'It looks so professional.'

I am mesmerised. 'How much oil is there here?'

The Scotsman preens himself. 'Fifteen litres. It's a good start. Just look at that colour.'

'Of course it has to stand for another month but it tastes good already,' says Pep.

The Scotsman fetches four glasses and together we sample the oil. It tastes warm and peppery and there's a distinct flavour of grass and even of lemon.

'It might only be a small production but you can't get much better than that,' says Pep happily. He raises his glass. '*Molt d'anys*!'

We all clink glasses.

'Many happy years to you and Juana, too. Happy Christmas!' beams the Scotsman.

Pep gives a wry grin. 'And now to end the evening in glorious style, we can look forward to a little entertainment.'

The Scotsman offers a puzzled expression. 'Really?'

Pep pulls out his mobile phone and a second later the heavy beat of 'Dancing in the Street' rings out.

'Of course, I forgot about your dancing debut for Focus Films!' cries Juana in delight. 'Show us your moves.'

The Scotsman pours himself a sizeable glass of *patxaran* and, sitting down heavily on the sofa, narrows his eyes at Pep. 'In the words of the great Scrooge I have only this to say, "Bah humbug!"'

Sixteen

LIQUID GOLD

I'm halfway up our rickety old wooden ladder, collecting the new season's crop of oranges from a tree in the orchard, when my mobile phone rings. It is a cool January morning and icy dew clings to the rough silvery bark. Propping the wicker basket between two branches, I fumble for the phone in my pocket and catch it on the fourth ring. I sigh inwardly for it is none other than my mad client Manuel Ramirez of H Hotels. He is breathing heavily down the line.

'Are you in a safe zone?' he enquires.

'I'm on a ladder in a leafy arbour gathering oranges from one of my trees. Happy New Year, by the way!'

'The new year is surely about work not happiness,' he counters.

'I like to think one can combine the two, Manuel.'

'That is why you are up a tree living the life of a humble peasant and I am in a chauffeur-driven limousine heading for my Learjet.'

I want to add 'and that is also why you are a friendless, paranoic and delusional lunatic living in bulletproof vests and unable to enjoy the simplest pleasures of life.' Instead I chicken out and mumble, 'Each to their own, Manuel.'

He offers an impatient hiss. 'Now listen. I am in Moscow with the Russian Philharmonic Orchestra. Their members have just finished rehearsals for the grand opening sequence for Le Coq d'Or. As you suggested, when they complete the overture of *The Golden Cockerel* by Rimsky-Korsakov, tiny gold cockerels will descend from an ingeniously concealed net rigged to the ceiling of the grand ballroom. These cockerels will prove an interesting keepsake for the guests.'

I clear my throat. 'Well I'm not sure a gold-foil cockerel will last too long, Manuel.'

He gives a manic laugh. 'Gold foil? Did I not tell you? They are made of gold. Real gold.'

'What?! But that would cost a fortune.'

He gives an impatient sigh. 'I have a good gold buyer back in Panama – the gold is only nine carat.'

I'm momentarily speechless. 'But we've already organised a fairly substantial goodie bag for the guests.'

'This is unimportant. To create the most spectacular launch Moscow has ever witnessed is all that matters.'

'All the same, you don't want costs to spiral out of control.'

Adrenalin pumps through his words. 'Ask yourself, what would you rather be? A sticker or a quitter, loser or a mover?'

There's a pause. 'Life is for living,' he practically screeches down the line.

This is one of Manuel's favourite platitudes. It's a shame he doesn't always take heed of his own mantras.

I shrug. 'It's your money, Manuel. The media will of course love it.'

'How many are we flying over from Britain for the launch?'

'Six, plus your VIP guests and political contacts.'

'My Learjet and private security team will be at their disposal. You will make the necessary arrangements directly with my head of protocol at H Hotels in Panama.'

'All in hand, Manuel.'

'As I would have expected. Remember, trust no one. Adios.'

I lean against the damp tree wondering whether Manuel is on medication. I sincerely hope so or he might just self-combust before the hotel launch in March. We already have a substantial guest list of leading press, a TV crew and an impressive selection of Hollywood A-listers who always stay at Manuel's luxurious properties. As an uneasy flyer, I am not in the least enthralled at the idea of flying to Moscow on Manuel's private jet, but hopefully a few shots of his ice-cold Stoli Elit vodka should stiffen my resolve. I take the secateurs out of my pocket and snip off fifteen oranges before gingerly descending from my leafy eyrie. The Scotsman swishes through the damp, tall grasses of the orchard and alleviates me of my wicker basket.

'Who was that?'

'Mad Manuel.'

'Ah, in that case I'll make you a strong coffee.'

'Brandy might be better. He grows more insane every day.'

'Yes, but he's a good barometer for your own level of madness. It's always comforting to discover someone more unstable than oneself.'

He walks jauntily over to the steps that lead up to the back terrace. 'Our new Silkies seem very happy with life, and did you take a look at Carlos I in his dog house?'

'I did, he seems very happy with it. I see that he loves having his own exclusive supply of food scraps over there.'

'Funny you should mention that. He's suddenly developed a ravenous appetite and has taken to leftovers like...'

'Mad Manuel to flak jackets?'

He laughs. 'Come on, let's have a coffee with Catalina and then hit the road. Tiffany's expecting us late morning.'

'Our lives seem to revolve around olives at the moment.'

In the kitchen, Catalina looks up from her ironing. 'Who's making coffee?'

Dutifully the Scotsman busies himself with the task.

'Did you enjoy the three kings event in Fornalutx last week?' asks Catalina.

'I always love it. Seeing the faces of local children when they're presented with gifts from the kings is always so endearing.'

She nods. 'And they never realise that they're just locals dressed up in costume.'

'It's all part of the magic of Christmas in Spain,' I say.

She gives a sigh. 'All the same, more and more families are adopting your Father Christmas rather than the three kings.'

Unlike in the UK, Spanish children traditionally have to wait until 5 January to receive their Christmas gifts from the three kings. The problem is that local schools start just a few days later so that they barely have time to play with their toys. Most towns and villages enter into the festive spirit for this special event, each employing locals to dress up as the three kings who normally arrive into communities on the back of horses or donkeys. They are charged with presenting the children with gifts provided by their families.

The Scotsman hands round coffees. 'I'm sure the traditionalists will continue with the three kings. It's such a wonderful event for children.'

'And how is Ollie settling in back at school in England?'

I raise an eyebrow. 'Happy to see friends but already complaining about the early starts and lashings of homework.'

'He's only got to suffer another year. So where are you two going today?'

I take a sip of coffee. 'You remember meeting our friend Tiffany Blackman who works as ambassador for the Aubocassa Estate in Manacor?'

'Of course I remember her.'

'Well, the company is officially opening its new olive mill today, so she's invited us over for a tour and lunch.'

'Lucky you. I'm working all day.'

'No peace for the wicked,' smiles the Scotsman, draining his cup. 'I'll just get the map.'

'Not so fast!' She narrows her eyes. 'Before you go, please remove those gardening boots from the kitchen.'

Obediently he picks up the offending items and places them on the mat outside the back door, oblivious to the trail of mud he leaves behind on the terracotta tiles.

We have just arrived in the village of Costitx en route to Manacor. I have asked the Scotsman to deviate as I'm keen to take a peek at the island's planetarium, which is situated on the outskirts of the village. Mallorcan friends have told me that it's necessary to book a visit at night when one can observe the stars in style. To my disappointment we find it closed but there's a telephone number for enquiries posted on the gate. I write it in my diary and once again we set off for Manacor in the east of the island. We have an hour to spare so I persuade the Scotsman to pop by the little town of Sineu, which isn't really that much of a deviation. When it comes to markets, Santa Maria and Sineu excel. The former occurs on a Sunday morning and the latter every Wednesday. Today the town square is quiet and we easily find a café where we enjoy croissants and coffee.

'This is such a lovely town. It's probably one of the few that tourists actually visit from time to time.'

He yawns. 'The market is a big draw each week but I'm not sure how many visitors stay here. Mind you, John and Jo will be opening Son Rierra soon. A new hotel will no doubt attract visitors to the area.'

Our surveyor friends John and Jo Lucas have bought a beautiful old-town property, which they are converting into a bijoux hotel. It's a big project but promises to be stunning.

'What have they called the restaurant?' he asks.

'Number Ten – which doesn't present any linguistic problems,'
I say.

'Although some British visitors might expect to see two bobbies
stationed at the door.'

'Ooh you're a wit.' I cast a glance at my watch. 'Come on, let's
head over to Tiffany's.'

Thirty minutes later we arrive in the rural grounds of the
Aubocassa estate. The panoramic views to the Serra de Llevant
and the monastery, Monestir de Sant Salvador, perched high on
a distant hill, are spectacular. Tiffany stands next to us, her face
basking in the sunlight.

'I never get bored with this view. Every day I look out over the
hills and think how lucky I am to work in such a gorgeous setting.'

'And you've got plenty of sheep for company,' I reply.

She laughs. 'Oh yes. I've also got two dogs, a pig and a baby
donkey that I'll introduce you to later.'

Excusing herself, she rushes off to welcome some of her guests.
There are now about 80 or more people milling about the grounds,
drinking coffee and enjoying the blissfully warm weather. It's hard
to believe that we are in the grip of winter. When all the guests
have arrived, Tiffany and Agustín Santolaya, the director general of
Aubocassa, take to the microphone to welcome us all and to explain
a little about the history of the building and the purchase of the olive
mill. It has been 20 years since Aubocassa planted its healthy and
thriving olive trees that annually produce a handsome crop of fruit.
Previously, the olives were taken to local mills for making into oil
but now, with the inauguration of an exclusive, technically advanced
mill in the grounds, olives have no delay in being processed once
picked, allowing maximum taste and aroma of the oil to develop.

After the presentation, we walk around the extensive olive groves,
watching a demonstration of how, with a mechanised machine that

rapidly shakes the branches, the olives are quickly gathered in vast nets. Before visiting the new mill, Tiffany allows us to look in on the farm's resident baby donkey and black pig, both of which seem oblivious to the throng of guests pacing about the nearby orchards. Back at the grand old *finca*, we sit around large tables in the refurbished and cosy wine cellar, enjoying a selection of Aubocassa's fine wines from the peninsula, accompanied by locally sourced fare. A tasting of the new harvest of virgin olive oil follows and I close my eyes over the glass and breathe in the fresh and piquant aroma reminiscent of newly cut grass and zesty lemons. It is delicious to taste, with warm and peppery undertones and a freshness and velvety smoothness that easily persuades me to drain the glass. Somehow I can't see myself knocking back a half glass of my ordinary cooking olive oil back home with quite such vigour and enthusiasm.

After lunch we all troop off to see the new olive mill in action, a shining, silver, technological beast that gobbles the olives into its vast belly and extracts the oil in a manner that retains all the flavour. It is fascinating to watch in action, and a far cry from the ancient old mill operated by Can Det in Biniaraix. Back on the road, the Scotsman and I ponder the old and new ways of creating the island's liquid gold. It is impossible to say one is better than the other for both have very different purposes. Aubocassa, with its sleek new mill, operates on an international level, guaranteeing premium olive oil at a significant price per bottle. By contrast, Can Det serves a very localised market built on tradition and the olives it presses have been gathered mostly by families owning small *olivars*, olive groves in the Tramuntana hills.

'Both oils taste fantastic to me,' surmises the Scotsman. 'I suppose one is for more general use while the other you'd use for more special occasions, rather like indulging in a fine wine.'

I nod and am about to prolong the discussion when Judas rings. It is Ollie.

'How is school?' I dare to ask.

'The same. As I've told you before it follows the boarding-school three-Rs principle – rules, restrictions and reprisals.'

I wince. 'Well, it's not for much longer and just think how relieved prisoners from Alcatraz or Colditz must have felt when they finally managed to escape.'

There's a bubble of laughter in his voice. 'Are you suggesting I break free, mother? Dig a tunnel under the electric fence, drug the Rottweilers and somehow destroy the search lights in the watch towers?'

'That all sounds a bit too risky. The guards could have Kalashnikovs and if you're unarmed it could end badly. Instead, how about buying some more chocolate supplies in the local Co-op to cheer yourself up?'

He sighs. 'Good thinking but funds are low.'

I laugh. 'So you're ringing for more pocket money?'

'I'm glad you got there in the end, mother. That would be perfect. *Gracias*. Cheerio.'

I plop the mobile back in my bag, amused to see an anxious expression on the Scotsman's face. 'Is everything alright with Ollie? What the heck was that about guards with Kalashnikovs?'

'Oh just mother and son banter. We like our little jokes.'

He offers a tut. 'I sometimes wonder if I'm the only sane person in our household.'

As we take the turning from Santa Maria for Sóller, I give him a nudge. 'You're wrong, you know. The sanest person in our household is Johnny.'

He turns to me with a resigned grin. 'Of course. No one could possibly trump the lucidity and rationale of a talking toad.'

Seventeen

STAR STRUCK

The Scotsman marches into the sunny kitchen holding a trug teeming with oranges and broad beans. I roll my eyes at him as I hold the mobile phone to my ear, listening to Greedy George pontificating at the other end of the line.

'The thing is, guv, I've told Hennie that she can only bring four of her hens along to the Chick-Knit press launch and they must be kept in a cage. We can't have them pooping around the showroom or Richard will have a fit of the vapours, the old queen.'

'In fairness, poor Richard would be the one having to clean up after them,' I protest.

'Oh don't go all Mother Theresa on me, guv. He gets paid enough. So just to recap, on Friday night press arrive at six o'clock, speeches kick off an hour later and then everyone gets blitzed?' he asks.

'I'm not sure we want anyone getting blitzed. The event finishes at eight-thirty, remember. We don't want them hanging about.'

'You're a barrel of laughs, aren't you? I suppose you'll be on the water?'

'Heavens, no. Alcohol's the only way I can cope with you.'

He gives a cackle. 'Touché! See you at the showroom for the rehearsal at five o'clock on Friday. Have a good flight.'

I finish the call and cast a glance in the Scotsman's direction. 'I think everything's under control for the press launch. Once that's out of the way, the Chick-Knitathon on Saturday should be fairly relaxed.'

He nods. 'How many press and celebs have you got coming?'

'At least sixty, and there'll be other guests, too. We're estimating about a hundred in total. And then on Saturday, there'll be about eighty volunteer knitters at the event. There are even a few males taking part.'

He gives a sniff. 'God help them surrounded by all those clucking hens.' He points to his trug. 'What do you think of the new crop of broad beans?'

'Wonderful. I see that the jasmine buds are getting bigger.'

He is in cheery demeanour as he potters over to the coffee machine. 'The white broom is already beginning to flower, too, and the almond blossom is a sight to behold. Pity you're going back to London just as it's flowering.'

I laugh. 'I'm only away three nights. When I get back we can take a ride over to Binissalem and around Es Pla to see the almond blossom. There's such a profusion of orchards there.'

He hands me a coffee. 'That'll be a treat. I wouldn't mind popping by a few *bodegas* to stock up on some wine while we're there.'

'And I want to take a peek at the new Park Hyatt Hotel that's just opened in Canyamel. It's the first super-luxury five star to open on the east side of the island.'

'In that case we'll avoid dropping in for lunch.'

'Spoilsport.'

He finishes his espresso and, grasping a pair of secateurs from the table, ambles across the terrace. Taking my cup with me, I walk out to the front garden and sit on one of the stone steps by the pond enjoying the sun on my face. The soothing sound of trickling water merges with the distinctive song of a nearby blackbird and the characteristic tweet of a flittering goldfinch. The front lawn is in need of a good trim, its drooping grasses resembling long, unruly green tresses. Tiny new and silvery leaves have appeared on the old olive tree in its centre and Coronilla shrubs have started to flower once more in the borders. The annual cycle of nature never ceases to amaze me, although at times the weather can play tricks with the order of play, quickening the arrival of some plants and delaying others. Despite a slice of tangerine sun in the sky, the weather still isn't warm enough to coax Johnny and the frogs to return home to the pond, so I must be patient until next month. I am about to head into the house when the front-door buzzer sounds. It is Jorge, sitting astride his distinctive yellow *moto*. He flicks back his long hair and passes me a weighty package.

'Books,' he sighs.

'Cheers, Jorge. Nothing like a surprise!'

I tear back the wrapping and find five copies of a book entitled *Wildlife in Rotterdam* by Professor Jelle Reumer.

Jorge peers over my shoulder. 'Who's he?'

'A brilliant professor of Earth Sciences and director of the natural history museum in Rotterdam. He also happens to be an expert on Myotragus, which is, in fact, how we came to be friends.'

He groans. 'Not that old goat you're obsessed with?'

'The same. Jelle has sent scores of students from Holland to study and catalogue Myotragus bones here at our local natural history museum.'

'Well, if it makes you all happy…' he counters. He rumbles in his postbag and thumps an awkwardly shaped package in my hands. 'This one looks a bit more interesting. Let's hope it's not another chicken.'

I laugh. 'Hopefully not.'

Standing by his bike, he folds him arms. 'Well, come on, open it. Don't keep me in suspense!'

In some puzzlement I look at the York postmark and pull open the parcel. Inside is – oh no – a fluffy, white toy chicken with an enormous red beak and glassy blue eyes. An accompanying note reads: 'Good luck with the Chick-Knitathon. Hope the event will prove a feather in your cap! Only yokeing. Rachel.' I shake my head and giggle when I see Jorge's horrified expression.

'*Madre mia*!' He bangs his head with his hand. 'What's wrong with you English? Why do you keep sending each other stuffed hens?'

'It's from Rachel, the former director of my PR company in London. It's just a joke. She's wishing me luck with two associated events I have in London tomorrow night and on Saturday.'

'And what are the events?'

I pull a face. 'I don't know how to tell you this, Jorge, but eighty women and several men will be getting together to knit jumpers for abused battery-farm hens that have lost their feathers.'

He stares at me as though I'm mad and then, roaring with laughter, revs up his *moto*. 'I'll never get British humour. You know, for a moment there, I thought you were serious!'

And with a friendly wave he roars off along the stony track.

The soft charcoal sky is clear and a huddle of white stars blink down at us as we walk along the dark leafy pathways to the Planetarium from the car park. It is eight o'clock and we are here to spend a few hours learning about Mallorca's very own astronomical centre, the first in the Baleares, which opened its doors 25 years ago. The observatory, with accompanying planetarium, is a pioneer in Spain, tracking and monitoring asteroids, near-earth objects and stars and comets. Since its inception, its scientists have discovered more than 6,500 asteroids and have even named one after Rafael Nadal, Mallorca's home-grown tennis champion. We reach the planetarium, a futuristic dove-grey building, sitting plumb in the middle of scrubland on a wooded hill, a few kilometres south of the picturesque village of Costitx. It wouldn't look out of place on a James Bond film set, placed broodingly among the trees like some nefarious despot's secret laboratory. To the left of the structure are a series of white igloos, or cupolas, and the ghostly white observatory standing like an alien apparition in the piercing moonlight. Surrounding the planetarium are what look like brown monoliths. I turn to the Scotsman. 'Are they sculptures of some kind?'

He squints at them in the darkness. 'I'd hazard that they are some kind of astronomical aid for measuring changes to the sky.'

In the foyer, we are greeted warmly and directed towards a small huddle of visitors, guided by Joan Guillem, one of the observatory staff who, we discover, also speaks English. He offers us all an entertaining and informative presentation about the work of the centre, highlighting how its researchers have found potential threats to earth, such as the uninspiring sounding 2006WH1, and keep a beady eye on about 2,000 asteroids in the black void that we know as space.

'When can we look through the telescopes?' I whisper to the Scotsman.

'Just be patient,' he mumbles as a film about the origins of the universe is suddenly projected onto the great dome of the roof. Later, we wander among bubble-shaped display cabinets containing lunar rocks and samples of rocks from Mars and study the significant meteorites arranged around the foyer.

'It's good to know that these scientists are keeping a close watch on near-earth objects and potentially harmful asteroids,' says the Scotsman contemplatively.

'But in truth, what would they do if one did look as though it was heading to earth and going to obliterate us all? Wouldn't it be better to remain in blissful ignorance before we were all zapped?'

He gives a snort. 'That's a very defeatist attitude.'

'Realistic, I'd call it.'

The *pièce de résistance* comes when we head outside and are able to view Saturn, with its rings clearly visible, through telescopes in the external cupolas and, better still, the moon that looms into focus like a giant peppermint drop, luminous and pockmarked with craters. In the cool, dark woods, by a rocky outcrop, a full-scale model of the Apollo moon lander silently observes us as we creep back along the shady pathways to our car.

'It's been a very illuminating visit,' I say to the Scotsman.

'Is that an attempt at wit?' he grins.

'Actually I meant it. I'm not too happy about all those dastardly asteroids waiting to obliterate us, but what can one do?'

'Find a decent place to eat and enjoy a warming glass of *vino tinto*,' he says.

'Excellent. If we make haste, we might just make it for last orders at Es Turo in Fornalutx.'

We drive out of the car park and carefully make our way along the rough, uneven track that leads to the main road. I look in the rear mirror and, shivering in the chill, watch as the alien landscape disappears behind us, the shining observatory with its white cupolas melting in the moonlight.

It is eight o'clock on a crisp February evening in London and St James's discreet and exclusive shops have long been closed for business. All the same, one showroom breaks rank, its windows emitting an ambient glow, its chic interior flooded with people. Standing by a small, temporary stage in the showroom of Havana Leather, Greedy George shovels a salmon appetiser into his mouth and surveys the swell of animated guests. In the corner of the room, close to the till, a jazz trio croons softly, while waiters donned in extravagant hen and cockerel masks and black suits circulate among the attendees, serving champagne cocktails and canapés. The speeches have been delivered with aplomb, although George's, laboured with poultry puns and jokes, elicited the loudest applause. Hennie's moving tale of abused hens reduced a few female journalists to tears, as did the sight of four featherless victims, Molly, Gertrude, Paddy and Fenella, paraded about the showroom and modelling Havana Leather black cape-ons and knitted jerseys. Richard stood by anxiously, wearing rubber gloves and clutching a cleaning cloth in his hand. As soon as the demonstration was over and the hens and cockerel safely returned to their luxury pad of a cage, he rubbed at the wooden floor and disappeared into the showroom's tiny kitchen, presumably to purge himself of the memory with bleach and hot water.

Hennie waltzes towards me across the room, a manic smile on her lips. 'My dear girl! Hasn't this been so exciting?'

'Absolutely,' I enthuse.

'And to think I got to meet all those charming celebrities, though I've always had a soft spot for Nicholas Parsons. And that Henry Kelly was very funny. I remember him from one of those popular TV game shows.'

I smile encouragingly while watching George meandering his way towards us, a mischievous grin on his chops.

Hennie rattles on. 'I cannot believe how sympathetic the press has been to our cause. Paddy was such a star and the girls played to the cameras. Two young reporters have actually volunteered to come to the Chick-Knitathon tomorrow to knit some sweaters. Isn't that touching?'

Behind her, George kneads his eyes and silently feigns tears while she gabbles on, oblivious to his mockery.

I avert my eyes. 'How many jumpers do you think your volunteers will knit tomorrow?'

She shrugs. 'In the eight hours I'd hope we'd produce about five hundred.'

'That would keep a lot of your clucking wards happy.'

She takes an extravagant sip of champagne and coughs heartily. 'Indeed. It would be wonderful to have such a stock.'

Greedy George steps forward and offers her a hug. 'Bravo, old girl. You had the press eating out of your hand.'

She offers him a wary smile. 'Is that another attempt at a pun, George?'

He guffaws good naturedly and gives her a cheeky wink. 'Course not.'

Richard floats towards us with a full bottle of champagne. 'I thought you might all like a top up before the catering crew packs up.'

As the bubbles rise in our full glasses, George clinks my glass. 'By the way, guv, thanks for bringing me that *sobrasada* sausage. I'll tuck into it later when I get home.'

I bite my lip. 'I think you've had enough canapés to last you until at least breakfast.'

'You must be joking!' he quips. 'Anyway, well done, guv. Another successful event behind us. I'm sure tomorrow will go without a hitch, although we shouldn't count our chickens. And at least Bianca won't.'

We all exchange groans and, laughing, raise our glasses. A moment later there's a kerfuffle when a reporter, attempting to stroke one of the celebrity hens, opens the cage door, allowing the four creatures to escape. With a haughty toss of his dark, glossy locks and a determined look in his eye, Richard struts off towards the chaos and, grabbing his feather duster, corrals the birds safely back into their cage. As applause and whistles break out from the delighted onlookers, he offers a stiff bow and, with a look of pain on his face, makes all haste towards the bar area and knocks back a glass of fizz in one fell swoop.

As we drive up our rocky track in the dwindling light, I look out over the bluey-grey Tramuntanas that wear a stole of downy white clouds about their tips. An eagle swoops low over the orchards then forms a series of elegant loops before soaring up into the sky again and disappearing from view. Our *finca* glows like a hot coal, its windows emitting a soft and welcoming amber hue. I sigh contentedly to be home, having been picked up at the airport some forty minutes earlier by the Scotsman. It has been a frenetic, highly charged three days of work back in London and, although hugely enjoyable, I am relieved to be back in the tranquil hills. The Chick-Knitathon attracted scores of knitters and, by the end of the afternoon, 2,000 miniature jerseys had been knitted for the Chanticleer Chicken Trust, much to Hennie Driscoll's delight. After a pleasant evening spent with my old university chum and recent walking companion, Jane, I had set off back to Mallorca.

At this time of the year, the majority of local restaurants remain closed and the hotels in the port tight-lipped, their shutters and doors closed until mid-March. On our track, a light peeks out between the shutters of Rafael's living room and I am surprised to see a hire car stationed outside Wolfgang and Helge's house.

I smile. 'Oh how lovely! Are Wolfgang and Helge back for a holiday from Berlin? It's been such a long time since they visited.'

The Scotsman eyes me sorrowfully from the driver's seat.

'Helge's daughter, Luisa, is back from Germany for a few days with her boyfriend. I'm afraid she has brought very sad news. Last week Wolfgang died suddenly from a heart attack and Helge is naturally devastated.'

I am shocked to the core. Our German neighbours have always been so warm and companionable and we have spent countless jolly summer nights dining on each other's terraces.

I feel tears well up in my eyes. 'But Wolfgang was always so hale and hearty.'

He nods. 'Who knows why these things happen. At least he lived an active and happy life. He didn't look it, but he was seventy-nine years old. I suppose it just teaches us once again that we should make the best of every single day.'

The car stops in the courtyard and, in sombre mood, I step onto the gravel, my head filled with happy memories of our time with our neighbours. At Easter and during the summer, when they visited their *finca*, Helge would spend hours in the pulsating summer heat kicking a football about with Ollie in the garden. Wolfgang preferred to play cards and word games with him on their terrace and would ply him with chocolates and lemonade. The Scotsman carries my overnight case and rucksack into the house and distractedly I set about making supper. Thoughts pop into my head about my friend Margalida from Calabruix bookshop who died so unexpectedly the previous year. The Scotsman places some heavy logs in the fireplace and soon we have a roaring fire. I stand deep in thought, warming my hands, and am grateful when he pushes a glass of red wine into them. I take a few sips. 'I think I'll pop over to see Luisa. It seems the right thing to do.'

'I'm sure she'll be pleased to see you. She's only here briefly to check up on the house and to pop by the lawyer's office on behalf of her mother.'

The sky has darkened as I set off through the courtyard and soon comes the persistent patter of rain. I open the front gate, a cool trickle of water coursing down my cheek like a rogue teardrop as I knock at Luisa's front door. I hear footsteps and suddenly the porch is flooded with light. She offers me a wan smile and wordlessly I step forward to share a hug.

Eighteen

NEW ARRIVALS

A golden sun beams down at me as I stand panting at the mouth of the track, my face hot with the exertion of running. Gaspar is nowhere to be seen but a moment later I hear the familiar whining of his *moto* as it courses towards me, stopping with a jolt by the municipal bins.

'Beat you!' I taunt.

He pulls off his helmet and shakes his woolly head. 'That's not fair! I gave you a ten-minute head start from the port and would have beaten you if that old dear hadn't broken down on the American Road.'

I laugh. 'You were very gallant to stop to help her.'

He scratches his bearded chin. 'The engine had just overheated. Anyway, do you think I'm looking a bit slimmer?'

I examine the bulky frame. 'Hm. I think you could still lose a few more kilos.'

'*Poc a poc,*' he grins, using the reassuring Mallorcan mantra of 'little by little'.

'It would help if you got off the bike and used your feet more.'

'So you keep telling me!' He replaces his helmet and, with a wave, zooms off along the lane.

I walk up the track, stopping to talk to Silvia who is sitting in a rocking chair in her courtyard. She is suffering from backache and rheumatism and blames the humidity for her painful joints.

'But March is here,' I chirrup. 'I can smell spring in the air.'

She gives a small shrug. 'Thank God for small mercies. Now run along or you'll catch your death.'

As I reach our front gate, I cast a glance at Helge and Wolfgang's house, shrouded in darkness. It is likely that Helge will sell the property in time, the end of a chapter and the beginning of a new one. Whatever happens, I know we shall all remain good friends and in touch. In our courtyard, a stack of logs is piled up by the front door and Llorenç, the woodman, is engaged in animated discussion with the Scotsman. When he sees me, he breaks off conversation to give me a hug and kiss on both cheeks.

'Running again?'

'It's a perfect day for a run! Look at that canopy of a blue sky.'

He smiles. 'I love this time of year. The lavender starts to flower and it's the perfect conditions for planting.'

The Scotsman nods enthusiastically. 'Just look at our jasmine around the door. It's blossomed so early and the perfume is exquisite.'

'My favourite,' I add. 'All we need now is the return of Johnny and the frogs and spring will have officially arrived for me.'

Llorenç slams the back door of his white van and smacks his hands together. 'Still in love with your frogs?'

'My angelic choir.'

'Certainly more angelic than the cacophony your cockerels make,' he grins. 'Anyway, that should be enough wood to see you through until next autumn. If you have any left over you could always grill a few feathered fiends on the barbecue.'

He jumps into the driver's seat and, with a wave and a cheery '*Adeu!*', steers the car gingerly along our track.

The Scotsman peers up at our olive tree on the front lawn where Sergi Squint, our regular Siamese intruder, is attempting to camouflage himself among the bushy leaves. 'That cat is a menace. He broke one of my pots this morning, trying to jump onto the lid of the well.'

'I'm sure he's repentant.'

'I doubt that very much. So how was the run?'

'Wonderfully invigorating. I saw Gaspar in the port and he challenged me to a race back home. I won.'

'And he was on his *moto*?' he asks incredulously.

'In truth, he stopped to help a pensioner who'd broken down on the American Road.'

'A rather pyrrhic victory, then?' he teases.

In the kitchen I find Catalina and Miquela shaking our sheets for ironing. Catalina breaks off her work to offer me a coffee.

'So how are Ramon and the twins?'

'They're all fine, although the girls have a lot of homework now that they're fifteen.'

'Poor things. School wasn't my happiest time in life.'

She shrugs. 'We all had to suffer it. By the way, when are you getting the new lambs you bought from Emilio?'

I sit down at the table. 'He's bringing them over on Friday at lunchtime.'

The Scotsman strolls in and helps Miquela fold the last of the sheets. She thanks him and disappears up the stairs, dragging the vacuum cleaner along behind her.

'I'm happy to have two lambs,' he says. 'Hopefully they'll concentrate on the grass and not on my vegetable patch.'

'I'd still like to have a few goats,' I grumble.

'That won't happen unless we invest in a secure pen. That'll be the next little project.'

With the doors flung open, soft light floods the kitchen, casting lemony sunbeams on the old oak table. I walk over to the cake tin and, placing several cherry muffins on a plate, return with them to the table.

'These are good,' says Catalina approvingly. 'So when is Ollie home for Easter?'

'On Thursday night, in time for the arrival of the lambs,' I say. 'There'll be quite a party of us on Friday. Neus and Bernat and Juana and Pep are popping by and also our neighbour Fernando.'

'If Ramon and I have time, we'll join you, too. So what will you be serving?' she says with a mischievous smile. 'Roast lamb?'

The windows of the office are wide open and, with my bare feet balanced on the edge of the sill, I sit back in my chair, phone receiver propped against my ear, listening to Ed in full flow. Cordelia is nestling on my desk next to the computer, her head cocked as if in sympathy.

'So, imagine, Scatters. I arrive at the school late as I get lost finding my way there and am in a complete fluster.'

'Not a great start,' I observe.

'You can say that again. I thought I'd probably blown the interview, so just burbled away about my experience and felt totally relaxed.'

'Only way to be.'

'When I got up to leave, they asked me to wait outside and, five minutes later, offered me a full-time job in their technical department.'

'That's fantastic! I'm so happy for you.'

'Better still, the offer we put on a new house has been accepted and with my getting a full-time job, we'll be able to pay the mortgage.'

'Excellent news! It's funny how when things are at their bleakest, life can suddenly take a turn for the better.'

'So true.' He falters. 'Is that a cluck I can hear?'

'Just Cordelia. She's sitting on my desk.'

'That wretched hen? It's not normal behaviour, you know.'

'What is, Ed?'

'So how's life with you? How was Moscow?'

'An extravagant two-day experience. The opening of Le Coq d'Or was the most opulent event I've probably ever attended. We had the Moscow Philharmonic Orchestra playing and, at the end of the performance, tiny nine-carat gold cockerels descended on the guests.'

'You're kidding!'

'It was like a scene out of a Bond film. Anyway, my Panamanian client, Manuel, was unbelievably chilled. I think he actually enjoyed himself.'

'Did he give you a golden cockerel for your efforts?'

'Not quite, but he did present me with a beautiful hand-painted wooden version that is now proudly on display in the kitchen.'

'We live such different lives. My new school presented me with a pack of biros and pencils when I joined.'

I laugh. 'Everything's relative. Besides, life's back to normal here. Cinders has exchanged her ballgown for ragged old shorts and a crumpled T-shirt and I'm all the happier for it.'

He gives a sigh. 'I'm happy to report that the new school headmaster was totally understanding about my MEK and said it was fine for me to bring it to school. I think I'm going to be happy there.'

'Alleluia!'

When Ed takes his leave, I sit listening to the trickling water in the pond but, disappointingly, I fail to hear a croak or a chirrup. The frogs are still not home. As I'm ruminating on the matter, Catalina rushes into the room.

'Come quickly! You'll never believe it, but one of your Silkies has hatched some baby chicks and they're like little black-and-white fur balls.'

I jump from my chair and, seizing Cordelia, follow Catalina out of the house and down into the orchard. In the corral we find our two Silkies, AZ and Sunny, fussing over eight little chicks, all a mass of white-and-black fur and feathers. The Scotsman stands in the corner of the corral, absolutely mesmerised.

'Have you ever seen anything like them?' he chuckles.

'Just keep the cats away from them,' warns Catalina.

I crouch down on my haunches and lift one into my hand. It is as soft as gossamer and radiates a gentle warmth. AZ watches me warily and seems relieved when I return the little creature to the grass. Protectively, she shields them all under her wings and, cheeping plaintively, they disappear from view. Ridiculously I feel tears prick my eyes, so moved am I by the sight of these perfectly formed and vulnerable little bodies that will now need to rely on the protection of their mother in order to survive. Frustratingly, I cannot prevent any mishaps occurring during the day, such as the tiny wards inadvertently being snatched by passing eagles or Eleanora's falcons. All the same, I resolve to usher the whole brood into the safety of the hen house at night to keep prowling rats, weasels and genets at bay.

We close the corral door and plod back up the stone steps to the rear patio, but not before the Scotsman has offered us a tour of the sprouting artichokes, giant, blossoming Echiums and the jacaranda, now covered in mauve flowers. Inko and the twins, Orlando and Minky, follow us, their paws ploughing disdainfully through the jungle of towering grasses. As we head for the kitchen, they sit on the stone steps like silent sphinxes, observing our progress, before setting about cleaning their ears and paws.

Ollie and I are just finishing our breakfast in Café Paris when my friend Cristina Alcover rushes over to greet us.

'How's life?' I ask.

'Busy. The hotel has just opened and the first guests arrive this week. It's quite a shock to the system after the long winter break.' She turns to Ollie. 'How long are you home?'

'Not long enough,' he replies with a smirk. 'Three weeks.'

'That's hopefully enough time to catch up on some sleep and see your friends.'

'I wish. Holidays are merely exam-revision periods these days.'

She smiles. 'It's so different from when I was at school. We never had such pressures. I believe childhood is to be enjoyed.'

'Hear, hear,' I say.

'By the way, have you heard that a new bookshop is opening in Calle Serra? It's going to be called Calabruixa, in honour of Marga.'

I nearly leap from my seat. 'Are you sure?'

'Of course. The sign's just gone up. It's the brainchild of Ana. She's a local but for the last few years she's been studying and working in Belgium. She's a biologist but has always had a love of books.'

Cristina takes her leave and in haste I pop into the café to pay. Carmelo slaps my change down on the counter and smiles.

'Good to have Ollie home. He must be happy.'

'He certainly is, even if his mother drives him mad!'

Carmelo laughs and offers a wave as we set off across the square. Taking the first left-hand turning off Calle Sa Lluna we soon find the bijoux terraced property that is home to the new bookshop. By the traditional wooden front door the name Calabruixa in purple, elegant script adorns a simple and tasteful ceramic tile, accompanied by the image of a flower.

'You know *calabruix* means hailstones, but *Calabruixa* refers to a purple plant. A biologist would probably have thought of that. She's putting her own mark on the place.'

Ollie shrugs. 'As they say, what a difference an a makes.' He studies my face in some horror. 'You're not going to cry, are you?'

I turn to him. 'Of course not, but I was just thinking of Marga and how this is such a wonderful tribute to her.'

The door swings open and a smiling face peeps out. It is, I presume, Ana. She swishes her long dark hair back and welcomes us inside her tiny, open-plan emporium, set on two levels. The place is cosy and still smells of newness and paint even though it is housed in an old traditional stone house. Ana has displayed the books imaginatively and is excited about the opening, planned for the next day. We promise to join the festivities in order to raise a toast to her success.

'I do hope you'll pop by often,' she says warmly. 'I want this to be a hub for the community, just as Calabruix was when Marga was alive.'

Back in the street, Ollie and I walk home, dallying when we arrive at what we refer to as Duck Bridge, which is just a stone's throw from the car park at Plaça Teixidor. A congregation of assorted fowl splash and paddle about in the *torrente*, making a terrible din when we throw them gifts of old bread and sunflower seeds. I lean over the railings, deep in thought, fondly remembering my old friend Marga. Although my heart is still heavy at her loss, I feel genuine happiness that a new chapter dawns for our local literary community and that, thanks to Ana and her new pearl of a bookshop, Marga's memory will live on forever in our mountain town.

There's an urgent buzzing at the gate. In some anticipation I rush out onto the sunny porch to greet the arrival of Emilio's white van that narrowly misses Jorge's *moto* by a whisper.

'*Uep!*' he cries, using the handy little Mallorcan expression to denote surprise. 'I thought you were going to hit me.'

Emilio climbs out of his van and, with a grin, slaps Jorge on the shoulder. 'I thought you postmen were indestructible?'

'That may be but I've got to take care now that I'm going to be a father.'

'A what?' I say in delight. 'Is Beatriz expecting a baby?'

Jorge gives me a bashful smile. 'It's due in September.'

We exchange hugs while Ollie, the Scotsman and Emilio rush forward to shake his hand.

He offers a modest '*gracias*!' and, handing the Scotsman a pile of letters, is about to clamber back onto his bike when curiosity gets the better of him. 'What's in the van?'

'Two baby lambs,' replies Emilio. 'Want to see them?'

He nods and joins us all as we cluster at the rear of the vehicle. I can hear plaintive bleating coming from inside and suddenly two little heads bob up at the back window. A moment later the furry prisoners are freed and start running friskily about in the sunshine, their woolly cream coats warm to the touch and their tiny tails shivering with excitement. Emilio steers them down the steep concrete slope that runs from one corner of our courtyard to the orchard below. Once there, they skip about, bleating and frolicking in the long grasses.

'They're beautiful,' I gasp.

Ollie offers a pert smile. 'As long as they make you happy, mother.'

'Don't you love them?'

He pats my shoulder. 'They're adorable. Another two to add to your menagerie.'

As Jorge takes his leave, Neus and Bernat hobble through the gate at the same time as Pep, Juana and their son, Angel, arrive by car.

'This is getting busy,' laughs Emilio.

'Come into the house and have a drink,' I urge. 'I've made some fresh lemonade and there's plenty of red wine, cava and beer.'

'And food,' butts in the Scotsman.

Ollie, accompanied by Angel, takes Neus's arm and leads her slowly up the front steps to the *entrada* while Bernat chats with Pep and Juana. A moment later, Catalina and her husband Ramon drive up and together we walk down into the orchard to see the new arrivals before entering the house.

'They look healthy,' says Ramon approvingly. 'It's a great way to keep the grass down.'

'You have one *macho* and one female, I see,' says Catalina. 'What are you going to call them?'

'Bertie and Buttercup.'

Ramon shakes his head in laughter. 'Naming sheep, whatever next?!'

'I think that calls for a celebratory glass of wine,' announces Catalina and promptly heads off up the stone steps. Our guests have arranged themselves informally at a long trestle table on the rear terrace. They sit chatting, enjoying drinks and canapés while the cats circle round, in search of handouts. Cordelia blocks the back door and will only take her leave when I give her a handful of sunflower seeds. I watch as she waddles off across the terrace and descends the steps to the field.

Pep rises and, with glass in hand, yells, 'Here's to roast lamb!' and is promptly given a good thump by Juana, much to the mirth of our seated guests. He gives a mock swoon and takes a recuperative swig of his wine, a mischievous glint in his eye. 'Of course what I *really* meant to say is here's to a happy life for our furry little friends, the exquisitely British-sounding Bertie and Buttercup!'

Everyone raises their glasses while Catalina helpfully bustles round, offering bread and canapés as if it was her own home. I take a sip of cava and potter happily into the kitchen. As I pull a pitcher of lemonade from the fridge, I fancy that I can hear a chirrup, a croak or even a quack. In all haste I patter in bare feet through the *entrada* to the front garden and sit on the edge of the pond. There's a series of small plopping sounds and a second later I detect the telltale chattering of my musical frogs. Sitting serenely on a lily pad are two small amphibians, their tiny iridescent bodies gleaming in the sunlight. I watch as their throats pulsate and their tongues whip out as soon as a passing insect flits by. The frogs have returned home from their travels: spring has officially arrived. My eyes search out the crude rocks around the pond but my critical, opinionated and much loved corpulent friend is nowhere to be seen.

'Are you there?' I whisper, but all I can hear is the rhythmic song of the cicadas and the buzzing of a passing hornet. I rise and, with eyes closed, stretch out my arms to the glorious hot sun shimmering in a wild, blue sky. It's only then, as I'm walking towards the porch, that I hear what sounds like a snigger, a hiccup and possibly a quack. And before I have a chance to whoop with joy, a voice rings out seemingly from the very depths of the pond. 'It's Johnnnnnny. I'm home!'

ABOUT THE AUTHOR

As a freelance journalist, **Anna Nicholas** has contributed to titles that include *The Daily Telegraph*, *Financial Times*, *The Independent*, *Daily Mail*, *Daily Express*, *Evening Standard*, *Tatler* and *UltraTravel*. She contributes a monthly column to *Telegraph Expat* and a weekly column to *Majorca Daily Bulletin*. She is a fellow of the Royal Geographical Society and has been an international adjudicator for *The Guinness Book of Records*. Together with explorer Colonel John Blashford-Snell, OBE, she once organised an expedition to carry a grand piano to the remote Wai Wai tribe in Guyana which was the subject of a BBC2 TV documentary. Anna runs an international marathon annually on behalf of her favourite charities. Her author website is at www.anna-nicholas.com and she can be found tweeting @MajorcanPearls

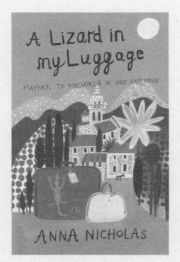

A LIZARD IN MY LUGGAGE
Mayfair to Mallorca in One Easy Move

Anna Nicholas

ISBN: 978 1 84024 565 3   Paperback   £9.99

Anna, a PR consultant to Mayfair's ritziest and most glamorous, had always thought Mallorca was for the disco and beer-swilling fraternity. That was until her sister hired an au pair from a rural part of the island who said it was the most beautiful place on earth. On a visit, Anna impulsively decided to buy a ruined farmhouse.

Despite her fear of flying, she kept a foot in both camps and commuted to central London to manage her PR company. But she found herself drawn away from the bustle and stress of life in the fast lane towards a more tranquil existence.

Told with piquant humour, *A Lizard in my Luggage* explores Mallorca's fiestas and traditions, as well as the ups and downs of living in a rural retreat. It is about learning to appreciate the simple things and take risks in pursuit of real happiness. Most importantly, it shows that life can be lived between two places.

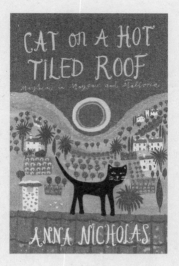

CAT ON A HOT TILED ROOF
Mayhem in Mayfair and Mallorca

Anna Nicholas

ISBN: 978 1 84024 683 4   Paperback   £8.99

Having moved to rural Mallorca to escape the stresses of London life, Anna Nicholas continues to commute back to her glitzy PR agency to earn a crust. But she is harbouring a bizarre dream to open a luxury cattery on the island – unbeknownst to her long-suffering family.

Life in the mountains is never uneventful as she gets to grips with phantom sheep, midnight snail hunts and Catalan lessons. Work also has its challenges, as she juggles demanding and often neurotic clients between Mayfair and Manhattan and is hotly pursued by lucrative deals. But increasingly Anna finds herself craving the simple life of her Spanish idyll because, as she discovers, you can take the girl out of Mallorca but you can't take Mallorca out of the girl.

GOATS FROM A SMALL ISLAND
Grabbing Mallorcan Life by the Horns

Anna Nicholas

ISBN: 978 1 84024 760 2   Paperback   £9.99

Life on the small island of Mallorca is entertaining and fascinating for Anna Nicholas, who moved her family to a rural mountain setting for a more *mañana* existence. But it's never simple.

She pursues her dream of opening a cattery, is devastated by the abduction of her beloved toad, and becomes fixated with Myotragus, the extinct goat that roamed Mallorca in ancient times. Meanwhile, trying to cut loose from her PR agency and its clients in London and New York, she finds herself among nutty Russian models and amorous rock climbers.

Hilarious, informative and brimming with memorable characters, *Goats From A Small Island* is a delightful tribute to Mallorca's rich way of life.

DONKEYS ON MY DOORSTEP
Hoofing it in the Mallorcan Hills

Anna Nicholas

ISBN: 978 1 84953 038 5   Paperback   £9.99

Anna wants to loosen the reins on her London-based PR company to spend more quiet time at home in sunny Mallorca with her family. But things don't work out quite as planned.

Amid ant and wasp infestations in the finca, she insists their menagerie of animals, including her new cattery, will only be complete with donkeys. Meanwhile she befriends an elderly Mallorcan poet, whose letters from his sweetheart during the Spanish Civil War waft into her garden, unveiling a poignant story of bravery and sacrifice.

In between all this she organises a Mad Hatter's Tea Party and survives a night in a haunted mansion. Brimming with hilarious and loveable characters, *Donkeys on my Doorstep* is a charming slice of the good life in rural Spain.

A BULL ON THE BEACH
Enjoying the Good Life in Mallorca

Anna Nicholas

ISBN: 978 1 84953 263 1   Paperback   £8.99

Having settled in a Mallorcan mountain idyll, Anna Nicholas, her husband the Scotsman and their son Ollie want to become as self-sufficient as possible. Anna teams up with organic farmers and smallholders to learn how to tend sheep, make cheese and honey and grind flour while the Scotsman creates havoc with his friend Pep in an attempt at winemaking, and tries to fathom what's troubling the wriggly inhabitants of his beloved wormery.

However, Anna can't quite shake off her old clients from the PR world, and is persuaded by Greedy George to create a media storm for his new Spanish leather store. The story of how a giant bull ends up on a Barcelona beach is enough to make her delighted to return to Mallorca, where talking to a toad and feeding porridge to her hens seems normal by comparison.

Have you enjoyed this book?
If so, why not write a review on your favourite website?

If you're interested in finding out more about our books,
find us on Facebook at **Summersdale Publishers** and
follow us on Twitter at **@Summersdale**.

Thanks very much for buying this Summersdale book.

www.summersdale.com